LOYOLA UNIVERSITY NEW ORLEANS
COLLEGE OF LAW

LOYOLA UNIVERSITY NEW ORLEANS COLLEGE OF LAW

A HISTORY

LOUISIANA STATE UNIVERSITY PRESS
BATON ROUGE

Published by Louisiana State University Press

Manufactured in the United States of America
First printing

Designer: Michelle A. Neustrom
Typefaces: Sina Nova, text; Friz Quadrata, display
Printer and binder: Maple Press (Digital)

Library of Congress Cataloging-in-Publication Data

Names: Medina, M. Isabel, author.
Title: Loyola University New Orleans College of Law : a history / Maria Isabel Medina.
Description: Baton Rouge : Louisiana State University Press, 2016. | Includes bibliographical references and index.
Identifiers: LCCN 2015043034 | ISBN 978-0-8071-6318-4 (coth : alk. paper) | ISBN 978-0-8071-6319-1 (pdf) | ISBN 978-0-8071-6320-7 (epub) | ISBN 978-0-8071-6321-4 (mobi)
Subjects: LCSH: Loyola University (New Orleans, La.). School of Law—History. | Law schools—Louisiana—History.
Classification: LCC KF292.L696 M43 2016 | DDC 340.071/176335—dc23
LC record available at http://lccn.loc.gov/2015043034

The paper in this book meets the guidelines for permanence and durability of the Committee on Production Guidelines for Book Longevity of the Council on Library Resources. ♾

For my children and my students

CONTENTS

PREFACE

The school opened in 1914, the year World War I began, and the year that a young man born in northern Louisiana destined to change the course of Louisiana history was admitted to the practice of law without having completed law school. Both the law school and the young man shared a commitment to social justice—to rectify the problems faced by the poor; neither perfectly realized that commitment. Huey P. Long's goals of frustrating increasing concentration of wealth and ensuring that the poor participated in the general wealth of the country were ultimately thwarted by the methods he used in his drive for power and an assassin's bullet. The first and only Jesuit law school to operate in the nation's southern region resisted a view of the legal profession as fitting only for the elite and instead aligned itself with those who sought to keep the law open to persons regardless of religion, class, or origin.

In keeping with its progressive origins, Loyola's law school throughout the twentieth century set a course that solidified its commitment to social justice: in its early years it sought to create opportunities for faculty and students to provide legal services for the poor. When legal education began to embrace clinical education on a national level, Loyola brought clinical education to Louisiana. In keeping with its view of legal education as a pathway to the profession, rather than as an academic discipline, Loyola emphasized professional training—it was the first law school in Louisiana to develop a comprehensive program of legal skills training. It was the first law school in the state to voluntarily integrate blacks. These initiatives did not bring to the school the success that their promise warranted, if success is to be measured by a school's national reputation. And law as an academic discipline and as a profession continues to reflect a hierarchy that reflects class, race, and gender differences.

But the law school's story is a work in progress. It is a story that reflects the battles and developments of legal education and the legal profession in the

United States. It is a story that reflects the story of the city of New Orleans, and, to an extent, Louisiana. Although founded long after slavery was abolished in the United States, and long after Reconstruction, it is a story about race. Although when the law school opened its doors it did not bar women from admission, it is a story about gender. Its past one hundred years need not define its future, but that past may help illuminate its present.

This is the story of that law school.

ACKNOWLEDGMENTS

This history is based on the available historical records, many of which are incomplete. The records, where possible, have been filled in through interviews, but where there are discrepancies between personal memories and available documents, I have rested my account on the documents. It is a history that reflects my own interest and particular focus: the role that class, race, and gender played in that history. I began writing this book in early 2012. Loyola had hired a new dean, the law school's centennial celebration was on the horizon, and the *Loyola Law Review* asked me to coauthor, with my colleague Kathryn Venturatos Lorio, a welcome to the new dean, Maria Pabón López. Lorio, the Reverend Lawrence Moore, S.J., and I, with the assistance of one of our recent graduates, Natasha Lacoste, wrote a brief history of the law school. That work led me to pursue a longer treatment of the subject, and I am grateful to the president of Loyola University New Orleans, the Reverend Kevin J. Wildes, S.J., and the New Orleans Province of the Society of Jesus, for granting me permission to work in their archives.

Writing this book has given me the opportunity to speak to large numbers of persons, both lawyers and nonlawyers. It is not possible to thank all of those who helped, but I am deeply grateful to everyone. In particular, I would like to thank Harold Baquet, Nona Beisenherz, Maria Calzada, Georgia Chadwick, Lolis Elie, Kyle Encar, Ramona Fernandez, Pamela Galindo, Marcel Garsaud, Joan Gaulene, Brian Huddleston, Elizabeth Kelly, Jessica Kelly, James Klebba, Maria Pabon Lopez, Kathryn Lorio, John Lovett, Victoria Luwisch, Nadia Moise, Lawrence Moore, David Normann, Robert A. Pascal, Andrew Piacun, Michele Pope, William Quigley, Thomas Sponsler, Barbara Wilson, James E. Wright III, and James S. Wright.

Bentley Anderson, Robert Garda, James Klebba, John Lovett, John Makdisi, William Quigley, and Thomas Sponsler read parts of the final manuscript, and for their insights and suggestions I am especially grateful. All would disagree with at least some of the interpretations and analyses of events, and, of course, mistakes are entirely my own.

The final version of this book has benefited from presentations I have given at the Mid-Atlantic People of Color Legal Scholarship Conference 2014 at the University of Baltimore School of Law; the Mississippi College of Law; the Tulane Forum on the Future of Law & Inequality, Tulane Law School; and the 2014 SALT Teaching Conference "Legal Education in a Time of Change: Challenges and Opportunities," at the University of Nevada–Las Vegas. Parts of this book rest on work that originally appeared as "Making History—Loyola University New Orleans College of Law Welcomes Dean Maria Pabon Lopez," in 2012 in the *Loyola Law Review;* as "The Missing and Misplaced History in Shelby County, Alabama v. Holder—Through the Lens of the Louisiana Experience with Jim Crow and Voting Rights in the 1890s," in 2014 in the *Mississippi College Law Review;* and as "Confronting the Rights Deficit at Home: Is the Nation Prepared in the Aftermath of Katrina? Confronting the Myth of Efficiency," in 2006 in the *California Western Law Review.*

I am indebted to Bernard Cook's history of Loyola University, *Founded on Faith: A History of Loyola University New Orleans,* and to Robert Stevens's *Law School: Legal Education in America from the 1850s to the 1980s.*

For excellent research assistance, I want to thank Melissa Aldape, Lauren Baudot, Rebecca Holmes, Natasha Lacoste, Hope Phelps, Aisha Pujadas, Chelsea Rice, and Cory Thornton. Special thanks to Nicholas Borkowski for assistance with the endnotes and bibliography.

I would like to thank the library and archive staffs at the Library of Congress, the J. Edgar and Louise S. Monroe Library at Loyola University New Orleans, the New Orleans Province of the Society of Jesus, the Loyola University New Orleans College of Law Library, the Louisiana Supreme Court Law Library, the New Orleans Public Library, the Earl K. Long Library at the University of New Orleans, the Amistad Research Center at Tulane University, the Howard-Tilton Memorial Library at Tulane University, in particular its Louisiana Research Collection, the University Library at the University of Illinois at Urbana-Champaign, the American Bar Association, and the Association of American Law Schools.

Finally, I thank Alisa Plant, Susan Murray and the staff at LSU Press for their encouragement, editing, and help with the project.

LOYOLA UNIVERSITY NEW ORLEANS
COLLEGE OF LAW

1

THE FOUNDING

A LAW SCHOOL FOR WORKERS

LAWYER'S WIFE (2 a.m.): John, there's a burglar downstairs.
LAWYER: Ask him if he's got $20 with him—I won't bother with him for less.
—*Times-Picayune,* October 4, 1914

As the Loyola Law School was a night school, it afforded a number of young men in New Orleans who were the bread winners of the family to take this night course in Law, while holding a day job that was the support of the family.
—REV. P. A. RYAN, S.J., "The Beginnings of Loyola University, New Orleans"

The story of the law school begins in October 1914, the year World War I began in Europe. Newspaper headlines in New Orleans that October were dominated by news of the war and the *Times-Picayune*'s self-described efforts "to do justice to both sides in this great European struggle."[1] News stories about the German, Russian, and English campaigns in Europe, and the civil war brewing in Mexico, commanded the front pages of local papers. Tucked away in the middle of the October 4, 1914, Sunday edition of the *Times-Picayune,* however, was a short article marking the opening of Loyola's law and dental divisions, with law's opening Monday, October 5, 1914, at eight o'clock in the evening, and a distinguished slate of religious, political, and legal leaders of the community scheduled to speak, including Louisiana's governor at the time, Luther Egbert Hall; New Orleans city mayor (and "boss") Martin Behrman; Joseph Arsenne Breaux, retired in April 1914 from serving as chief justice of the Louisiana Supreme Court; the Most Reverend James Hubert Blenk, archbishop of New Orleans; the Reverend Alphonse E. Otis, S.J., second president of Loyola University of the South; the evening's principal speaker, St. Clair Adams, former district attorney for the city and on the faculty at the new law school to teach criminal law; and Judge John St. Paul, sitting judge on the Court of Appeal for the Parish of Orleans and the new law school's founding dean.[2]

Much reported in that Sunday edition reads as if it could be from a Sunday newspaper in 2013. A tract of land in Grand Chenier had been set aside for a wildlife refuge. The community was engaged in a debate about teacher standards and how best to rate teachers. A child shot another child accidentally. Two black men had been sentenced to death for murder, and a white man sentenced to life for the same crime.

But much placed it squarely in the reality of life in 1914. The black men sentenced to death were referred to as "Negroes." The same edition of the paper noted that twenty-one ex-soldiers still resided in the Confederate Soldiers' Home. Police in Shreveport had shot another "Negro" caught with a stolen pair of boots and a saddle. His body contained thirty shots. Women in Cleveland, Ohio, paraded in support of suffrage, while women in New Orleans held a suffrage party meeting. The nation debated enactment of the Clayton Anti-Trust bill. A Spanish-language magazine published by the New Orleans Wholesale Merchants and Manufacturer's Bureau, the *Mercurio,* expanded its distribution, with the publishers claiming it added to the prestige of the city and helped to facilitate trade with Latin America. A four-year-old child had been diagnosed with a case of plague, and the city urged the community to combat rats.

Monday, October 5, 1914, emerged as a hot day for the time of year with a high of 88°F and a low of 68°F.[3] The thin *Times-Picayune* morning paper, only fourteen pages for the Monday edition in contrast to the Sunday edition's fifty-two pages, made no reference to the law school's opening that night. The paper noted, however, that Leland University, a school for the education of "Negroes," had announced its opening for October 7. Gun control was in the news with "two hundred persons gathered . . . [in Shreveport] to protest indiscriminate sale of pistols and deadly weapons."[4] And a sheriff, the newspaper claimed, had successfully stymied an attempted lynching of a "Negro" accused of attempting to rape a white woman.[5] War news dominated the front page, and Tennessee faced default. New Orleans churches organized peace prayers, and the community continued to deal with a small outbreak of plague.

The Tuesday, October 6, edition of the *Times-Picayune,* however, noted the opening of the school and predicted success for the law school of the Jesuits, reporting that thirty-seven students had enrolled. Father Otis, Loyola's president, was quoted as noting that 120 other law schools were then in existence in the nation, with a combined enrollment of more than twenty thousand. The *New Orleans Item* reported that Father Otis had stressed that Loyola's was a "nonsectarian law school" and that several members of the faculty were not Catholics.[6] According to the *Times-Picayune,* St. Clair Adams's address claimed that "better law schools [were] needed" and that Loyola's law school would be "a patent of integrity and merit."[7] The *Item*'s story explained further: St. Clair Adams had noted that people were "too critical of lawyers because of their strict adherence to technicalities." Thus, a "broader study of the law is advisable," and Loyola's law school would "meet the demand for better and able lawyers."[8]

Other news of the day reflected the national debate on alcohol and noted that ten Connecticut towns had voted to go "dry" and thirty-one to allow licensing, making Connecticut a majority "dry" state but still leaving almost half the state "wet." Several individuals were sent to jail for failing to pay child support. On the issue of cotton and the decreased European demand for cotton as a result of the war, the paper noted increased calls for restrictions on planting the crop. The first ship to sail to New Orleans from Chile and to pass through the recently completed Panama Canal arrived, and a fugitive in neighboring Mississippi was jailed in a manner that to the modern reader appears a relic of the antebellum past but was still part of the 1914 reality of life in the progressive South: "Bloodhounds Catch Planter's Slayer: Dogs Run down Negro Murderer of Hugh Russum: Fugitive Jailed."[9]

But the story of the law school's founding begins much earlier, with the Reverend John O'Shanahan, S.J., the superior of the New Orleans Mission for the Jesuits from 1888 to 1891; the Reverend William Power, S.J., the superior from 1897 to 1906; and the Reverend Albert H. Biever, S.J., Loyola's first president, men whose vision was to establish a major Jesuit institution of higher learning in New Orleans, modeled after Georgetown University, the country's oldest Catholic college and law school in the nation's capital.[10]

In 1889, Father O'Shanahan purchased a tract of land along St. Charles Avenue, opposite what is now known as Audubon Park, the site of the 1884 World's Industrial and Cotton Centennial Exposition, his goal to establish a Catholic institution of higher learning in the city.[11] Edward Douglass White, a graduate of the College of the Immaculate Conception and a former student and friend of Father O'Shanahan's who went on to serve as chief justice of the

U.S. Supreme Court from 1910 to 1921, arranged for the purchase. The new Jesuit college, however, was not established until 1904. Father William Power, then the Jesuit superior, asked Father Biever, then pastor of Holy Name parish in New Orleans, to set up the new college.

Biever had entered the novitiate at Grand Coteau as an adolescent and pursued further studies at Stonyhurst and St. Beuno's in Wales. He had emerged from his travels and studies with an interest in the sciences and natural life. His writings and public lectures reveal him as an engaged, creative, and dynamic visionary. Newspaper reports make clear his talent for communicating what must have been challenging concepts to the mostly illiterate New Orleans audiences of the time. Although his writings establish his interest in the sciences and he actively corresponded with other scientists, his overarching interest at least during his time as pastor of Holy Name and as president of Loyola was education and bringing to fruition the vision of many earlier Jesuits in establishing a Jesuit university in New Orleans.

ALBERT BIEVER'S JOURNEY TO FOUNDING A UNIVERSITY WITH A LAW SCHOOL

Albert Biever journeyed to south Louisiana very early in his life, after a brief time in Belgium at the Jesuit College at Turnhout in 1874. He was born in Luxembourg in 1859, into a large family, and his journal notes the impact of the outbreak of war between France and Germany on him and his family.[12] He left Belgium for New Orleans at the age of seventeen, as an aspirant to the Society of Jesus to train at the Jesuit College at Grand Coteau, boarding a ship at Liverpool. Travelling with him was a fellow student from Turnhout, Mr. Koch, "a South American, a linguist of note and ex-captain of an ocean vessel."[13] On his journey to New Orleans, going through Washington, D.C., he commented on his experiences with a greater variety of humanity and nature than previously encountered in Europe:

> All was strangely new to us. The quaint locomotives, the large and peculiar railroad coaches, the cosmopolitan population, passed before us like a kaleidoscope. I had never seen a black man, and as we neared Washington, I was bewildered by the variety of colors, from the yellow saffron and chocolate, to the ebony black.

> Every-day revealed new wonders to us. Mighty rivers and lakes, dense forests, century old trees draped with grey moss, swamps with alligators basking in the sun, long tressels spanning great lakes, continuously excited our admiration.[14]

Father Biever did not realize it, but his journey down had been made in the company of a man Louisiana southerners would consider black. Upon their arrival at Grand Coteau, he noted the strange reaction the group received from the other students already at Grand Coteau:

> The big bell accompanied by the howling of dogs awoke us about four o'clock next morning. After mass we were ushered into the dining hall of the students and breakfasted with them. All eyes were turned towards us especially towards Mr. Koch the faithful mariner of our little band. The faces of the students showed surprise and dissatisfaction, and sundry remarks were passed which I did not understand.
>
> When dinner bell sounded, the students refused to enter the dining hall, stating that they would never sit at the same table with a Negro. In fact, Mr. Koch was of dark complexion, had kinky hair and possessed other clear symptoms peculiar to the negro race.
>
> Our European Superiors, not knowing the social conditions of the Southern States where the Negro had just emerged from slavery, thought that Mr. Koch because of his dark complexion and South American origin would prove a most valuable subject. Unfortunately this was not the case. The house doctor was called in for consultation and after close scrutiny declared Mr. Koch to be of the colored race. Poor young man who but yesterday was supremely happy in the hope that he had reached the goal of all his ambitions had now to pack up and tearfully resume the return trip to Europe. Mr. Koch himself stated that his Father was a German physician and that his Mother was a colored woman.[15]

Later, after being received as a novice on December 13, 1875, Biever reflected on Koch: "I felt very happy at this initial step in religious life though I tearfully remembered our fellow traveler Captain Koch who had been coerced by the exigencies of time and place to retrace his steps and return to Europe."[16]

At Grand Coteau, Biever, with other novices, taught catechism to former slaves still residing in "the old plantation cabins."[17] He found them unfamiliar with reading and writing, "and the prayers and catechism lessons had to be orally drilled into their ears and memories. . . . [H]undreds were prepared for their first Holy Communion and were taught to love the Catholic Church as the true friend of the colored race."[18] It is unclear from his writings whether he was aware of the restrictions on education of slaves common throughout the southern states until after the Civil War.

Biever wrote his "Reminiscence" long after his experiences at Grand Coteau, and they may have been influenced by the decisions the Catholic Church made in Louisiana later, but his account of working to convert former slaves in the 1870s in southern Louisiana reflected on the Church's failure to provide priests willing to do this kind of ministry after the Civil War: "If shortly after emancipation of the negroes, priests had been found to take care of these unfortunate men and women who wandered about like sheep without a shepherd, the colored population of Louisiana would be today largely catholic."[19]

The racism to which he had been introduced at Grand Coteau also expressed itself through violence, and it is plain from his journal that the ministry to blacks sometimes drew the threat of violence to the priests themselves.[20] Later in the journal, he recounts an incident involving the threatened lynching of a black man who had insulted a white woman that was averted by one of the Grand Coteau priests.[21]

Biever's first impressions of New Orleans convey a sense of the city in 1875. While he regarded it a "great Southern metropolis," he noted that "Baronne Street was still paved with cobble stones, and the street was lined with stables where planters came to buy mules for their farms."[22] Like many visitors to the city, he noted its similarity to European cities: "We were surprised to notice a remarkable likeness between New Orleans and the cities of Europe, and were most surprised when we heard French spoken almost everywhere."[23] Biever left Grand Coteau after taking his first vows in August 1878, but his return to New Orleans was delayed until October—the city was quarantined because of an outbreak of yellow fewer. When he finally arrived in New Orleans, he was assigned to Spring Hill College in Mobile, Alabama, where he taught German and French grammar, among other things, to twenty-four students, only three of them Americans, the rest Cubans and Mexicans.[24] He was twenty-one years old, and some of his students were older and bigger than he. It was at Spring Hill that he learned to work with and observe bees, as he was assigned to be in charge of the apiary.[25] His journal entries from this period suggest that it was the wildness of the Louisiana countryside, where he encountered alligators, water moccasins, and old forest, that awakened his lifelong interest in nature and science. His interest in nature was clear from his days at Grand Coteau, where he enjoyed opportunities to explore the Louisiana country: "Birds of all colors abounded and the forests were made vocal with their various minstrels. Great flocks of snowy aigrettes and blue herons stood solemn and peaceful near open water spaces where unmolested they found food in abundance.... Through the watery lanes of almost primeval forests, beneath entangling vines and giant hackberries, gum, oaks and magnolia trees festooned with Spanish moss, we rowed to our hearts content."[26]

His journal entries describing the bees he worked with at Spring Hill reveal him as a self-trained naturalist while still a young man. Biever taught at Spring Hill for six years. He then travelled to England to pursue studies in philosophy at the Jesuit College at Stonyhurst, and theology at St. Beuno's in North Wales. He was ordained in 1891 and returned to North America. After brief stints in Georgia, Texas, Canada, and Florida, he returned to New Orleans in 1897, where by 1904 he served as the fourth pastor of Holy Name parish.[27]

In 1904, Biever began to realize Father O'Shanahan's project with the establishment of a Jesuit high school and college.[28] The project culminated with the founding of Loyola University of the South in 1912. Louisiana's grant of a state charter to the University to award professional degrees paved the way for the establishment of a law school.[29] That Father Biever's vision for Loyola included a law school was clear by 1907, when New Orleans newspapers reported it.[30] But the initial focus of the plans was the development and construction of an undergraduate institution on an undeveloped parcel of land along St. Charles Avenue, next to Tulane University and across from Audubon Park. And lawyers played prominent roles in assisting with those plans, in particular Judge John St. Paul, a graduate of Spring Hill College (the Jesuit institution in Mobile, Alabama, where Biever taught for some years) and an 1886 Tulane University law graduate, and William H. Byrnes Jr., a graduate of Georgetown University and a Louisiana state senator. St. Paul and Byrnes, both Catholics and both devoted to Loyola, were instrumental in the founding of the undergraduate program at Loyola and were vital to the founding of Loyola's law program. St. Paul was the founding dean of the law program and Byrnes served on the founding faculty and went on to serve as its fourth dean.

In March 1906, St. Paul, then a judge on the Louisiana Court of Appeals for Orleans Parish, drew up the charter for the Marquette Association for Higher Education, a group designed to assist the Jesuit fathers to further "the cause of higher education and to establish and maintain Loyola University."[31] Its first objective was to raise funds to develop buildings on the Loyola campus. St. Paul served on the building committee that selected the architect to build Loyola College and helped raise funds for the fledgling university.[32] He served on Loyola's Board of Directors and as chair of the Committee on the Charter and its By-Laws.[33] In 1912, St. Paul was selected to speak at the opening of Thomas Hall, at the time the Jesuit residence built alongside Marquette Hall.[34] St. Paul was also one of the featured speakers at the January 1913 Alumni Banquet, at which the affiliation with the Pharmacy School was announced.[35]

St. Paul was born in Mobile, Alabama, in 1867, according to family members, after his parents' land in Louisiana was confiscated as a result of the Civil War. His father, Henry St. Paul, born in Belgium, had emigrated from France in the early 1830s after serving in Napoleon's army. Henry St. Paul worked as a newspaper reporter in New Orleans prior to pursuing legal studies at Transylvania University in Kentucky.[36] His wife's family came to New Orleans as refugees from the Haitian slave uprising of the 1790s. They married, set up life in New Orleans, and had five daughters before the Civil War. Henry St. Paul took up arms against the Union, and his wife, Honore, the family remembers, refused to swear allegiance to the United States when Union forces took over New Orleans. Instead, she moved the family to Mobile, Alabama. When the war was over, St. Paul joined her and set up his law practice in Mobile. They had two sons in Mobile, one of them John. St. Paul's heritage, perhaps, makes understandable the role he was to play as a political and juridical leader in Louisiana.

John grew up in Mobile and graduated from Spring Hill College, but when it came time to attend law school he returned to New Orleans and attended Tulane University. Upon graduating, he moved back to Mobile, where he married Florence Gertrude Townsley, and then returned to New Orleans to practice law from 1891 to 1896. He was elected to the state senate in 1896 and appointed to the Louisiana Civil District Court for Orleans Parish in 1899, and to the Louisiana Court of Appeals for Orleans Parish in 1909. John and Florence had eight children; one died in infancy. Two of the children became attorneys, one of them, John St. Paul Jr., a member of the new law school's first graduating class.[37]

State senator William H. Byrnes Jr. introduced the act securing the University's charter and shepherded its passage through the Louisiana legislature.[38] The University's charter gave the University the right to confer degrees in "all learned professions."[39] As early as 1907, when Father Biever publicly proposed the new university opposite Audubon Park, it was clear that a law division was an integral part of Biever's plan.[40]

NEW ORLEANS, LOUISIANA, THE PROGRESSIVE ERA, AND JOHN ST. PAUL

The New Orleans that entered the twentieth century had changed dramatically from the city that Albert Biever encountered in 1874 and that formed the backdrop to the infamous *Slaughterhouse Cases,* a constitutional law case studied by modern law students because it constricted the reach of the Reconstruction Amendments.[41] New Orleans then reflected the paradox that the city perhaps continues to be in the twenty-first century: "at once the shabbiest and most alluring of American cities,"[42] with a reputation for being liberal on race relations that it may not have deserved. New Orleans was unique—it was southern and it was Catholic. The city was racially and ethnically diverse, and its racial and ethnic heritage was complicated. Blacks made up approximately 27 percent of the city's population;[43] creoles of color, descendants of freed or free blacks usually of mixed ancestry, viewed themselves as distinct from recently freed slaves or darker descendants of former slaves.[44] Chinese made up the second-largest ethnically and racially distinct group in the city,[45] although Irish, German, and Italian immigrants were sizable enough groups that they impacted the development of the city and left their own ethnic stamp on residential neighborhoods.[46]

The city's acceptance of creoles, before and after the Civil War, created a more tolerant racial climate than available in other southern cities. Even after Reconstruction ended in 1877, New Orleans appeared to be slightly more accommodating to people of color than the rest of Louisiana and the South; its streetcars were integrated, and blacks and whites often lived alongside each other in the poorer areas of the city.[47] Jazz, alcohol, cocaine, and sex perhaps facilitated a more tolerant attitude to black-white interactions. It was not uncommon for interracial couples to share lives and raise children, for music halls and houses of prostitution to facilitate interracial socialization, and for blacks to shop in clothing establishments alongside whites.[48] As William Ivy Hair notes in his history of the Robert Charles riot, many New Orleans neighborhoods were racially mixed at the turn of the century.[49] When Robert Charles set out on his ill-fated visit to a young woman residing on Dryades Street, before his encounter with a New Orleans police officer set off race riots in the city in late July 1900, he and a friend waited on the steps of a white family's home because it was a few houses down from his girlfriend's house.

The city clung fervently to its French heritage but tended to deny its Spanish one, although the latter defined its architecture and much of its history.[50] It was the nation's second-largest port, attracting not just goods but immigrants. Although Louisiana saw a drop in the number of immigrants as a whole from 1870 to 1900, it continued to be one of four southern states with the highest number of immigrants and Catholics.[51] Its decadence was reflected in Storyville, a twenty square block next to the French Quarter featuring houses of prostitution, saloons, gambling establishments, and dance halls;[52] Mardi Gras, a Catholic celebration to usher in the Lenten season of French and Spanish origin that featured parades, balls, and pretend kings, queens, and royal courts; and its mostly tolerant attitude toward gambling, alcohol, and corruption. It lacked a safe water supply until 1909, tolerating the dumping of raw sewage into the Mississippi River, the source of its drinking water. Yellow fever, smallpox, and cholera plagued the city throughout the nineteenth century; the city experienced its last major outbreak of yellow fever in 1905 and an outbreak of plague as late as 1914.

Jim Crow affected the city's reputation as a more welcoming space for southern blacks or free people of color. When the federal government abandoned Reconstruction policies in 1877 under President Rutherford B. Hayes, Louisiana and other southern states responded aggressively to undo the political, economic, and social gains of blacks after the Civil War and enactment of the Thirteenth, Fourteenth, and Fifteenth Amendments to the United States Constitution.[53] Any distinctions that Louisiana culture had drawn between creoles of color and darker-skinned blacks evaporated; all were targeted. As the state's largest metropolitan area with a substantial Catholic creole population, many of whom had provided political leadership during the state's Reconstruction government, New Orleans was at the center of the battle over the mechanisms designed to deprive blacks and creoles of political power—mandated segregation of the races and disenfranchisement of blacks and people of color.

Louisiana began its formal rejection of the Reconstruction Amendments with enactment of a statute mandating segregation of the races in railroad cars, upheld in 1896 by the U.S. Supreme Court in *Plessy v. Ferguson.*[54] The challenge to the law was mounted in New Orleans by creoles, who traditionally had enjoyed a more privileged status in New Orleans society than slaves or darker-skinned blacks.[55] Light-skinned creoles, many of whom passed for white, strongly resisted racial segregation and the increasing rigidity of racial castes that made it more and more difficult for interracial relationships of any kind. It took over six decades in the twentieth century to restore legal protections to blacks in the South, but even at the height of the era of segregation, blacks and black community organizations, like the Comite des Citoyens, which organized Plessy's challenge to the railroad car statute, tried to battle Jim Crow's grossest abuses. Those abuses and increasing competition for low-skilled work, largely as a result of the 1890s depression, domestic migration to the city, and an influx of immigrants, led to racial tension that often erupted into racial violence, like the Robert Charles riot.[56]

Notwithstanding the naked racism of the era and the incidents of racial violence in the city itself, historians like Adam Fairclough maintain that the incidence of racial violence, including lynchings, and the overall attitudes to blacks in Louisiana were "harsh, but not as harsh as in Alabama or Mississippi."[57] Fairclough attributes this difference in attitude to the influence of Catholicism in the southern half of the state, and New Orleans:

> Catholicism itself, for all its conformity to the practices of white supremacy, softened, albeit slightly, the harder edges of racism. The ameliorative influence of the Catholic Church was discernible, for example, in the lynching statistics. Between 1889 and 1922, the peak years, the north Louisiana parishes of Caddo, Quachita, and Morehouse, all overwhelmingly Protestant, witnessed more lynchings than any other counties in the nation. Over half the lynchings that occurred in Louisiana between 1900 and 1931 took place in seven parishes, all of them mainly Protestant, and all but one in the northern part of the state.[58]

Louisiana as a whole had a relatively high number of Catholics, as Fairclough notes, most residing in the southern part of the state and New Orleans. It was the only southern state to emerge in a religious census done by the U.S.

government in 1906 with a significant percentage of Catholics: 31 percent of church members in Louisiana reported themselves as Catholic, with only 19.4 percent self-reporting as Protestant.[59] The high number of Catholics in the state and the city was due not just to the area's founding by Catholic countries, France and Spain, but to the Acadian migration of the late 1700s, the influx of refugees from the Haitian Revolution, and heavy Irish and Italian immigration during the nineteenth century.[60]

The majority of Louisiana's black population was rural and resided in north Louisiana—Huey Long country. The city and the state were poor, and the populations of both were overwhelmingly illiterate. Race in the state was linked to religion. Blacks tended to be Protestant, and creoles or people of mixed racial ancestry tended to be Catholic.[61]

In the 1890s, with a majority of blacks making up the state's population (51 percent), Louisiana set about the task of disenfranchising blacks.[62] It accomplished a change to its state constitution, with the express intent to disenfranchise blacks, by allowing changes to the state constitution to be made without approval by voters. In 1896, Louisiana voters approved an act calling for a constitutional convention "with power to frame and adopt, without submission to the people, a new Constitution for the State."[63] John St. Paul, a state senator at the time, was elected delegate-at-large, one of nine from Orleans Parish—the largest parish in the state. At the convention, St. Paul served on the Committee on Suffrage and Elections. The convention proceedings make clear his participation; he submitted his own proposal on suffrage, ultimately defeated.[64]

Delegates met at Tulane Hall, on University Place, in the central business district of New Orleans on February 8, 1898. The convention's newly elected president, Ernest Benjamin Kruttschnitt, made clear its primary goal in his opening statements:

> We know that this convention has been called together by the people of the State to eliminate from the electorate the mass of corrupt and illiterate voters who have during the last quarter of a century degraded our politics.... Only a few years back, it might have been considered impolite to say what I am now saying, but there are men standing high to-day in the councils of the nation, who have seen the doors of the White House barred to them by the ignorant and corrupt delegations of Southern negroes.... May this

> hall, where, thirty-two years ago, the negro first entered upon the unequal contest for supremacy, and which has been reddened with his blood, now witness the evolution of our organic law which will establish the relations between the races upon an everlasting foundation of right and justice.[65]

The goals of the proposed constitutional changes in 1898 were plainly stated. Kruttschnitt claimed they were necessary to "protect the purity of the ballot box and to perpetuate the supremacy of the Anglo-Saxon race in Louisiana."[66]

Women in Louisiana had been pushing for the franchise since at least 1879.[67] This initial push for the franchise did not align itself explicitly with white supremacy and sought the vote for women on the grounds that they deserved it and would use it wisely. Again, in 1898, women attempted to persuade the conventioneers to give them the suffrage, this time by aligning themselves with the white supremacy movement; even that, however, failed to persuade a majority in the convention to grant the suffrage to women.[68] Subsequently, the women's movement in Louisiana became divided between groups who wanted the suffrage for all women, black and white, and those who aligned themselves with white supremacy. Louisiana women did not obtain the vote until passage of the Nineteenth Amendment to the U.S. Constitution in 1920.

The convention debated a number of measures designed to deprive blacks of the vote including a proposal to restrict the suffrage to persons who were voters on January 1, 1868, before the adoption of the Fourteenth and Fifteenth Amendments to the U.S. Constitution, a proposal rejected because it was plainly inconsistent with the Fifteenth Amendment. The Fifteenth Amendment prohibited states from denying citizens the vote on account of race, color, or previous condition of servitude. The proposal would have immediately disenfranchised all black voters, since none could have been voters on January 1, 1868. Instead, the convention delegates adopted ostensibly racially neutral rigorous registration requirements, including a two-year residency period, literacy tests and/or property requirements, and a poll tax. Most whites would be exempted from the new requirements through a "grandfather clause" that provided that any males entitled to vote on January 1, 1867, and their male descendants over the age of twenty-one at the date of adoption of the new Constitution, did not have to comply with the new, burdensome educational or property qualifications.[69] The measure was similar enough to the previous measure, through the working of the exemption, to pose a similar conflict with the mandate of the Fourteenth and Fifteenth Amendments. Nonetheless, the measure passed by a strong majority, with John St. Paul voting in its favor: "I vote yes upon my own individual personal and political responsibility. I vote yes because the bill is right and for the reason given orally to the Convention last evening, and which the Convention has heard. To repeat them now would be only for the benefit of the galleries, as to whose approval or disapproval (since the bill is right and my conscience clear thereon), I am indifferent, whether they be filled from the slums or from the clubs."[70] Approximately one-fourth of the delegates to the convention voted against the measure, most expressing concerns about its constitutionality, and many expressing concerns over its morality and what they called its undemocratic nature.[71] It is difficult to ascertain how many objected to the intentional disenfranchisement of blacks and how many objected because of its effect on poor, illiterate, white voters, and creoles of color, and because its plain language directly conflicted with the Fifteenth Amendment and thus was likely to be held unconstitutional by the U.S. Supreme Court.

The new constitution was soon challenged in court, and the challenge ended up before one of the new judges on the Civil District Court of New Orleans: John St. Paul. David J. Ryanes, a sixty-year-old former slave, born in Tennessee but a resident of Louisiana since 1860 and freed in 1863, filed an action challenging the grandfather clause, and the property and literacy requirements. Ryanes had been a registered voter for thirty years, a beneficiary of the Louisiana Constitution of 1868, which guaranteed that all citizens of the state enjoyed "the same civil, political and public rights and privileges, and be subject to the same pains and penalties."[72] Through his attorney, Armand Romain, Ryanes alleged that the intent and effect of the new constitutional provisions was to deny him and other "Negroes" or colored citizens the vote. Ryanes could read and write only a little—not enough to fill out the registration form and to demonstrate literacy to the registrar of voters. He did not own property. And as a slave until freed by the Emancipation Proclamation, not able to vote in Louisiana until 1867, he was not exempt from the onerous literacy and property requirements. He could not qualify to vote in Louisiana.

To prove the impact of the grandfather clause on black voters, Romain introduced voter records for 1896, 1897, and 1900 to show a dramatic reduction in the number of blacks registered to vote: in 1896, Louisiana showed 164,088 white registered voters and 130,344 colored; by 1900, Louisiana had 125,437 white registered voters and only 5,320 colored. The New Orleans numbers were staggering as well: in 1896, there were 45,907 white registered voters and 14,177 colored; by 1900, white registered voters had dropped to 37,491, but colored voters had dropped to 1,493. To prove that the intent of the constitutional provisions was to deprive blacks of their votes, Romain tried to introduce the *Official Journal of the Convention Proceedings*, which proved "that the Constitutional Convention . . . was called together for the purpose principally of disfranchising the colored citizens of this state, and to adopt a plan . . . of suffrage qualifications, by which all white men in the state could . . . be retained in the Electorate, and all the colored men in the state, as far as possible should be excluded from the said Electorate."[73]

The attorneys representing the defendant, the supervisor of voter registration for the parish of Orleans, objected to the admission of the *Journal* on the grounds that it was immaterial and irrelevant, since the language of the relevant constitutional provisions was clear, and thus there was no need to resort to questions about legislative intent. Judge St. Paul agreed and refused to consider the evidence. One of the defense attorneys was the former chair of the Louisiana Constitutional Convention of 1898, E. B. Kruttschnitt. The suit was filed on April 30, 1902. The case went to trial on July 28, 1902, and Judge St. Paul issued his decision the same day. Judge St. Paul ruled that a prior action filed by Mr. Ryanes in the same court but before a different judge barred reconsideration of the issues since the dismissal of the prior suit constituted a ruling on the merits. On appeal, the Louisiana Supreme Court decided it lacked jurisdiction to review the dismissal of the case because the new constitution did not specifically provide for appeals when the only question was one of the alleged invasion of political rights, like the right to vote.[74] Mr. Ryanes, a voter for thirty years, like many other black voters, was left without a vote and with no recourse.

Other southern states adopted Louisiana's grandfather-clause approach to reduce black suffrage. A year after law school classes at Loyola started, in 1915, in the case of *Guinn v. United States,*[75] the U.S. Supreme Court held that this kind of grandfather clause, plainly adopted to disenfranchise blacks, violated the Fifteenth Amendment. In response to the *Guinn* decision, Louisiana amended its constitution in 1921 to adopt the "interpretation test," which continued to vest almost complete discretion in the hands of registrars to determine who would be allowed to register to vote based on a potential voter's ability to "give a reasonable interpretation" of any clause in the Louisiana or United States constitutions. This provision remained in place until the U.S. Supreme Court struck it down in 1965 in *Louisiana v. United States.*[76] Black voters in Louisiana, as across the South, had to wait for Congress to enact the Voting Rights Act of 1965 and for the activism of the 1960s and 1970s before their votes were counted again.

But the goals of the proposed constitutional changes in 1898, as Mr. Ryanes had attempted to prove, had been achieved. By the time Loyola's law school began its evening classes, Louisiana had effectively disenfranchised black citizens and accepted "the supremacy of the Anglo-Saxon race."[77] Having settled the racial issue, the convention turned its attention to education. Delegates viewed public education as the means to facilitate voter registration for poor, illiterate whites. Although Louisiana's public education system was initiated in 1845, it was not developed until the 1890s and then only for whites. The state's long-term neglect of public education reflected the state's poverty and its lack of interest in providing services to the poor, even the white poor. By 1910, while plans for Loyola's law school were being developed, Louisiana did not provide a single public high school for blacks.[78] It was not until 1920 that the state first provided a public high school for black students. Louisiana provided few public primary or secondary schools for blacks until the mid-twentieth century.

The paucity of public education in Louisiana made religious and private institutions the primary providers of education in the state at the turn of the twentieth century. Religious institutions were the first entities to provide formal education in the city. In New Orleans, the Jesuits had established a secondary school in 1849, the College of the Immaculate Conception, at the corner of Common and Baronne Streets, under a charter granted to the Jesuits in Louisiana, the Catholic Society for Religious and Literary Education (La Société Catholique de L'education religieuse et litteraire).[79] Prior to this, few educational opportunities were available for boys or young men in New Orleans. The Ursuline Sisters, invited by the Jesuits to the New Orleans province in 1727, undertook education of young girls and women in New Orleans upon their arrival in August 1727, including black slaves, native American Indians, and orphans.[80] In their formal school, however, the Ursulines educated only young, Catholic, white girls.[81]

In 1823, Sister Ste. Marthe Fontiere, living within the Ursuline community, opened a school for free girls of color.[82] One of the school's pupils, Henriette Delille, together with Juliette Gaudin and Josephine Charles, founded the Congregation of the Sisters of the Holy Family, an order to minister specifically to persons of color, in 1842.[83] Even Catholic women, however, lacked an avenue for higher education. The Sisters of Mercy wanted to start a women's college in New Orleans in the latter part of the nineteenth century, but church authorities refused amid concerns about finances.[84]

After the Civil War, blacks in the South increasingly sought to form and control their own religious congregations.[85] Although New Orleans contained a substantial number of Catholics, the state of Louisiana was predominantly Protestant. In the aftermath of the Civil War, Protestant parishes, traditionally segregated, facilitated black leadership and control.[86] The Catholic Church's highly centralized hierarchy, as well as its clerical celibacy requirement, made the formation of black-controlled congregations difficult. Few blacks or persons of color were admitted to or trained for the priesthood.[87]

Protestant churches also provided for the education of blacks; Catholic parishes, however, failed to do so, in part, perhaps, because they faced financial bankruptcy during the 1880s.[88] Concerned that black Catholics were converting to Protestantism, and recognizing that in order to continue to attract and retain black Catholics the Church would have to provide them with educational opportunities, the Catholic Church similarly began to provide for racially segregated parishes.[89]

Catholic churches in New Orleans were racially integrated up until the 1890s, although inside the churches worshipers would have been segregated in seating.[90] Other Catholic institutions, however, like hospitals and schools, were racially segregated, including the first Jesuit high school in New Orleans for boys, the College of the Immaculate Conception that, in 1914, provided the first home to Loyola's law school.

The push to segregate Catholic parishes in the New Orleans area was controversial and encountered resistance, particularly by creoles who feared the Church wanted "to separate the races and widen the gap which exists between the white and colored population."[91] R. Bentley Anderson explains in his study of race and the Jesuit order in New Orleans during 1947 to 1956 that Church leaders sought racial segregation of parishes to accommodate the wider Louisiana trend in Protestant churches to allow for black leadership and independence in Protestant parishes. Segregation led to black churches and, as important, the growth and development of Catholic schools for blacks and creoles.[92] Although Archbishop Francis Janssens established the first black parish in Louisiana in 1892, it was not until 1916 that the Church established the first black parish in New Orleans, two years after the law school's official opening.[93] Thus, at the time of the law school's founding, in 1914, Catholic churches were still integrated.

But the Church's decision to adhere to segregation norms was consistent with the majority sentiment of the time. Some New Orleans political leaders pushed for enforcement of complete segregation of the races, even in the streetcars.[94] As Alecia Long notes, even in Storyville, the district established to segregate prostitutes from the rest of the city's population in 1897, the year after the Supreme Court upheld segregation in railroad cars, the 1909 Gay-Shattuck Law, adopted to avoid prohibition by regulating alcohol and prostitution, made it increasingly difficult for interracial socialization of any kind.[95]

Thus, New Orleans in 1914 was a city firmly in the grip of Jim Crow: entrenched racial segregation, race riots, and formal disenfranchisement of blacks, creoles, and poor whites. Reform movements associated with the Progressive Era like the prohibition of child labor, compulsory school attendance laws, Prohibition, and women's suffrage still reflected the region's commitment, in the post-Reconstruction era, to deny full equality to blacks, creoles, and other persons of color.

A political machine, the Choctaw Club, also known as the Regular Democratic Organization or "Ring" machine, ruled the city, with Martin Behrman, mayor of the city for five terms between 1904 and 1926, at its head. Behrman was a political leader unabashedly racist, corrupt, and supportive of business, including the business of gambling, prostitution, and alcohol, but nonetheless in the historical narrative an effective administrator who oversaw the modernization of the city's infrastructure.

By 1914, New Orleans had signified its entry into modernity by providing for a massive water and sewerage system. Its press reported regularly on international events—its coverage of the outbreak of war in Europe was extensive and suggested the city was sophisticated and engaged in global affairs. The heart of the city was still the French Quarter, and much of what is modern-day New Orleans, like the Midcity, Carrollton, New Orleans East, and Lakeview neighborhoods, had still to be developed. The individual the Jesuits selected to head the new law school was regarded well by the city's political leaders and reflected deeply his city's commitment to Jim Crow.

THE FOUNDING OF A LAW SCHOOL

At the time of the law school's founding, Louisiana already had two other law schools: Tulane's law school in New Orleans and the law school at Louisiana State University and Agricultural and Mechanical College (LSU) in Baton Rouge. Tulane was the oldest surviving Louisiana law school, having taken over the Louisiana Law School, a proprietary law school owned by Gustavus Schmidt, in 1847, as the University of Louisiana and, then, in 1884, as Tulane University.[96] Tulane's law school had moved to its uptown campus on St. Charles in 1906. By 1914, both Tulane and LSU operated as day schools, and although students attending LSU paid no tuition and attended classes for only three hours a day, both schools were beyond the reach of working-class New Orleans residents.

Straight College, now known as Dillard University, had offered law studies to both white and black students in the latter part of the nineteenth century, from 1874 to 1886.[97] Straight College educated a number of black attorneys in Louisiana, including Louis A. Martinet, Rodolphe L. Desdunes, and Renee C. Metoyer, but by the 1900s its law program had ceased to exist.[98] Neither Tulane nor LSU admitted blacks, so blacks who hoped to practice law in Louisiana either had to attend law school out of state or serve an apprenticeship; they then had to take the Louisiana bar examination, at the time an oral test administered by a Board of Examiners.[99] Between 1898 and 1923, the committee admitted only one "colored" attorney, Joseph A. Thornton, in 1914, and only two women, Mollie M. Parker in 1918 and Judith H. Douglas in 1920. The committee minutes record two other black attorneys seeking admission to the bar—Albert Wicken in 1898 and E. J. Rosborough in 1917—both of whom failed to gain the committee's approval. Mr. Wicken returned before the committee in 1900, but it is not clear whether he was admitted at that time. The advantage to attending an in-state law school was substantial due to the "diploma privilege." Students completing the law course at any of the three law schools were essentially "waived" into the bar without taking an examination.

By 1914, a national push to improve the legal profession by embracing more rigorous training and systematic bar examinations had succeeded in establishing law schools as the optimum method of training lawyers, rather than apprenticeships, although an apprenticeship would continue to be part of an attorney's legal training.[100] Although Harvard and Pennsylvania treated law as a graduate degree, most law programs operating at the turn of the twentieth century offered law as a three-year undergraduate degree program.[101] Law was not viewed as an academically rigorous discipline. Robert Stevens in his history of legal education discusses the "unpleasantness at Georgetown," which resulted when "opponents of Georgetown's athletic programs" discovered that "a disproportionate number of Georgetown's athletes enrolled in the law school."[102] Georgetown did not require a high school diploma for admission to its law division at the time.

Law's emergence as an academic discipline yielded serious discussion and controversy over admissions, curriculum, methodology, and faculty. Law schools debated the extent to which the study of law should reflect its character as an academic discipline rather than training for the profession, and whether students should be taught legal reasoning rather than the law of their particular jurisdiction. Stevens credits Charles Eliot, appointed president of Harvard College in 1869, and Christopher Columbus Langdell, appointed dean of Harvard Law School in 1870, with establishing the curriculum and methodology ultimately adopted by American law schools in the twentieth century. Some of the reforms included raising admission standards for law to be at least equivalent to other disciplines; making law a three-year graduate program; instituting a system of teaching that emphasized analysis of appellate cases, the "case method"; and the hiring of law professors who had limited, or no, experience with the practice of law. This approach to law teaching, Stevens noted, created a division between academics and practitioners, a difference that Stevens suggests inevitably led to the formation of the Association of American Law Schools (AALS) in 1890 as an entity separate and apart from the American Bar Association (ABA), established in 1878, with one of its objectives the raising of the standards of the profession.[103]

At least two types of law schools had emerged by 1914: trend-setting, prestigious institutions like Columbia, Harvard, and Yale, and other, "lesser," law schools whose more immediate objective was to train lawyers for the practice of law in their state. Some critics expressed concerns about the relationship between law schools and corporate interests, but most, according to Stevens, viewed the relationship as a salutary one.[104] A parallel discussion about the role of lawyers and law schools in the community centered around admission to law school, with some favoring the view that "the gates to the bar should be wide open, and easy admission allowed to all applicants,"[105] but others, like Lewis Delafield, president of the American Social Science Association, urging that law be treated as a public calling, with those deemed "'unworthy' to be 'excluded' and 'rejected.'"[106]

Thus, the controversies concerning legal education and the legal profession that dominated discourse at the dawning of formal legal education and that continue to provoke controversy today, and the stratification of law schools into a hierarchy that reflected prestige and elitism were apparent by the time the Jesuits in New Orleans thought about offering legal studies to the New Orleans community.[107]

New Orleans contained the largest Catholic population in the South, and tensions in the city arose between the Catholic community and the majority Protestant community. The Reverend P. A. Ryan, S.J., first vice president of Loyola, recorded in his journal religious attacks on the Church and the difficulties encountered by students graduating from the Jesuit high school in gaining acceptance to Tulane University's undergraduate program.[108] "Preachers in their Sunday sermons and religious bigots generally made frequent attacks on the Church," he wrote in his journal.[109]

Prior to Loyola's founding, the relationship between Tulane and the Jesuits had been cordial. Biever had given the blessing at Tulane's May 1898 graduation, a ceremony that is of note because it marked the first woman law graduate in Louisiana—Bettie Runnels. Even after Loyola's founding, Biever continued to enjoy a scholarly relationship with Tulane, and the discord that Ryan notes eventually was resolved, although it appears to have reappeared when Loyola's law school sought accreditation from the ABA and AALS.

In discussions with Catholic community members, Ryan noted a request for evening courses; the New Orleans adult Catholic community felt its own ignorance and desired a way to rectify it. Ryan responded with a series of evening lectures, thus, paving the way for evening programs at Loyola.[110] Although Tulane was eventually persuaded to accept Jesuit high school graduates, to the Jesuits these difficulties justified plans for a Catholic university in the South, and a law school offering an evening program was one way of addressing adult needs for further educational opportunities.

Black workers, however, would continue to lack access to a Louisiana law school. Black Catholics continued to lack local access to a Catholic institution of higher learning until Xavier University of Louisiana, established by Katherine Drexel and the Sisters of the Blessed Sacrament, opened its doors in 1915.[111] Black law students of whatever faith continued to lack access to a legal education in Louisiana until the state, in response to litigation challenging LSU law school's admission policies barring blacks, established a separate law school for blacks at Southern University in 1946, and Loyola's law school voluntarily segregated in 1952. Blacks had to leave the state to go to law school, and many, like A. P. Tureaud, attended Howard Law School in the District of Columbia.[112]

A LAW SCHOOL FOR WORKERS

Loyola's law school offered workers, including immigrants, a way into the legal profession through a part-time evening program. Not all Jesuits favored such a program, and conflicts in the Jesuit leadership threatened to thwart realization of the proposed law program.

Formal planning for Loyola's law school began in the summer of 1911, in meetings of the Jesuit Alumni Association and the Marquette Association for Higher Education.[113] Shortly after those discussions began, the Jesuit Province consultors, the local leadership for the Society of Jesus in New Orleans, met on December 28, 1911, to discuss the proposed law school.[114] The consultors at that meeting agreed that the Superior General, the head of the Society of Jesus worldwide in Rome, "should be asked for permission to take preliminary steps at least in this direction."[115] The Superior General appears to have approved the plans to start a law school, but the next reference to the law school in the consultors' minutes does not appear until March 1914, the spring before classes were scheduled to start in the fall, and after the 1913–14 *University Bulletin* announced the opening of the law school, under the leadership of Judge St. Paul, as well as its first faculty and its proposed curriculum. Despite the public commitment to a law school, Biever's push to expand Loyola soon met a foe in the New Orleans provincial—the Reverend Michael Moynihan, S.J.

According to Father Ryan's journal, Judge John St. Paul was the obvious choice to lead the law school from the start. Biever's journal makes clear his trust and confidence in St. Paul, and St. Paul, through his strong support for Loyola throughout the founding of the undergraduate program, certainly seemed to merit that trust. In fall 1912, Biever asked St. Paul to serve as founding dean.[116] The *Bulletin* notes that St. Paul agreed to serve as dean in the fall of 1913.[117]

St. Paul's descendants credit him with convincing the Jesuit Fathers to proceed with an evening program, and it is possible that Father Biever initially preferred to institute a day program. By 1914, many institutions were offering law as a full-time day program. But it is likely that given Georgetown's model, Father Biever was open to pursuing law as a discipline to be offered through a night program, rather than a day program.

Evening or part-time law school programs became prevalent in the United States after the Civil War. Georgetown's evening program, established in 1870, thrived by 1920 with a population of one thousand students.[118] Evening programs made it possible for persons who had to support themselves or other family members to attend law school while continuing to provide for their families through a daytime job. New Orleans's Jesuit law school would make it easier for individuals who worked during the day and could afford to attend school only in the evening to gain access to the profession.

Few Loyola records survive from this period, and the account of the law school's founding is based primarily on Jesuit consultors' minutes, Father Biever's journal, Father Ryan's journal, newspaper articles, and the *University Bulletin,* which described the curriculum and faculty to be offered in the new law program, as well as the curriculum and faculty who taught in the first year of classes. From the beginning, however, concerns emerged about funding and control of the professional programs, which led to severe friction between Biever and Moynihan, the Jesuit provincial, and threatened to block establishment of the programs. The concern that threatened to thwart the law school's establishment involved its funding and the financial liabilities that it might pose to the University. Moynihan was reluctant to establish professional programs, in particular, a law school, primarily due to concerns about financial liabilities and, in regard to the law school, faculty compensation. If Biever was the visionary, Moynihan provided the limits to the vision: the conflicts between the two escalated to the point where they ceased to communicate, and—according to Father Ryan, first vice president of Loyola—Biever relied on Ryan as an intermediary to reach compromises that allowed expansion of the University to move forward.

Most of the undergraduate faculty at Loyola consisted of Jesuit priests; initially, it was a relatively small faculty with a very small student body. The addition of the pharmacy school added lay faculty, but the pharmacy school had been in existence prior to its incorporation into Loyola, and was perceived as self-sufficient. Nonetheless, according to Ryan, Moynihan approved the addition of the pharmacy school in July 1912, only after the school agreed to relieve Loyola of any financial losses. The acquisition or addition of the pharmacy division, thus, was described not as a purchase but an affiliation.[119]

The law division, on the other hand, was a completely new entity: few Jesuit priests were available to serve as law faculty. Moreover, in Louisiana as in most other states at the time, law faculties were being recruited from the profession rather than straight out of prestigious academic institutions like Yale or Harvard. The expectation for a law division, then, was that lay faculty, practicing members of the bar, would be used. Moynihan was concerned that they would have to be compensated and, thus, that the costs of offering a law division would be too high to make the program viable for Loyola.[120]

The Jesuits in the United States had dealt with similar issues at the founding of Georgetown—finances and control. The Georgetown law school's evening program initially operated as a proprietary school taught by part-time faculty. Only one of the six lawyers who served as faculty, an associate justice of the U.S. Supreme Court, Samuel Freeman Miller, was paid a salary.[121] The rest were reimbursed by sharing any profits brought in by tuition. At some point in its early years, the law school had to borrow money from the undergraduate college to meet its obligations. By the late 1870s, however, professors received salaries, which ranged, by 1883, from $200 to $450.[122] By the 1890s, after the D.C. Bar Commission decided to require a three-year course of studies for admission to the bar, Georgetown's law school had become the largest school within the University.[123]

At Georgetown's law school founding, Georgetown's president insisted on serving as the law school's president, to prevent the law school from following the model of Georgetown's medical school, styled as an independent affiliate, the model followed at Loyola for the pharmacy school.[124] Loyola's law school adopted a similar model. Later, Georgetown's law school was put under Jesuit direction in the form of a "regent" appointed to represent their schools on the University's highest authoritative body.[125] Loyola's law school similarly instituted the office of regent who served as the school's leading Jesuit authority, alongside the dean, until the latter half of the twentieth century.

Moynihan insisted that law dean and faculty serve without compensation, on a volunteer basis, something that appears to have been the subject of negotiation and discussion between Biever and Moynihan, but that St. Paul and the original faculty he recruited to serve had agreed to from the start. Volunteer professional faculty would have to continue fulfilling the demands of their regular day jobs; an evening program could easily accommodate the needs of the volunteer faculty and provide an as yet unmet need in the city of New Orleans and the state of Louisiana for an evening program in law—a law school for workers. Similarly, the fact that it was a night school made it possible for judges and lawyers with a full-time, successful private practice to teach the courses at night. Judge St. Paul would have finished work at the courts and walked over to the College of the Immaculate Conception on the corner of Baronne and Common, the law school's first home, every weeknight to teach classes.

Although it was his vision that led to the founding of the law school, Biever did not preside over its opening; he was relieved of his office as president of Loyola and assigned to missionary duties at other Jesuit missions in 1913. Biever ended his term of office as rector-president at Loyola having served six years on March 5, 1913.

Moynihan insisted that law faculty guarantee in writing that they would donate their services to the law school. Biever refused to entertain this request, and Ryan, Loyola's vice president, undertook to relay the request to John St. Paul. According to Ryan, Judge St. Paul took great umbrage at the request because all the faculty were gentlemen and knew that they would serve without pay. To ask them to sign a contract, he felt, signaled disrespect. While the 1913–14 *Bulletin* announced the start of the law school in fall 1914, and Biever had secured Judge St. Paul's service as dean, the behind-the-scenes reality was that the actual establishment of the law school was precarious. It was not until after Biever's dismissal that Moynihan approved proceeding with the law school. The March 28, 1914, consultors' minutes record the approval of the law school on certain conditions:

1. The professors are not to exact any salary until the school is on a paying basis.
2. As soon as the school is on a paying basis the salaries of the various professors are to be determined.
3. The salaries of the secretary and of the janitor are to be paid from the beginning.

4. These conditions should be approved in a meeting held between the Trustees of the university and the members of the faculty of the Law School.

Thus it was the Reverend Alphonse E. Otis, S.J., second president of Loyola University, who presided over the law school's opening-night ceremonies on October 5, 1914. A year later, the consultors considered whether the founding dean, Judge St. Paul, should be paid a salary, given the strong performance of the law school in its first year, but the consultors, still under the cautious leadership of Moynihan, "decided to wait until we see what the enrollment for next year will be."[126]

Judge St. Paul served as dean until 1918 without financial compensation. That same year the University awarded him an honorary doctor of law. He also had the pleasure of awarding his son, John St. Paul Jr., his diploma as one of the first graduates of the new law school.[127] He continued to teach at the law school until shortly after being elected Associate Justice to the Louisiana Supreme Court in 1922.

Although the Jesuits maintained overall control of the law school to some extent, Judge St. Paul selected the faculty, not all of whom were Catholics, and he and the faculty plainly exercised control over the curriculum. At the law school's founding ceremony, Loyola's then president, the Reverend Alphonse E. Otis, S.J., addressed the role of religion in the context of legal education:

> Since Loyola is under Catholic direction, is religion to play a part in its professional training? The professional courses must of necessity be nonsectarian in character, and Loyola's full appreciation of this is shown by the fact that she numbers among her faculty many non-Catholics and has enrolled among her students those who differ greatly in their religious beliefs. However, God will not be debarred from our professional schools, and religion will be our guiding star, to the extent, at least, of preventing us from treading on the dangerous ground of skepticism and materialism and of coming into conflict with Divine revelation. God's holy Commandments will be esteemed and reverenced, and our young men will be taught a code of ethics which will acknowledge God's rights and supreme dominion over man.[128]

Loyola's *Bulletin* for academic year 1913–14 included as officers of the University and faculty: Judge John St. Paul, as dean of the law school, and Alfred J. Bonomo, as secretary, the only salaried position, as well as the Reverend Patrick A. Ryan, S.J., as vice president and lecturer on ethics. Included in University faculty as law faculty were St. Clair Adams, as professor of criminal and trial law; Joseph A. Breaux, recently retired as chief justice of the Louisiana Supreme Court, teaching civil code, successions, and testaments; William H. Byrnes Jr., teaching insurance and torts; Donelson Caffery, teaching constitutional and international law; Hugh C. Cage, to follow St. Paul as second dean of the law school, teaching civil code and contracts in general; Charles I. Denechaud, who had served in the Marquette Association, teaching civil code, personal relations, and property rights; William C. Dufour, teaching corporations and receivers; Clarence S. Hebert, teaching civil code; Gustave Llambias, teaching civil code, accessory contracts, privileges, and prescriptions; Eugene J. McGivney, teaching insurance and torts; James J. McLoughlin, who had served alongside St. Paul in the Marquette Association and its charter and by-laws committee and who had contributed the last one thousand dollars to the building of Marquette Hall,[129] teaching municipal corporations, public offices, and taxation; Henry Mooney, teaching commerce factors and traders, bills and notes, and banking; Theodore Roehl, teaching theory of law; Irving R. Saal, teaching code of practice; William J. Waguespack, teaching federal jurisdiction and procedure; and W. W. Westerfield, teaching warehousemen and carriers, and shipping.

Law school classes were scheduled every evening of the workweek from 6:00 to 9:00 p.m., "thus affording an excellent opportunity for students to combine the advantages of practical experience in a law office with those of a thorough scientific law course."[130] The evening program was designed as an undergraduate three-year program, consistent with many of the evening programs offered throughout the nation at the time. The location of the school in its first year, in what today is known as the central business district of the city and in 1914 was "the heart of the business section, and in the vicinity of the local courts," offered to prospective students "exceptional advantages of location and convenience."[131]

The *Bulletin* assured students that they would be prepared for practice "not only in Louisiana, but also in common law states," and a special feature of the school was its commitment to "practical training in legal reasoning, pleading, practice and forensic oratory."[132] As a practical matter, like many other law schools at the time, the curriculum focused primarily on local law—Louisiana law, something that proved an impediment to accreditation in later years.

Consistent with the requirements for admission followed at most law schools, all that was required to be admitted to Loyola's law division was a high school diploma or its equivalent and that the applicant be at least eighteen years old.[133] Students paid twenty-five dollars in fees on a quarterly basis.

Students in the first year started every Monday evening at 6:00 p.m. with a class on theory of laws, which would have included history of law, statutory construction, conflict of laws, and the nature of equity. At 7:00 p.m., they had civil law "A," dealing with personal relations. On Tuesday, they started with criminal law and finished with civil law "B," on successions. On Wednesday, they took public law "A," which included international law and constitutional law, and finished with civil law "C," on contracts. On Thursday, first-years started with commercial law "A" and finished with civil law "D" on particular contracts, and on Friday, they started the night with civil practice of state courts, studying Louisiana Code of Practice, and finished with civil law "E" on accessory contracts. The 8:00 to 9:00 p.m. time slot on the schedule was reserved for third-years; thus it was not used until academic year 1916–17.

The entering class appears to have consisted of 42 students who attended evening classes at the University's first campus downtown, on Baronne and Common, at the Jesuit "Alumni Hall." Felix W. Gaudin, a graduate from the 1917 graduating class, the first class to graduate from the law school, noted, "At least 50 percent of the class would not have been able to study law if it had not been for the night school at Loyola."[134] Twenty-six students made up this first graduating class.[135]

At the end of its first year, in 1915, the law school moved classes to Marquette Hall on the uptown campus, where it remained for almost two decades. Shortly before law classes were due to start that fall, on September 29, 1915, a hurricane struck the city. "A terrific wind and rain storm devastated the whole city. Much damage reported," the Jesuit minister's diary recorded.[136] The morning edition of the *Times-Picayune* warned the city of the storm, expected to hit the coast near the mouth of the Mississippi River.[137] The headlines on the morning of Thursday, September 30, assured its readers that the city had come through safely what it considered the "worst hurricane experienced" in the city, with nominal property damage. Subsequent reports revealed the damages to be more severe, with more than 350 fatalities and many injured.[138] The weather continued to be bad into October, and the greatest disruption appeared to be to the communications and power infrastructure of the city. Law classes were scheduled to begin the evening of October 4, but Loyola's campus still did not have electricity. Nonetheless, law classes opened as scheduled, with "good attendance" despite the bad weather, and classes were held by candlelight.

Also in 1915, the Jesuits decided to admit women to the law school. Women would not be admitted to the undergraduate program or to the dental school until much later in the century.[139] It was not until 1918, shortly before the end of World War I, that the law school admitted its first woman candidate. The United States' entry into the war in April 1917 had a devastating impact on the law school; classes during the war years were sharply reduced in size.

In fall 1918, Alice Agnes Allen joined a class of eleven young men. The war ended on November 11, 1918. Ms. Allen earned her LLB in 1921 and enjoys the honor of being the first woman to graduate from Loyola's law school, coming in fourth in her class.[140] Irene J. Barrios, Ella G. Hickman, Anna J. Veters, and Marie Washburn are listed as students, alongside Ms. Allen, in the 1920–21 *Bulletin*. It is difficult to know whether more women applied than were admitted; certainly, it appears that the loss of male candidates due to the war effort may have encouraged women to apply and may have facilitated their admission to the law school.

The Jesuits' law school had set its course in the history of New Orleans. It was the law school that paved the way for workers to access a profession that often led to affluence, prestige, and power. A profession that had two images in the public eye: that of the sophist and shyster, reflected in the humor at the start of this chapter; and that of the moral leader charged with braving popular opinion in an effort to ensure justice, epitomized to many by Abraham Lincoln, and later, the fictional Atticus Finch, a character perhaps more palatable to the South. It took several decades to correct the moral flaw at its founding. That the correction came in part through the efforts of two Loyola Jesuits and some of its graduates makes it clear that it is the individual who decides what kind of attorney she or he will be, and that individuals can and do shape the institution.

2

ACCREDITATION

> Night schools enrolled a very large proportion of foreign names . . . emigrants [*sic*] covet the title [of attorney] as a badge of distinction. The result is a host of shrewd young men, imperfectly educated . . . all deeply impressed with the philosophy of getting on, but viewing the Code of Ethics with uncomprehending eyes.
>
> —SUSAN K. BOYD, *Assuring a Qualified Bar*

At its inception, Loyola's law school was a local school, founded by Jesuits and Catholic leaders of the bar to facilitate a Catholic legal education to persons for whom a part-time evening program created access to the legal profession. The diploma privilege, available in Louisiana until 1924, as a practical matter rendered law school a surer way to earn admission to the bar than an apprenticeship under a practicing lawyer and passing a bar examination. Candidates still had to get through law school, and that, Loyola's law school found, increasingly, was a challenge to many of their students, some of whom entered the program at a young age, some as early as seventeen, with insufficient preparation to undertake law studies. The law school was essentially a local phenomenon, put together by a full-time judge and practicing attorneys, none of whom had any expertise or familiarity with legal education and none of whom were paid for their efforts. And by 1914, legal education had already undergone substantial developments, so that by 1909, Tulane's law school had hired full-time law faculty (both of whom had completed master of laws programs from highly regarded national law schools); had adopted the "case-method"; and had tightened the requirements for entering law students. LSU's law school, begun in 1906, employed full-time compensated law professors from the start, and although some of their classes were held at night, their program was styled a full-time day program, where students were expected to study the law when not in classes. LSU's first faculty all had graduate degrees and some experience in legal or university education.[1]

Loyola's transformative moment in becoming an established and nationally recognized law program came when the American Bar Association (ABA) and the Association of American Law Schools (AALS) accepted it for membership in the 1930s. Ironically, it was Loyola University's desire to solidify its own standing in the national and regional educational community that led to the strengthening of the law school's program.

Loyola University itself had started as an institution of higher learning chartered by the state, its undergraduate faculty originally composed of Jesuits. By the beginning of the twentieth century, however, higher education had developed its own evaluation standards and mechanisms, designed to ensure a certain level of competence. To ensure that a degree would be recognized not just locally, but nationally, universities and colleges had to qualify for membership in a regional association. For Loyola, that meant it had to secure membership in the Association of Colleges and Secondary Schools of the Southern States (ACSSSS).

The Association's membership standards at the time required that professional schools of member universities be "of approved grade, national standards being used when available." In the case of law schools, that meant approval by the ABA and membership in the AALS. The effort to secure that approval fundamentally transformed Loyola's law school from a night law school staffed by volunteers to a full-time day and evening program staffed by a combination of full-time legal educators and part-time professionals. Indisputably, the transition to a full-time day program made it possible for the school to develop aspects of legal education that would have been very difficult for an evening-only program like professional skills training and clinical education. Loyola became the first law school in the state to initiate clinical legal education and provide free legal services to those unable to pay for them.

LOYOLA'S ACCREDITATION

Two events impacted New Orleans during this early period that caused enrollment at Loyola to plummet: the United States' entry into World War I on April 6, 1917, and the 1918 influenza epidemic. American participation in the war was of relatively short duration, but two months after the armistice on November 11,

1918, Loyola had only 20 students left in the University.[2] After the war, Loyola's enrollment at both the University level and the law school quickly increased; by 1922–23, enrollment had increased to 600 (including part-time programs, like law), with 209 full-time students.

As the University recovered from its drop in enrollment, its students encountered difficulty being admitted to graduate programs like the medical school at Tulane University. Loyola, the University learned, was not on the American Medical Association's list of approved undergraduate programs. Loyola's Board of Directors, at the time all members of the Society of Jesus, noted that other universities were denying Loyola students academic credit earned at Loyola. Consultation with other Jesuit universities convinced then Loyola president, the Reverend Edward A. Cummings, S.J., that membership in the Association of Colleges and Secondary Schools of the Southern States was necessary to ensure the continued viability of the institution. Accordingly, in 1920 Loyola began the arduous pursuit of membership in the Association.[3]

The initial response from the Association deferred Loyola's application and raised numerous concerns about the institution, including entrance requirements; insufficient numbers of faculty with doctorate degrees or its professional equivalent; faculty compensation (most faculty were unpaid); insufficient endowment; irregular students (students who did not satisfy the traditional admission criteria); the athletics program (at the time in the hands of an alumnus); and the professional schools, in particular the law school, which as a night school was "of a type not recognized by this Commission."[4] The professional schools, Loyola was advised, would have to be recognized or accredited by their respective professional accrediting bodies. The pharmacy school was not a problem, but the law school, run by an all-volunteer faculty, was a long way from coming into compliance with the recently adopted ABA and AALS standards. The Association also counseled that accreditation was a lengthy process that often took five or more years.

The Association's response to Loyola reflected the battle over evening schools being fought in the legal education arena, as well as the institution of the ABA as an accrediting entity. Loyola's law school had been founded alongside many other night schools. Both the bar and established full-time day schools reacted strongly to the trend, communicating concerns about the dilution of standards and the incapacity of night schools to adequately prepare students working full-time day jobs for a competent practice in law.[5]

In the words of one of the earliest American studies of legal education, sponsored by the Carnegie Foundation for the Advancement of Teaching and published in 1921: "Part-time schools offering instruction during evening or afternoon hours, outwardly the equal of full-time schools having courses of equal length, were really much more superficial in their work, without anybody—not even themselves—fully realizing their inferiority. Thus they reached the deplorable position that they occupy today—that of being merely cheapened copies of the regular full-time model."[6] Alfred Reed acknowledged the benefits of night schools in creating access to the profession for the working poor; however, he concluded, "they have done more harm than good to legal education."[7] Reed's concerns focused on the fact that evening programs would lack access to practical training because students would be busy during the day primarily with non-law-related work and on concerns over the length of time the various programs required. Reed preferred three- or four-year programs, as the majority of law schools offering a night program required, but nine schools offered a two-year program. At the same time, Reed was concerned not only about the length of time required but also about the quality of the courses and work required of the students, which he thought was weakened in the night school setting.

The debate over night schools coincided with the formation of the AALS, the development of standards for legal education by both the ABA and the AALS, and the institution of an accreditation process for law schools. Although the Southern Association had required Loyola to secure accreditation for its law school, the ABA's accreditation function was just getting off the ground. The ABA first adopted standards for legal education in 1921 and began implementation of those standards in subsequent years, employing its first advisor, H. Claude Horack, in 1927. Professor Horack, retiring as president of the Iowa State Bar Association at the time of his appointment, a professor at the University of Iowa Law School and practitioner, oversaw the accreditation process at Loyola.

In 1920–21, Loyola's law school was one of 62 schools offering a night program. Forty-one of the schools offered a night program alone, and the remaining 21 offered an evening program in conjunction with a full-time day course. Eighty law schools, however, the majority, offered a pure day program, for a total of 142 law schools operating in the country by 1921. At its 1916 meeting, the AALS debated a resolution not to recognize any night work after 1920. It adopted a requirement that member schools have three "substantially" full-time faculty members, despite the threats from member schools, including Marquette University, another Jesuit institution of higher learning, to resign their membership in protest.[8]

Loyola could have opted to abolish the law school rather than bring it up to par, but the Reverend Florence Sullivan, S.J., appointed Loyola's president in 1925, was resolute: "As you well know, the night school was the great object of attack, and we were not prepared to give up our excellent night school, which is doing such efficient work, because of arbitrary standard."[9] The law faculty were "convinced that the abandonment of night classes will work undue hardship on many worthy citizens of this State and Parish who, as Americans, are entitled to an opportunity of making themselves better citizens and better equipped servants of the people by the study of law."[10] Ultimately, the AALS abandoned the push to prohibit part-time night programs.

Father Sullivan, however, was experiencing difficulty in persuading the law faculty to make other necessary changes to achieve membership in the ABA and AALS. The law school had an all-volunteer faculty with full-time professional commitments, and they had joined in the creation of the enterprise as a part-time night school providing easy access to the legal profession. Faced with the demand to radically change the nature of the enterprise, according to Sullivan, they resisted change.[11] Sullivan explained to the Association, "[Y]ou cannot imagine the difficulty I am having in persuading these legal men to abandon their viewpoint." What was that viewpoint? "Louisiana law seems to be a peculiar thing," Sullivan wrote, "and these men feel that they have evolved a proper method. Besides, they are strong for giving every young man a chance, so that the practice of law may not be restricted to those only of the wealthier class who can afford college preparation."[12] If only they were Jesuits, Sullivan lamented, "we could adjust ourselves by a simple command in military fashion," but they were leaders of the bar, not so easily herded. Subsequent events at the law school proved that Jesuits themselves were similarly not always so easily led. In 1923, when Loyola asked for more time to develop the full-time day program, Washington & Lee dean H. D. Campbell, then chairman of the Association's Commission on Institutions of Higher Education, suggested that Loyola abolish the night program.[13]

Instead, Sullivan sent Judge Hugh Cage, then dean of the law school, and the law school regent, the Reverend Michael Kenny, S.J., to visit a number of eastern law schools with part-time schools, to determine how best to proceed. Responding to Dean Campbell later that year, Sullivan warranted, "The Faculty of law are determined on a gradual raising of the entrance requirements and the lengthening of the course."[14] The letter makes clear the lengthy shadow of the Civil War:

> I have tried to tell you . . . the attitude of our department of Law. They are earnest, serious men of high caliber, and as they have had excellent results, they are slow to make radical changes, especially as they believe that the Southern States are not in position to accept dictation from the larger cities in Northern States, where higher education has been fostered and developed under many favorable circumstances. . . .
>
> Louisiana cannot do what Massachusetts, New York, Michigan and Iowa have achieved, after very many years of well-financed organizations. But as educators, they feel that they must meet the needs of our own citizens, as they find them, even though we may suffer a little by comparison with the achievements of others, which has been the sad story of the South since the War.[15]

In all likelihood, Sullivan was speaking not only of the law school faculty but also of the financial challenge to Loyola of replacing a volunteer law faculty with full-time legal academics who would have to be compensated, and developing and instituting a full-time day program in addition to the night program. Providing adequate space for the law school and library resources were additional financial expenditures that loomed on the horizon because by 1927 the ABA had adopted a standard requiring law schools to have an adequate law library. The University newspaper, the *Maroon,* ran a story in spring 1924 noting that the law school was holding a dance to raise funds for the law school library. It is doubtful that such fund-raising would have sufficed to bring the law library into compliance with ABA standards.

Thus, for Loyola, gaining membership in the ABA and AALS, in order to gain membership in the Association, would mean drastically revising the law school program and increasing the financial resources devoted to the program.

Loyola's push to earn membership in the Association proved a lengthy and arduous process, far longer than Campbell had predicted. It took almost ten years for the University to be provisionally admitted to the Association, and the efforts of four Loyola presidents: the Reverend Edward A. Cummings, S.J., the Reverend Francis X. Twellmeyer, S.J.,[16] the Reverend Florence D. Sullivan, S.J., and the Reverend John W. Hynes, S.J. It appears to have taken a letter-writing campaign by Jesuits, organized by Hynes, to the officials of the ACSSSS in 1929 to secure the initial admission in 1929. Although the Association's formal response to Hynes was that it was "as far as possible from being the right way to approach these gentlemen," the campaign worked: Loyola was admitted to membership.[17] Not until the law school was accepted by the ABA in 1931 and the AALS in 1934, however, did the accreditation cease to be provisional. Father Hynes went on to serve as vice president of the ACSSSS in 1932.

CHANGE AT THE LAW SCHOOL

Judge St. Paul retired as dean in 1918, and Judge Hugh Cage, also on the city's civil district court, succeeded him. While Judge Cage was highly respected by the bar, he served as a part-time dean, like Judge St. Paul. As Leon Sarpy, Loyola graduate and law faculty member later recalled, "He had the saying from time to time that he ran two law schools: one uptown at Loyola and the other in civil district court on motion day."[18] Notwithstanding his part-time status, Judge Cage presided over a number of changes at the law school before stepping down as dean in 1924.

Control over the law school, however, remained squarely under Jesuit supervision, in the hands of Loyola's president and Board of Directors, all Jesuits, in turn, all under the control of the Jesuit provincial. In 1920, the University instituted the office of regent, intended to function as the Jesuit administrator of the law school, serving alongside the dean. Although the Jesuits deferred to the dean and faculty with regard to the curriculum, most decisions about the law program appear to have been made by the central university administration, through the office of the regent. The costs of running a law school, at that point, were minimal, since only one person, the secretary, Alfred Bonomo, was compensated, and the school relied primarily on donations for the law school library.[19] Kenny, the first law school regent, was the primary full-time presence at the law school, in addition to Bonomo. Unsurprisingly, he appears to have been regarded as carrying administrative authority at the law school. Indeed, a story in the student newspaper in spring 1924 describes him as the dean of the law school.[20] And through the regent, moreover, Jesuit philosophy influenced the curriculum. Kenny introduced the teaching of fundamental law and legal ethics at Loyola in 1916.[21]

It was not uncommon for the law school to admit individuals who did not satisfy the admission requirements. Herbert Christenberry was one of those applicants who were exempted from the regular admissions requirements: he was admitted without a high school diploma. Christenberry worked at a brokerage house and attended a local business school. At some point he approached Father Kenny for help getting into the law program at Loyola. According to his son, with Kenny's tutorials and assistance, the elder Christenberry was admitted and worked his way through the evening program, graduating in 1924. Christenberry was a member of what appears to have been the first student law club at Loyola, the Law School Debating Society.[22] Father Kenny's instincts proved true: Herbert Christenberry went on to an illustrious career and was the first Loyola Law graduate to be appointed to the federal bench. President Franklin Roosevelt appointed him as U.S. attorney for the Eastern District of Louisiana in New Orleans in 1942. Five years later, in 1947, President Harry Truman appointed Christenberry to serve in the United States District Court for the Eastern District of Louisiana.[23]

To deal with the problem of weak or poor preparation, "especially in English composition," the University began a pre-law program in the Arts and Sciences division; students who earned credit in this program earned credit toward the bachelor of laws degree (the LLB).[24] In 1921, the school inaugurated a summer session to make it easier for night students to complete their studies but also as a way for "conditioned students" (students who had failed a course) to qualify for the fall term.[25] A short-lived master of laws (LLM) was instituted in 1920.[26] Both of these programs, however, created problems for accreditation.

The LLB program consisted of a three-year course of study with the regular session beginning on the first Monday in October of each year and continuing to the end of the following May, for a total of thirty full weeks. Final examinations were scheduled for the first half of the month. Classes were offered for two hours each evening (from 7:00 to 9:00 p.m.) five days a week, Monday through Friday.[27]

Throughout this early period, the curriculum consisted of courses on the Louisiana Civil Code, including successions, property, persons, contracts, and obligations; courses on Louisiana law, including civil and criminal procedure, torts, insurance, bills and notes, banking law, and criminal law; courses with a federal focus, including constitutional law, federal procedure, admiralty, bankruptcy; and other general courses on the common law, international law, legal history, legal ethics, statutory construction, equity, and conflict of laws. Occasionally, the school offered interdisciplinary offerings, like "History and Literature."

In addition, beginning in 1920 the school offered "Practice Court" in conjunction with the evidence and code of practice courses. Judge Cage presided over what appears to have been a "moot" courtroom for a weekly session, in the University Auditorium, that offered students the opportunity to observe and participate in actual court practice "including the routine of examining the jurors, impaneling juries, opening the case to the jury, examining and cross-examining witnesses, making objections and motions, and presenting arguments to court and jury."[28]

It is difficult to ascertain how "Practice Court" actually worked, but the *University Bulletin* makes clear the aim was to give students actual practice experience: "Officers of the Court and Clerks are appointed from among the student body, thereby giving them a clearer insight into the working of all machinery of justice."[29]

Another innovation in 1920 was the establishment of the *Loyola Law Journal,* the first student publication at Loyola and the second law review in the state, following the *Tulane Law Review,* which began publication in 1916. LSU's *Louisiana Law Review* was first published in 1938. The *Loyola Law Journal* was a quarterly publication and primarily a venue for Loyola faculty publications and short commentary by Loyola students. To some extent, the *Journal* functioned as a newsletter or yearbook, including news about individual students and alumni. The 1922–23 *Bulletin* states that faculty assisted students in the production of the *Journal* to give it "a text-book value," a function quite different from that ascribed to most law journals today.[30] This early law journal was discontinued in 1932 and reintroduced in 1940 as the *Loyola Law Review.*

Law students also started a student newspaper called *Pep Juris* at some point in the early 1920s, which was abandoned in 1923 to adopt and support the *Maroon* as the official school newspaper.

Reflecting the national trend, by 1920 the school had begun to suggest that a high school degree might not be enough for admission. The 1920 *Bulletin* specified: "Collegiate training is always desirable, and College credits of at least one year may be demanded should lack of maturity or other deficiencies in the applicant so require."

In 1921, the ABA adopted the first set of standards for legal education.[31] The Root Report standards required two full years of college work for admission to law school and a three-year full-time course of study or its equivalent (for part-time or night programs). The ABA also declared that graduation from law school alone was not sufficient to admit students to the bar—every candidate should be subject to examination by public authority to determine fitness for the practice of law.[32] In 1924, the Louisiana legislature accommodated this ABA requirement and enacted a statute requiring students to pass an examination before being admitted to practice in the state.[33] Law students at Loyola expressed concern through an editorial in the February 1, 1924, *Maroon,* urging the Louisiana legislature not to enact the bill. Application to the law program, the *Maroon* noted next fall, had not been deterred by the prospect of having to pass a bar examination, in addition to successfully completing law studies.

In 1927, the ABA's standard on law school libraries required "not less than 7,500 well-selected, usable volumes . . . owned and controlled by the law school or university."[34] Faculty was to constitute "a sufficient number giving their entire time to the school to ensure actual personal acquaintance and influence with the whole student body," and the teacher-student ratio was a minimum of one to one hundred: "In no case shall the number of such full-time instructors be less than three." The Council would publish the names of law schools in compliance with the standards, labeling them either "Approved" or "Unapproved."[35]

In 1931, the National Conference of Bar Examiners (NCBE) was founded at the suggestion of the ABA's Section on Legal Education, its mission to increase the efficiency of the state boards of admission to the bar, but in response to concerns that too many lawyers were being admitted to the practice of law. Susan Boyd, in her history of the ABA's Section of Legal Education and Admission to the Bar, quotes John T. DeGraff, former chairman of the NCBE, in a 1967 report that discussed the history of the NCBE: "It's hard for us to remember that in those days the main emphasis of the bar was on limitation, on overcrowding, and, to be perfectly frank, the motives of the examiners were not entirely altruistic. I think that each one of them was faced with the problem in his own state where the bar was complaining that they were admitting too many new lawyers, and I think they sought solace and companionship from the examiners in other states."[36] By 1931, when Loyola's law school gained accreditation, the ABA had inspected eighty-four law schools and approved seventy-seven.

At Loyola, the administration took as a model the Jesuit law schools at St. Louis University and Loyola University Chicago.[37] By 1923, President Sullivan reported to the Southern Conference that the school had begun to require some first-year students to complete four years of part-time studies in order to receive their degree.[38] In 1924, both Cage and Kenny left Loyola, and Mark Boatner, also a judge on the Orleans Civil District Court, took over as dean of the law school, and the Reverend John D. Foulkes, S.J., was appointed regent. The school began requiring one year of college for admission.[39] The law school's enrollment increased considerably: its first-year class in 1922–23 numbered 82 (not counting those students enrolled in the pre-legal course); in 1923–24, the first-year class totaled 114. By the third year, however, almost half the class had been eliminated: in 1925–26, there were only 36 seniors in attendance, and in 1926–27, only 77. The school's total enrollment for academic year 1923–24 was 289 (including postgraduate students and pre-legal students).[40] The law faculty still consisted of part-time and uncompensated judges and practitioners, and the law school continued to hold classes at Marquette Hall, a building that had grown too small for the law school; the caption of a photograph of Marquette in the *Law School Bulletin* identifies it the "Law School Building."

In academic year 1925–26, under Dean Boatner, the law school began to offer a full-time, three-year day program and a four-year night program.[41] The school charged $120 for the year (payable thirty dollars per quarter), and generally the cost of books did not exceed thirty dollars.[42] Although the *Bulletin* indicated that only one year of college work was required, in the provisions for the day school, the 1925–26 *Bulletin* notified prospective applicants that: "In accordance with the standards of the Association of American Law Schools and the American Bar Association, students entering upon Law will be required to present credit for two years' work in a College of Arts."[43]

The day classes were scheduled from 8:00 to 11:00 a.m., Monday through Friday. The trend to increase enrollment continued with the entering class for 1924–25 at 126, but the graduating senior class (which would have been made up of the entering class of 1923–24 at 114) was down to less than one-third at 36. The first day class for fall 1925 consisted of 30 students.

The 1926–27 *Bulletin* formally required two years of prior college work for admission to law studies. Classes, day and night, continued to be taught by part-time professionals, something that must have challenged both the institution and the professionals who continued to teach without compensation. The school increased tuition in 1927–28 by twenty dollars, perhaps anticipating the need to begin to hire full-time faculty. The night school continued to be most attractive to applicants: in 1926–27, the entering day class, in its second year of operating, consisted of 15 men and 2 women, as compared to 41 students in the first-year night class (2 of them women). The big jump that year was in the number of seniors set to graduate (77) at the end of that academic year. The curriculum itself does not appear to have changed dramatically, and the course of study continued to be described as the "textbook and lecture system." The school appeared to have dropped any effort to include "skills"- or "practice"-oriented courses, such as that offered by former Dean Cage.

Enrollment dropped in both the day and night courses: the first-year day entering class in 1927–28 numbered 7, and the night entering class consisted of only 11 (including 1 woman). The first senior day class to graduate consisted of 29 graduating students including 3 women. Some of these students had begun in the night program and transferred to the day, a trend that would continue in the years to come. Alfred Bonomo, the school's original secretary and the only compensated person in the administration, was appointed assistant dean and began to be listed as a full-time instructor on the law school faculty.[44] Two other individuals, Sandford E. Owen and Rene J. Waguespack, were listed as full-time instructors as well. Owen and Waguespack appear to have been compensated, and their annual salaries are listed as $2,500.[45]

In 1929–30, the Honorable William H. Byrnes Jr., like all of his predecessors a judge on the Civil District Court for Orleans Parish, became dean of the law school. Judge Byrnes had earned a bachelor of arts degree (AB) from Georgetown and his law degree, an LLB, from Tulane. He had been instrumental in the founding of the University and had taught on the faculty at the law school since its founding. The school also hired a law librarian, and Natalie Phillpott, the first woman to serve in an administrative role at the law school, was chosen as librarian. The entering day class for 1928–29 consisted of 12 young men, of whom one, Leon Sarpy, went on to serve on the law faculty, eventually moving to full-time practice.[46] The 1929–30 entering day class included Robert Andrew Ainsworth Jr., the third Loyola Law graduate to be appointed to the federal bench.[47] President John F. Kennedy appointed Ainsworth to the United States District Court for the Eastern District of Louisiana in 1961. On June 28, 1966, President Lyndon B. Johnson appointed Ainsworth to the United States Court of Appeals for the Fifth Circuit, the second Loyola law graduate to serve on a federal circuit court of appeal.[48] For many years, Loyola sponsored the Judge Robert A. Ainsworth, Jr. Memorial Lecture Series in his honor. The last Ainsworth Lecturer was the Honorable Ruth Bader Ginsburg, United States Supreme Court associate justice.[49]

As a result of Loyola's pursuit of ABA and AALS membership, the AALS conducted an inspection of the school in November 1929. The inspection report noted as deficiencies at the school that the majority of courses were taught by part-time instructors; that full-time faculty/administrators were not really "full-time" at the law school; that the school lacked sufficient office space for faculty-student interactions; concerns over whether the school was consistently applying its admission standards; and concerns over the curriculum in that some core courses received scant attention, in the view of the inspector, like contracts, with the most time and attention devoted to local law courses, the civil code courses. The inspector, H. W. Arant, also found an inordinate focus on memorization, and insufficient exploration of "the economical, sociological, psychological, historical and other factors that cause courts to decide cases," as well as insufficient focus on developing critical analysis and logic.[50]

Whether as a result of the Arant Report or the University's own review of other law schools, 1931 witnessed substantial change at Loyola's law school, still under the deanship of Judge Byrnes, with the Reverend John D. Foulkes, S.J., serving as regent. The law school announced a new course of instruction, completely revised to meet the requirements of the ABA and AALS, which appears to have been modeled after that in use at LSU's law school.[51] The law school moved from Marquette Hall to Bobet Hall, where the school would enjoy six offices for the deans and full-time professors, and a new space for its library with an additional $1,200 worth of new books. Most importantly, perhaps, the school hired three new full-time professors: Frank Hyatt Jr., from LSU; James Connor, with an LLM from Northwestern University; and Antonio Papale, with an LLB from Catholic University. Both Connor and Papale would go on to serve as deans of the law school.[52]

The ABA granted the school accreditation in 1931. Membership in the AALS, however, necessitated greater changes. The law school's announcement of the changes in 1931 in the *Times-Picayune* was telling—it referenced the new system as being "decided upon by Father Foulkes." The lack of a full-time dean familiar with legal education continued to be a stumbling block to membership in the AALS.

To that end, the University hired Paul M. Hebert, former Loyola Law faculty member and on the LSU faculty at the time of his appointment to Loyola, as the first full-time dean of the law school.[53] Hebert had earned an AB and LLB degree from LSU and an SJD from Yale in 1930. He was young at twenty-five, with two years' experience in legal education. His addition meant that the law school had five full-time faculty members. Dean Hebert appears to have taught the same number of courses as other full-time faculty: negotiable instruments, bankruptcy, corporations, taxation, and Louisiana Civil Code. By comparison, Professor Papale taught contracts, sales, equity, and conflict of laws.

More important, the hiring of a full-time legal academic as top administrator of the law school meant that it was no longer led, primarily, by the regent. Announcements at the law school came from the office of the dean, not the regent, so that a September 11, 1932, *Times-Picayune* article reported Dean Hebert's announcement of two new courses at the law school: a general survey of the law and a complete course in taxation; the former apparently designed to respond directly to the criticism of the Arant Report, as it "emphasize[d] the study of the science of jurisprudence and to correlate certain phases of the several branches of the law." Dean Hebert also noted the additional space and resources made available to the law library.[54]

The 1932 inspection, conducted by H. C. Horack on October 31 and November 1, found substantial changes for the better but recommended that the school continue to operate in accordance with AALS guidelines for two years, prior to urging its application for membership in the organization.[55] The focus of the visit was to make sure that the administration, faculty, and course of instruction at Loyola were consistent with those of law schools already members of the AALS. The report singled out the hiring of a full-time dean as meaningful change, reporting that prior to Dean Hebert's hiring, "active management of the school seems to have been in the actual control of the Regent, a member of the Jesuit Order, without law training or experience." The inspector sounded caution, however, as it was too early to determine whether the new dean was "only in nominal control or [wa]s in actual control with power to build up the law school along the lines marked out by modern legal education." Horack found it promising that the dean had direct access to the president and also that the new Loyola president, the Reverend John W. Hynes, S.J., "seems earnest and thoughtful and very desirous of having the school measure up to recognized standards."

The leadership provided by a full-time dean with experience in legal education undoubtedly yielded additional benefits to law students and law faculty, particularly in providing opportunities for professional and academic activities. Law faculty members began to attend the Louisiana State Bar Association as members of a law faculty.[56]

In accordance with Horack's 1932 report, Loyola applied for membership in the AALS in 1934, and Horack returned for another inspection on December 6 and 7, 1934. The school had hired an additional faculty member, for a total of six full-time faculty and eight part-time instructors, most of whom taught only one course. The report showed law school enrollment as between 83 to 87 students, with a deficit from operation each year. Tuition had gone up to $175 for the first year and $170 for the remaining years, with tuition the same for the day and evening divisions. In 1934, $175 was worth $3,106.90 in 2014 dollars, a substantial amount of money for someone making the 1935 hourly wage (between 42 to 78 cents).[57] Most of the school's students were from New Orleans.

This time Horack found the regent's involvement in the administration of the law school minimal and reported that the dean had immediate and active control over the law school, with "direct contact with the President to present any and all matters which concern the administration of the school."[58] Although the report found small deficiencies in secretarial support and in the physical furnishings of the law school, overall Horack found that the school was functioning well, with dean and faculty in control of the school and its curriculum, and operating it in accordance with AALS standards. Although some courses, primarily the civil code courses, still were taught through lectures, the majority of courses were taught through the case method. The report found that the school was, for the most part, fully enforcing its admissions requirements and scholarship standards, finding problematic the fact that most students in two part-time professors' classes earned the grade of A. The report was overwhelmingly positive and recommended that the school be elected for membership in the AALS. Accordingly, the AALS granted membership to Loyola in 1934.

As in many law schools, the tradition of volunteer faculty continued throughout the years and is still in use today, with many practitioners and jurists serving to teach practice-oriented or specialty courses. Many Loyola law graduates, including the Honorable Herbert Christenberry, the Honorable James Skelly Wright, the Honorable Adrian Duplantier, and the Honorable Calvin Johnson, among others, taught Loyola law school students while serving on the bench.

But having faculty who would commit their time and focus fully and primarily to the law school itself and to active scholarship made a great difference to the school and its position in the University and the legal academy—membership in the professional associations gave it not just national (and local) credibility but made it possible for its faculty and student body to benefit from the national conversation on legal education and how to best produce individuals competent and ready for practice. Perhaps because of its origins, squarely in the world of practice, Loyola's law school embraced practice-oriented courses, including skills courses and clinical education, while many in the legal education community lagged behind.

From the University's perspective, it meant subsidizing the law school because law faculty had to be compensated, books bought for the law library, and sufficient space and other support made available. The investment would prove wise, and eventually the law school would, perhaps, double the returns on the investment, something that would benefit the University greatly, sometimes at the law school's expense. But primarily, the law school's accreditation meant full accreditation for Loyola as a whole and acceptance of its undergraduates into other universities' graduate programs.[59]

3

THE LAW SCHOOL IN ITS FORMATIVE YEARS

> The first time that Huey P. Long campaigned in rural, Latin, Catholic south Louisiana, the local boss... said at the beginning of the tour: "Huey, you ought to remember one thing in your speeches today. You're from north Louisiana, but now you're in south Louisiana. And we got a lot of Catholic voters down here." "I know," Huey answered. And throughout the day in every small town Long would begin by saying: "When I was a boy, I would get up at six o'clock in the morning on Sunday, and I would hitch our old horse up to the buggy and I would take my Catholic grandparents to mass. I would bring them home, and at ten o'clock I would hitch the old horse up again, and I would take my Baptist grandparents to church." The effect of the anecdote on the audiences was obvious, and on the way back to Baton Rouge that night the local leader said admiringly: "Why Huey, you've been holding out on us. I didn't know you had any Catholic grandparents." "Don't be a damn fool," replied Huey. "We didn't even have a horse."
>
> —T. HARRY WILLIAMS, *Huey Long*

Notwithstanding the Great Depression, a global economic depression that began in September 1929 and ended at some point in the late 1930s or early 1940s, by 1934 the University had succeeded in the accreditation of its law school with a compensated, full-time faculty and a full-time day and part-time evening program. While the stock market collapsed on Wall Street on October 29, 1929, Adolf Hitler's Nazi party came to power in Germany. In the Pacific, Japan took Manchuria from China in 1931; by 1937, Japan and China were at war, with Japan advancing steadily into China. In 1933, Adolf Hitler became chancellor of Germany. Hitler opened the first concentration camp at Dachau in 1933 and declared himself Führer in 1934. In 1938, Hitler's Germany annexed Austria. The following year, Hitler invaded Poland. The invasion of Poland led Britain and France to declare war on Germany. World War II had begun.

In Louisiana, Huey Long rose to power on a promise to address the needs of the poor and to end the dominion of the oil and gas companies. Long had been admitted to the Louisiana bar the year of the law school's founding. He had attended classes at Tulane briefly, but rather than take advantage of the diploma privilege, he had studied intensely to brave the bar examination without the benefit of a law degree. Unsurprisingly, he passed.

As the law school worked to earn accreditation, Long amassed strong public support, despite the steadfast opposition of Louisiana's wealthy ruling class to his reform agenda, at least to the extent that it called for sharing their wealth. Louisiana voters elected him governor in 1928. Unfazed by his opposition, Long built a Louisiana political machine whose reach persisted long after his death. Many Loyola law graduates were heirs to that machine and legacy, and Loyola itself at times relied on Long for assistance and at times chafed at the reach of his power. The University counted on Long's support in securing a full-time license for its radio station from the Federal Radio Commission in the early 1930s.[1] Loyola granted Governor Long an honorary doctor of laws degree in 1931. The honorary degree was awarded for the state law making free textbooks available to all students, including students at Catholic schools. Loyola historian Bernard Cook contends that in reality it was awarded for his help with the radio station.[2] Long's commitment to making available free textbooks to all Louisiana students, black or white, attending public or private schools, was a significant benefit to Louisiana residents and justified the honor on its own terms.

Long had already been elected U.S. senator, albeit while serving as governor, but he deferred taking his Senate seat until 1932, when he had successfully arranged for a successor as governor. The University was not thrilled, however, when Long's initiatives adversely affected the law school.

In spring 1935, Loyola's Board considered a request by Dean Paul Hebert to be released from his contract to accept an offer of the deanship at LSU Law School. While "desirous of advancing himself . . . [he] expressed himself, if Loyola needed him, as willing to remain with us with perfect good grace and contentment."[3] LSU's push to hire Hebert, the Board stated, arose out of "the activities of Senator Huey P. Long." Long's zeal to enhance the national position of LSU by pouring resources into the university and directly intervening in its administration have been well documented by T. Harry Williams in his Long biography.[4] Several members of the Board strongly opposed allowing Hebert to accept the LSU offer, explaining that "it would be suicidal on our part to let Mr. Hebert go" and that "it would appear to the public as a political sell-out to Long." The Board was unanimous to retain Dean Hebert.[5] The challenge to the law school, of course, was matching the LSU salary offer. That fall, an assassin shot Huey Long in the State Capitol.

LSU persisted, returning with an offer in 1936 to Hebert to become dean of administration of LSU as a whole, not just the law school. Again, Hebert "expressed himself as quite willing to abide by the decision" of the Board, but this time the Board agreed unanimously "that it would not be fair and equitable and honorable to stand in the way of such advancement for a man whom we admire and treasure so much."[6] As his replacement, Hebert had suggested one of the professors already on the faculty, James T. Connor, a graduate of St. Viator College and Northwestern University, whose brother John Connor served as chair of Loyola's department of economics. The Board voted to offer Connor the position of dean for a period of three years at a salary of $4,000 per year.[7] Connor accepted the position and took over as dean in 1936. Local media reported the start of the new academic year with full optimism: "Loyola Foresees Successful Year."[8] Loyola's inability to keep Hebert was prophetic of things to come. No challenge facing the law school throughout the twentieth century was as persistent and consistent as the lack of adequate financial resources.

Connor was not the only change at the law school that year. Leon Sarpy, a Loyola law alumni, replaced Professor McMahon on the law faculty.[9] Mr. Sarpy also acted as law librarian until the law school appointed Solange Mille as law librarian on July 1, 1939. Mille was the first woman to hold a significant leadership position at the law school.

During this time, the law school operated primarily as a local school, its faculty and student body focused on Louisiana law and on its Catholic character. Faculty and deans were expected to be Catholic and to some extent to act consistently with Church doctrine and policies. Thus, Connor in 1939 addressed the community as part of a Catholic Church campaign announced by the archdiocese "to ban indecent literature" and "promote the reading of good literature."[10]

Although led by a full-time dean, the Loyola Board continued to exercise substantial control over the law school. Most activities at the law school appear to have required formal approval by the Board, regardless of how significant. In early years, students established clubs without Board involvement. But, in 1938, when students wanted to establish a chapter of a national legal fraternity at Loyola, the matter came before the Board for approval.[11] Later that year, the matter of student clubs again returned to the Board, when Connor asked for authority to disband the national law fraternity in favor of the Saint Thomas More Club.[12] The Board refused the request "unless additional reasons for doing so were brought forward," suggesting instead that the school "make the two organizations mutually exclusive in their membership."[13]

The first *Law School Bulletin* to recognize student organizations was for the academic year 1937–38. That *Bulletin* lists both the Saint Thomas More Club and the Delta Theta Phi, National Legal Fraternity, as the only student organizations at the law school, so it appears that the students were able to organize first and then seek board approval of the organizations.[14] The St. Thomas More Club, currently known as the St. Thomas More Law Society, was open to all law students, but the Delta Theta Phi was open only to men. By 1940, the law school had a chapter of the national women's legal fraternity, Phi Delta Delta.[15] The law student clubs active during the mid- and late 1920s, the debating society and Alpha Phi Delta and Sigma Nu Phi, appear to have disbanded by the late 1930s.

The Board exercised some degree of control over curriculum. When Dean Connor wanted to initiate a course in the common law at the law school, the request was made through the regent at the time, the Reverend Michael J. Walsh, S.J. The Board concurred that "if Dean Connor thought he could conduct such a course without overburdening his teachers or increasing the expense accounts of his school, he should be given a free hand to develop such a course."[16] Even as slight a matter as the case of a law student requesting to be excused from attending graduation came before the Board.[17]

The Board exercised control over law faculty decisions as well. Law deans had little discretion in the setting of salaries or even in the final selection of faculty. When Connor sought to replace Mr. Bonomo in May 1940, originally hired to serve as secretary at the law school but eventually promoted to the law faculty, the Board denied his request, given Mr. Bonomo's long service to the University and law school, and troubled by the fact that Dean Connor had failed to discuss any perceived problems with Bonomo.[18] The Board's response to Connor was a primer on modern procedural due process, suggesting to the dean that if he wanted to dismiss Bonomo, he give him notice, include a written statement of any problems that Connor had identified, and give him an opportunity over the course of the year to correct the problems.[19] Subsequently, the president appointed Bonomo director of radio script work and educational projects in connection with the University's radio station.[20]

As a practical matter, after accreditation the Board exercised substantial control over the law school, and although the Board tended to defer to the law school dean and faculty on matters of curriculum and, for the most part, the hiring of law faculty, it considered and exercised final decision-making authority over most actions taken at the law school, including hiring and firing of faculty, student organizations, and publications like the law review. By at least 1939, the law school dean was submitting annual budgets for the law school to the president and the Board for approval.[21]

That same May, the Board considered the employment of one of the law school's most esteemed graduates in the Louisiana legal academy, Robert Anthony Pascal. Pascal, the Board considered, "had gone off to do graduate work in Law with the understanding between himself and Connor and the Reverend Gaudin [the former Loyola president] that he would be given a position on the Faculty this coming school year."[22] Pascal, Connor had assumed, could take the position left open by Bonomo.

The Board decided that the president, not the dean of the law school, should confer with Pascal, "and that if Mr. Pascal felt that the University should give him a place on the Faculty there was nothing left for the University to do but so to honor the promises of Father Gaudin; but that if Mr. Pascal wished to seek employment on another Faculty he should feel free to do so."[23] Although the Board minutes report that negotiations with Pascal over salary were proceeding, with the Board authorizing a salary of $2,000 a year,[24] less than that initially promised, Pascal rejected the offer and accepted a position at a law firm.[25] When Connor learned of the outcome, he communicated to the president profound regret since "Pascal is one in a thousand and his like will not be turned out in our School of Law for another generation."[26]

Pascal went on to a highly successful career as a scholar and law professor at the LSU School of Law, where he inadvertently created some tension between the law school and the University administration. The incident also exemplifies the degree to which law faculty were expected to adhere to the positions of the Catholic Church during this period. In May 1948, the new law school regent, the Reverend Louis J. Twomey, S.J., responded in defense of the law school to a charge that its graduates were not adhering to Catholic dogma. The incident involved the work of James A. Bugea, a Loyola law faculty member, and Pascal, by that time at LSU working with LSU law professor Harriet Daggert on revisions to Louisiana's law on divorces. The Catholic Church wanted "to remove all divorce laws from the statutes of our state," which was Bugea's aim as well. In fact, Bugea "has taken no step without prior consultation with Monsignor Plauche [the chancellor of the archdiocese]."[27] The legislation actually proposed as a result of the revisions, however, was not to the Church's liking, and the president wrote to Father Twomey in complaint. Twomey's response, while not offering staunch adherence to the principle of academic freedom, made it clear that if Pascal's suggestions had not been consistent with Catholic teachings, they had been made "in spite of his training in the Loyola Law School," not because of it. Bugea, meanwhile, would continue to consult with the chancellor of the archdiocese in his work on the revisions.

The law school had missed an opportunity when it failed to persuade Pascal to join the law faculty. In his stead, the Board approved the employment of John J. McAulay, another recent Loyola law graduate. McAulay, however, the Board suggested, should be offered a salary of from $1,600 to $1,700.[28] Subsequent efforts to persuade Pascal to join the faculty at Loyola proved unsuccessful.

Despite the financial strictures under which the law school operated, Connor and Loyola's small but full-time faculty devoted considerable energy to legal reforms and enhancement of the school's program and reputation. During this period, deans continued to teach a full load of courses, in addition to their administrative duties.[29] Connor participated in the formation and work of the Louisiana State Law Institute (LSLI), formed by act of the Louisiana legislature in 1938 to consider reform and revisions to Louisiana law.[30] The legislature envisioned the LSLI as an entity that would act in collaboration with the legislature to advise it on the advisability of reforms and changes to Louisiana law. Six Loyola law faculty served in the original Council of the LSLI.[31] Connor put Pascal, then a young Loyola Law student about to graduate, to work on LSLI matters.

Connor also served as commissioner for Louisiana to the National Conference of Commissioners on Uniform State Laws (National Conference) in 1939. The National Conference arose from the efforts of the ABA to develop uniform national legal standards in various subject matter areas for the states to consider and adopt. As Connor explained in an article written to educate the New Orleans community as to the work of the commissioners, published in the city's daily newspaper: "Business and commerce is nationwide rather than statewide. . . . The growth of the automotive industry with its attendant system of nationwide highways has contributed its part to the unification of the nation and its people. . . . So long as individual state legislatures continue to enact laws effective only within their respective borders but upon subjects of national significance it was apparent that conflicts and controversies would arise."[32]

As Connor explained to his readers, in 1889 the ABA had proposed a committee to act in an "advisory capacity and as a clearing house of ideas among the states," and in 1890 New York led the other states in appointing commissioners to come up with uniform legislation on a number of subjects. Louisiana had provided for its commissioners in 1902, and the first appointed to serve were the three Louisiana law deans: Loyola's Connor, Robert Lee Tullis, dean emeritus of LSU law school, and Dr. Paul Brosman, dean of Tulane's law school. In 1940, Connor was appointed chair of the Committee on Public Information of the National Conference.

In addition, Loyola law faculty members began to participate in AALS activities and annual meetings. In 1936, Foulkes, then law school regent and secretary to the Loyola Board, reported attending the AALS annual meeting in New Orleans during Christmas week. At the time Tulane's dean served as president of the AALS. Loyola had offered to co-host the meeting with Tulane, and apparently Tulane had agreed. Although the Loyola law faculty was eager to participate in the AALS committees, Foulkes regretted that "our Faculty men were left entirely off all of the committees."[33]

Subsequently, however, both Connor and law faculty member Vernon X. Miller became more active in AALS proceedings, as the school authorized their attendance at AALS meetings. Miller had joined the Loyola law faculty in September 1938, at that time a full-time faculty of six, including Bonomo, Papale, Sarpy and John Mort Walker, Jr. Miller's credentials were strong. He was a graduate of the law school at the University of Minnesota and had earned an SJD (doctorate of law) in 1929 from Yale. Miller would become the first and only Loyola law faculty member to be elected to the Executive Committee of the AALS, serving as president of the organization the year after his departure from Loyola. Connor served on the Nominating Committee for the Executive Committee of the AALS.[34]

In addition to its six full-time faculty, the school benefited from the services of eight part-time volunteer faculty including Judge William Byrnes Jr., former dean and original law faculty member. Fourteen faculty members taught a total enrollment for the 1938–39 academic year of 98 day and evening students.[35] By this time, law faculty met on a regular monthly basis, and two faculty committees, the library administration committee and the special students committee, were established at the law school.

The law school expected some scholarship from its faculty, but when Dean Connor reported to the president on faculty publications that more had not been done, he explained that "law teaching requires constant attention to new developments... which make heavy demands upon the Faculty in the preparation of their class work and... because of meager stenographic assistance and negligible research assistance." Connor urged that such assistance be provided, for "there is no other medium which brings so much prestige to the School of Law and... to the University as a whole."

The school also sought to improve the strength of its entering classes, as well as the discipline of its students. Faculty exacted discipline through a variety of measures, including pecuniary ones. The law school charged students taking make-up examinations five dollars. The practice of taking make-ups had become so prevalent that the faculty felt the need for a financial sanction "to prevent this practice from becoming an abuse."[36]

By 1939, the law school had begun to hold annual moot court competitions between the Delta Theta Phi Legal Fraternity and the Saint Thomas More Law Club. This early moot court competition appears to have been wholly local and more in the nature of a trial than an appellate moot court competition.[37]

In fall 1939, as Europe endured the horrors unleashed by Nazi Germany, the law school formed the Loyola Law School of the Air, to be broadcast over the University's radio station, WWL. Faculty member Antonio Papale served as director, and during its life the Loyola Law School of the Air presented programs on, for example, the oil industry in Louisiana (airing October 19, 1939); the Social Security Act (November 2, 1939), and the life of Chief Justice Edward Douglass White (November 16, 1939). In his report to the president, Dean Connor complained that the law school had "not enjoyed the kind of cooperation from some of the staff of the radio station... [who] seem to view the activity as definitely 'second rate' the function of which is only a 'fill-in.'"[38] Loyola Law School of the Air went on to produce programs on government control of business, the National Labor Relations Act, a dramatization of the Langles case,[39] and a dramatization of the life of Edward Livingston.[40] The Loyola Law School of the Air ceased to exist in spring 1940. The last broadcast appears to have been "The Signing of the Magna Carta." The law school continued to provide programs as part of the *University Time* radio program series.

Connor also initiated the practice of writing directly to law alumni with a view to fund-raising activities. His first letter to the alumni went out on November 7, 1938, and its purpose was to fully inform alumni about the state of the law school, the facilities available to them for their use, and some of the problems facing the law school, such as the need for "a separate building devoted exclusively to the School of Law."[41]

After its opening at the College of the Immaculate Conception on Baronne Street, the law school spent most of its early years in Marquette Hall. Gaining accreditation meant a move to Bobet Hall, where the law school soon found itself at odds with other departments using the building, including athletes on the field adjacent to Bobet. Students practicing athletics tended to be loud, and, the law school complained, their activities disrupted classes. As the law school enrollment had grown, so had its need for space, not just for classes but also for law faculty and staff office space, as well as the library. The solution was to provide a building for the law school's sole use. The University decided to renovate an existing structure, a former private residence on St. Charles Avenue, to accommodate law school needs. For a brief period between its move from Bobet to Thomas More Hall, the law school was housed at the Old Biever Hall.[42] As the renovations began, the law school regent, Father Walsh, urged the president to "go into the plans more fully with the Dean and Acting Dean of the Law school." The law school wanted a two-story building rather than a one-story structure, but the president was concerned about the additional expense to renovating a two-story building.[43] The law school was able to convince the president that they needed the space.

The naming of Thomas More Hall was the subject of a contest by the Alpha Sigma Nu Fraternity. Of the student-submitted names, the Board selected two as winners: William Byrnes Hall and John St. Paul Hall. Notwithstanding, the Board chose a different name altogether for the new building: Thomas More Hall, in honor of St. Thomas More, the patron saint of lawyers.[44] Connor, still serving in the Army, objected to the naming of Thomas More Hall on the grounds that St. Thomas More had practiced the common law, not the civil law "as it is followed in Louisiana."[45] The law school building today houses a memorial to St. Thomas More, erected during the deanship of John Makdisi in academic year 1997–98.

In early fall of 1940, the University granted Connor leave to serve in the Army. The United States instituted the Selective Training and Service Act of 1940 on September 16, 1940, and Connor appears to have been one of the first to be called to duty.[46] The act required all men between the ages of twenty-one and forty-five to register for the draft. Connor suggested Vernon Miller as acting dean, and although the Board considered several individuals presented by the regent of the law school, Father Walsh,[47] the Board chose Miller to replace Connor, who returned briefly for a term in 1941, after his initial release. In February 1942, Connor returned to active duty and Miller became acting dean again. Miller continued to serve as dean until his departure in 1951.

The war in Europe and Asia had an impact on enrollment. The law school graduated 20 students in June 1941.[48] Total enrollment at the school that year was eighty-seven.

Japan attacked Pearl Harbor on December 7, 1941. Life in the United States changed when it formally entered the war. The Board minutes for its first meeting after the attack on Pearl Harbor reflect the Board's consensus that "the University should hold itself ready to cooperate with the Government in every possible way."[49] The University and law school began plans to abridge courses and to face serious enrollment shortfalls as a result of the war.[50] The law school anticipated possible cessation of the day school on account of the draft because it expected most law school students would be affected,[51] and it determined that the best course of action was to conform to the responses of the other law schools in the state. The Board deferred action on whether to accelerate the curriculum until the Commission on Higher Education of the Southern Association of Colleges and Secondary Schools had considered the matter. Ultimately, the Board adopted a plan to accelerate its academic programs by conducting two regular semesters of sixteen weeks each, with twelve weeks of summer school divided into two six-week periods. Entering first-year classes were to start in the summer "so as to begin acceleration at once."[52] The accelerated program would allow law students to complete the three-year full-time day course in six trimesters over the course of two calendar years. Night students would complete the law course in three calendar years, rather than the normal four-year program. The law school began its accelerated program in academic year 1942–43.[53]

All Loyola colleges were expected to respond to the war crisis. The University appointed a committee to make recommendations of a practical nature to assist the war effort by promoting the war on the educational front.[54] At the law school, this meant offering a course in military law open to law students in its first semester, and to all University students in its second semester.

During the war years, Connor lost the support of the faculty, apparently over his style of leadership. The matter came to light when Connor attempted to retain the position of dean while serving in the military. The Board politely refused his request, and Acting Dean Miller continued as dean.[55] Notwithstanding his falling out with the faculty, Connor's leadership of the law school was strong and beneficial to the institution. He advocated strenuously for his faculty and for the law school; he was vigorously engaged in national, regional, and local professional associations; and despite his teaching load and professional engagements, he continued to publish and write for a variety of venues. The loss of his services as dean did not negatively affect the law school because his successor was strong in his own right.

During Vernon X. Miller's tenure, the Board continued to play a meaningful role in the decision making for law school matters.[56] As predicted, law school enrollment dropped substantially during the war years. Miller's first report to the president on February 8, 1941, signaled the change: he reported that the starting enrollment of 83 had dropped to 72 by the end of the year.[57] In September 1942, Miller recommended only 4 students to the Board for the degree of bachelor of laws; total enrollment in 1942-43 dropped to 45.[58] The Board minutes for October 5, 1942, report a drop in student enrollment at the law school of 52.4 percent, the highest drop in enrollment for all the colleges.[59] The draft, up to that point, had applied only to twenty-one-year-olds. In November 1942, the Board noted pending federal legislation changing the age for the draft to eighteen, and worried over what this might mean to the University during the coming years. Further collaboration with the Armed Forces was envisioned, including the establishment of a chemical warfare school at Loyola for civilian defense.[60]

In view of the drop in enrollment, Miller asked the president and Board to consider allowing women to be admitted to the undergraduate programs, to facilitate their admission to the law school. Most of the law school's students, he noted, took their pre-legal work at Loyola. For Loyola to refuse women admission to the undergraduate program, he explained, would have an adverse effect on law school admissions. He cautioned the Board: "I believe that we must recognize that in the future women will enroll in the law schools of the country in increasing numbers. The law schools' functions will not be merely to train persons to practice law, but to train persons for some of the branches of the public service."[61] He concluded, "I wish that it could be the policy of the University to encourage the registration of women in the Arts College as pre-legal students." Miller's advice went unheeded.

In 1942, Miller asked the Board for permission to institute a Council of the School of Law. The Board concurred.[62] The Council was composed of representatives from the student body and the faculty and appears to have been the precursor to the current student body association, the Student Bar Association (SBA).[63] The Student Bar Association, a member of the American Law Student Association, was established ten years later in spring 1952 and was recognized in the *Law School Bulletin* for academic year 1952–53.

Like his predecessor, Miller sought to institute a course in the common law to attract out-of-state students. The Board approved the course and some expenditures but refused to authorize hiring an additional faculty member to teach the course. The proposed salary, $6,500, the Board explained, "is contrary to the scale for salaries established in the law school."[64] Miller could hire a new professor to teach the common law, but the salary would have to be within the salaries established for the law school. That those salaries were inadequate to attract candidates competitive at the national level did not preoccupy the Board.

In 1940 the state contemplated removing authority for admission to the bar from the Louisiana Supreme Court to an elected board of governors. The proposal was not successful, and control over admission to the bar remained with the Louisiana Supreme Court, as it does today. During the war years, however, veterans were granted relief from the bar examination; all military personnel were granted the "diploma privilege" that had been abandoned in the early decades of the twentieth century.

Bar performance by law school graduates continued to disappoint; the law school's results tended to place it third when considered against the other law schools in the state. Miller reported to the president in fall 1942: "Forty two persons took the examinations including ten of our own graduates. Eight of these were successful. The two men who failed were good students. We do not try to explain their failures. I would recommend either one of them as a good prospect for any law firm."[65]

The Louisiana bar examination, in Miller's view, produced somewhat arbitrary results. He noted in October 1944:

> During the summer five of our graduates and certified special students took bar examinations, four in Louisiana and one in New York. Two of the four passed and the one applicant in New York passed his examinations. The results in the recent Louisiana bar examinations among law school people show no uniformity. Three persons from Louisiana State University took the examinations and all of them failed. Three from Tulane took the examinations and all of them passed. The people from Tulane [must have meant LSU] were unusually good students. They should have passed. One of our two failures is a good man. He should have passed. The other person from Loyola who failed was a mediocre law student. He was able to pass his courses in the law school with nothing to spare and he made no special preparation for the bar examination. This man who failed earned also four credits in the law school at Tulane.[66]

Prior to his departure, Dean Connor had proposed publishing a law review again. The new publication would not be a reincarnation of the original *Loyola Law Journal* but a law review more along the lines of other law review publications. Connor sought the support of the president because the publication required financial support until it became self-supporting.[67] Publication of the new law review began in academic year 1940–41.[68] Upon his return from military service for a term, Connor reported to the president that the faculty had determined that "too many of the contemporary United States law reviews purport to be put out by the faculty and students of the school whose name it bears... [but] strive by every device to secure manuscripts from 'name' scholars."[69] Loyola's law review, the Dean stated, would be different, publishing primarily Loyola law faculty publications: "Only in exceptional circumstances would contributions from other scholars be sought or accepted."[70]

Miller echoed Connor's sentiments concerning the need for faculty resources in his communications to the president; he stressed that law faculty could not produce quality scholarship for the review while dealing with heavy teaching responsibilities. At the time the school had 68 students registered at the law school, 32 in the day and 36 in the night division, with only four full-time faculty. Miller noted the impact of offering the accelerated program and explained to the president that this meant that in order to produce the law review, law faculty had to make contributing to the law review their priority, second only to teaching.

By February 1943, almost two years after the United States entered the war, law school enrollment was down to 38, with only two full-time faculty members, one of them the dean.[71] Like students, law faculty had gone into the service. In fall of 1945, after the war ended, the enrollment at the law school began to return to prewar numbers.[72] In spring 1946, Miller reported to the president that the law school could expect an enrollment of up to 100 students for fall 1946.[73] The school started the 1947–48 academic term with an enrollment of 131 students, 77 of them in the day division.[74] By 1948, Thomas More Hall had proved too small to accommodate the student enrollment. Dean Miller noted 165 students enrolled at the law school that year, "a heavy load for our building."[75]

Nineteen forty-nine was a banner year for the law school, which welcomed the largest student body since earning membership in the AALS, with 183 enrolled students, at least 5 of them women, including Janet Mary Riley. Miller had hired Riley as law librarian in 1945, replacing Solange Mille. He had encouraged Riley to attend law classes while she served as law librarian and had supported her request for an increase in salary later in 1949. When she completed law studies, Miller urged Loyola's president to consider employing her as an assistant professor in law.[76] In 1950, however, the Korean War precipitated a loss in enrollment.[77]

Throughout Miller's tenure, as throughout Connor's, the law faculty engaged actively in regional, local, and national organizations, including the AALS, the ABA, and the Louisiana and New Orleans Bar Associations. In the postwar years, the Board approved the employment of six full-time faculty, the number of law faculty employed at the start of the war. Miller experienced difficulty finding the "sixth man." The problem appears to have been that the faculty member had to be Catholic, hold a graduate degree, and be happy to relocate to New Orleans for a Loyola salary.[78]

On issues to do with the curriculum, Miller, in explaining to the president why a particular undergraduate instructor had not worked out as an instructor at the law school, conveyed a view of Louisiana's civil law: "Louisiana law is peculiar, and even in those fields where the Civil Law is important, Louisiana law is intensely practical. It is not civilian in the same sense that continental law may be."[79] This question concerning the extent to which Louisiana's legal heritage under the French and Spanish civil codes meant that it had a uniquely distinct legal system from that found in the rest of the states, even those with a similar civil law heritage like California, the Southwest, and Florida, continued to be a source of tension for the Louisiana law schools, including Loyola, as well as for the Louisiana bar. To date, this view of Louisiana law is the basis for administering a bar examination process for admission to the Louisiana bar that is completely different from that used by the other forty-nine states.

Miller also expressed views concerning Loyola's night school. Enrollment in the night program, he acknowledged, often fell below that of the day program. He explained to then Loyola president the Reverend Thomas Shields, S.J.:

> Enrollment in this division never will be large. Many people who want to study law at night do not have the pre-legal requirements. . . . The night school program is rugged and many students who do enroll cannot keep up with it. That is why so many students withdraw from the evening division. But our night school is a necessity. Without it we would invite competition from sub-standard proprietary schools. The night school helped us during the war. We have graduated some good people from it and they are our friends.[80]

The challenge of maintaining a separate program for a small group of students was being felt. The law school may have been under pressure to discontinue the program. Later in 1949, he expressed strong sentiments for maintaining the evening program despite the fact that it "costs us more than we get out of it through tuition."[81] He continued: "We think we must keep it. We do offer a service to a relatively small number of good people in the community and we cannot afford to open the evening school field to a sub-standard school." He reminded the president that it was due to the evening division that the school had managed to survive during the war years.

Among the matters discussed in faculty meetings was a proposal to raise the number of years required for admission to the law school from two to three years. The faculty was concerned about the immaturity of many of the students.[82] During this period, the school changed the total number of hours required to earn the bachelor of laws degree. Prior to 1946, students had to complete 72 credit hours in order to graduate. Between 1946 and 1948, the school increased the minimum number of hours required to graduate to 75. Students entering the law school in fall 1948, however, had to earn a minimum of 78 credit hours to graduate with a law degree.[83] The law school, like many other law schools, set a higher number of credit hours for the degree than suggested by the ABA or AALS.

Miller also thought the appointment of the Reverend Louis J. Twomey, S.J., as law school regent in 1948 felicitous:

> There is something else which I think helps to make this the best year we have had since I have been at Loyola. Father Twomey is working with us to make this law school something more than a professional school. We are becoming a Catholic law school. . . . Although some of us on this faculty have been working toward that goal, I doubt that we could have gone far without the guidance and support that Father Twomey's presence in this school gives us. And I might add that it is not everyone of the Fathers who could have helped me as Father Twomey has. He and I understand one another as few co-administrators do.[84]

In 1948, Loyola dealt comprehensively with the question of faculty salaries, which as regards the law school, the Board determined, were out of step with those of other professional schools. At the time, the law school employed three law faculty on a ten-month basis: Antonio Papale had been earning $4,800; James A. Bugea, $4,300 and John McAulay, $3,800. The Board approved an increase for the 1948–49 academic year on a ten-month basis of $5,400 for Papale; $4,850 for Bugea, and $4,300 for McAulay.[85]

But when the University raised tuition in 1948 for most of the programs, law tuition was left at $350 per year.[86] Salary issues continued to be a problem for the law school, and it came to the forefront again over the question of retaining Miller, who had been offered initially $12,000 to serve as dean at another Jesuit law school. The Board confessed to being mystified at how the schools were in a position to make such offers.[87] Unable to match the $15,000 offered by the University of San Francisco (USF) law school, almost double

Miller's salary at Loyola, the school lost Vernon X. Miller to USF; Miller would become president of the AALS in 1951.[88]

In his stead, the Board appointed Antonio Papale the new dean at the law school.[89] Papale had joined the Loyola faculty in 1931 as an associate professor after earning an undergraduate degree in law in 1928 from the University of Pennsylvania and a doctorate in law from Catholic University in 1931. He had been promoted to full professor in 1932 and served as assistant dean under Dean Miller.

In 1950, Miller informed the president about the ABA requirement that approved schools require applicants to have completed three years of pre-law or undergraduate studies beginning in fall 1952.[90] The school began to recruit applicants from out of state. Father Twomey, in particular, traveled to Jesuit parishes in Georgia and Florida. The law school began to develop a dual curriculum to cater both to Louisiana applicants intending to stay in Louisiana, and students from other states with an interest in the common law.[91]

Miller advised the president that the school was considering adopting an honor system for examinations. They were not asking for approval yet but thought "there is something missing in a Catholic law school when the honor system is not observed."[92]

The year Miller left, Loyola adopted a system of tenure.[93] University and law faculty benefited from national recognition of the principles of tenure and academic freedom. The American Association of University Professors' (AAUP) "1940 Statement of Principles on Academic Freedom and Tenure" laid the groundwork for national acceptance by both secular and many faith-based colleges and universities that in order to thrive as institutions of higher education, faculty, including law faculty, had to be free to engage fully within their area of expertise and exercise autonomy and independence in scholarship and teaching.[94] In the post–World War II years, when the country faced the turmoil of the McCarthy era and the Cold War, universities accepted the principle that faculty had a meaningful role to play in academic decision making, and tenure and academic freedom principles became established attributes of American higher education.[95]

Although the Board approved recognition of tenure at Loyola in 1950, a formal policy on tenure was not part of University process until several years later, when the first *Faculty Handbook* was formulated and published in 1956. At that time, Loyola was composed of six schools or colleges, including the

School of Law. The early version of the *Handbook* also included the protection of academic freedom, with provisions that made it unclear the extent to which faculty enjoyed full academic freedom to teach in areas that departed from "the teaching of the Catholic Church."[96]

Whether as a result of the abandonment of the regent system, to come in 1955, changes in legal education and Jesuit institutions in general, or the growing professionalization of the legal academy, more of the decision making at the law school was made by the law school in the latter half of the twentieth century than in the first half. Budgets, faculty, and decanal hiring and salaries tended to be decisions ultimately made by the University, but much of the administration of the law school came within the control of the law school itself. Continuing concerns about budgeting and resources at the law school eventually led to a more formal financial relationship between the law school and the University.

As Miller left in 1951, the country faced another war, and the school experienced a drop in enrollment and instituted an accelerated program much as had been adopted during World War II. With only one exception, none of the deans' reports filed during this era reflect, consider, discuss, or memorialize the most momentous question that the institution faced in the decade before and the one to come: the admission of African Americans. Only Papale's first report of November 6, 1951, reminds Loyola's president that he will receive a copy of the report of the Special Committee on Racial Discrimination from the president of the AALS. Papale makes clear to the president that the law faculty "will want to vote in favor of the recommendation of the committee." He ends his report with a final admonition: "If the recommendation is adopted by the Association I suggest that you weigh carefully its implications and instruct me accordingly."[97] It would take considerable advocacy and efforts to persuade the New Orleans Society of Jesus leadership to change its mind about segregation.

4

ENDING RACIAL SEGREGATION

> The problems attendant desegregation in the deep South are considerably more serious than generally appreciated in some sections of our country. The problem of changing a people's mores, particularly those with an emotional overlay, is not to be taken lightly. It is a problem which will require the utmost patience, understanding, generosity and forbearance from all of us, of whatever race. But the magnitude of the problem may not nullify the principle. And that principle is that we are, all of us, freeborn Americans, with a right to make our way, unfettered by sanctions imposed by man because of the work of God.
>
> —*Bush v. Orleans Parish School Board* (1956)

> We can admit colored students to Loyola if we want to do it.
>
> —DEAN VERNON X. MILLER to Rev. Joseph H. Fichter, 1947

Before the Civil War, New Orleans had enjoyed what some perceived as a more hospitable posture toward an integrated society than other southern cities, with a robust and active free black presence in the city that suggested that its acceptance of Reconstruction might be amenable to real integration of blacks and whites. As some scholars have suggested, that hospitality may have hidden a one-way acceptance premised on white male superiority that tolerated or accepted white male/black women relationships, and white employer/black servant relationships but no others. Whether through the implacable adherence to male white supremacy, a principle adhered to not just by men but by some women, or because of federal abandonment of full equality for blacks, segregation took hold in the city and state. The easiness of New Orleans society might have led some to expect that the commitment to segregation would be less fervent in the city than elsewhere in the Deep South. Whether because of its leadership, its student body, its Catholic nature, or its commitment to the public interest, Loyola's law school abandoned segregation in the early 1950s with little trauma and almost no public opposition.[1] Not so the public schools of New Orleans and not so the city.

Perhaps no event played as significant a role in the push to integrate blacks into American society as World War II. The war brought racial discrimination into national view, not just because of events overseas but within the United States itself. Hitler's political philosophy hinged on premises about race; rejection of Nazi Germany at some level involved rejection of the morality of a legal or political system that declared one race superior to others and justified the segregation and genocide of others.[2] On the West Coast of the United States, the government's exclusion and internment of Japanese Americans forced the country to examine its racial attitudes in a context other than one linked to slavery.[3] During the war, the words "Japanese internment" were more likely to have evoked images of Americans interned in Japanese camps overseas than of Americans of Japanese origin interned in camps within the United States. News articles make clear, however, that even during the war, Americans had cause to understand that exclusion of American citizens from the Pacific Coast and their internment in camps in the United States had much to do with racial bias and prejudice. Even far from the West Coast, at Loyola, when the institution was asked to host Japanese American students to allow them to continue their studies, something impossible to do in the internment camps, it decided to deny admission to the Nisei youths.[4]

The military played a meaningful role in ending segregation. Although the Armed Forces were segregated during the war, in 1948 President Truman issued an executive order ending segregation in the armed forces, as well as in the federal government.[5] President Truman, the same president to appoint Loyola Law graduates Herbert W. Christenberry and James Skelly Wright to the United States District Court for the Eastern District of Louisiana, had set the nation on a course incompatible with that established in southern society. Acknowledging the role that private but publicly sanctioned violence played in maintaining entrenched racism in the South, President Truman urged Congress to pass an antilynching bill that it had been considering for over a decade.

The U.S. Supreme Court was also working its way through the repercussions of *Plessy v. Ferguson* and cases that had signaled to the South that it was free to continue its policies of violent racial repression and segregation. The National Association for the Advancement of Colored People (NAACP) in a number of contexts continued to challenge the Court's earlier facilitation of established racial oppression.[6] As at Loyola, desegregation of public institutions began in law schools and other professional programs, and the cases challenging segregation in public institutions in state and federal courts mirrored the discussion being pursued in the halls of Louisiana's only Catholic law school, and the only Jesuit law school in the Deep South. As a private, religious institution, Loyola's own segregation policies were unlikely to be the subject of litigation. Louisiana law did not mandate segregation at private educational institutions; in fact, at the time, Louisiana law did not mandate racial segregation in public educational institutions.[7] Loyola was free to admit African Americans or to continue to deny them admission. Tulane University, for example, resisted integration well into the 1960s.[8] The fact that law did not yet require educational institutions to desegregate, however, made it possible for Loyola to hesitate, and even delay the admission of black young men and women.

R. Bentley Anderson has described at length the efforts to desegregate the Catholic Church and Catholic institutions in New Orleans, including Loyola, in *Black, White, and Catholic: New Orleans Interracialism, 1947–1956*.[9] Anderson's work and Bernard Cook's history of Loyola make clear, moreover, that the Jesuits in charge of the University and the New Orleans province were torn on the question and for the most part resisted integration.

The law school played a unique role in the abandonment of segregation in New Orleans and Louisiana institutions. In successfully integrating its student body in 1952, the law school made it clear that even in the Deep South black and white young adults could and would go to school together without disruption to themselves, their studies, or their community, something that is self-evident today, but that segregationists at the time rejected.

Plainly, not all Loyola law graduates supported integration; just as plain, the law school was indisputably one of the earliest institutions in New Orleans to voluntarily stop discriminating on the basis of race, something that would not have happened without the support of the law dean and faculty. Many of the school's graduates, including Herbert Christenberry, Lolis Elie, Norman Francis, Moon Landrieu, Jack Nelson, Janet Mary Riley, and J. Skelly Wright, took leadership roles in ending racial segregation. Unsurprisingly, it was the first white Louisiana law school to voluntarily admit African Americans. Unsurprising as well, perhaps, is that its road to integration took a tortuous and lengthy path.

THE LAW SCHOOL: ON THE PATH TO INTEGRATION

The Supreme Court moved slowly but steadily in dismantling segregation in law schools. In *Missouri ex rel. Gaines v. Canada,* decided in 1938, the Court held that Missouri could not exclude blacks from its public law school because it did not otherwise provide for an equal in-state legal education for blacks.[10] Thus, *Gaines* established the principle that states that provided whites an in-state legal education were required to provide blacks with an in-state legal education as well.

Louisiana's flagship university, LSU, provided the only public legal education in the state, and admission to LSU was open only to whites. In 1946, Charles Hatfield sued to be admitted to LSU's law school.[11] The court dismissed the case, reasoning that the complaint should have included Southern University, the state's university for blacks, despite the fact that it did not have a law school at the time. In the court's view, the appropriate remedy for black students seeking a legal education in the state was not to admit them to the state law school but to have the state black institution set up, fairly immediately, a law school for blacks. Louisiana's Board of Education decided to preserve LSU as a white-only law school and, with the help of former Loyola dean and then dean of LSU Law School, Paul M. Hebert, set up Southern Law School to open in fall 1947.[12] W. Lee Hargrave, in his history of LSU Law School, claims that its law faculty voted to deny admission to a black candidate later in 1948. Mr. Turner, Hargrave writes, applied for admission to LSU Law School in 1948, arguing that he would not be entitled to an exemption from the state bar exam if he graduated from Southern, since Southern at the time was not accredited. Thus, in order to get a substantially equal education to that afforded whites, he should be admitted to LSU Law School. The law faculty did not agree.[13]

By 1950 a significant number of professional associations in the South had "dropped the color bar." Social workers, nurses, and librarians had led the way, and at least six southern states had bar associations that accepted African Americans as members, including Louisiana.[14] The experience of Louisiana librarians illustrates the challenges of integrating even institutions that were open and willing to change.

Janet Mary Riley served as a member and on the Board of Editors of the *Bulletin* published by the Louisiana Library Association. When the Association debated in 1947 whether to accept African Americans as members on the understanding that they would not be admitted to the annual meeting, she moved to amend that they be accepted as members without limitation. The motion passed, and the Louisiana Library Association became an organization open to whites and nonwhites. Riley wrote about the problems that state and municipal segregation laws posed for the organization in the *Library Journal* of September 15, 1950.[15] In her piece she concluded that there were few to no legal impediments except "the state law requiring separate entrances and ticket offices for circuses, shows, and tent exhibitions, and the New Orleans ordinance prohibiting the sale of alcoholic beverages to both races." The real problem lay with the reception they might meet at the hands of the community or the police:

> But under the police power and duty of maintaining order, any boisterousness at an interracial gathering could result in an arrest for disturbing the peace, as at any gathering of one race only. An overeager sheriff might hear a disturbance in what the participants considered reasonable moderation. In New Orleans about a year ago, sixty persons were arrested for disturbing the peace while attending an interracial social at a private home. They were found not guilty on appeal. I don't think any of us expect the addition of Negro members to our meeting to have any effect on the character of these conventions. . . . It is hard to imagine the Louisiana Library Association disturbing the peace.[16]

More practical problems consisted of finding meeting space open to biracial meetings and hospitable cities. Louisiana law might not prohibit restaurants and public places from serving blacks and whites together, but most establishments in the South at this time denied service to blacks, if they were open to whites. Generally, biracial groups avoided meetings where food was served.[17]

The first documented effort to integrate the law school came in 1942, approximately six months after the attack on Pearl Harbor and the United States' entry into World War II. The Loyola Board noted the "very persistent movement fostered by the American Association for the Advancement of the Colored Race to force negro students into white schools, and . . . cited an instance in which considerable pressure was exercised in regard to the Law School of

Loyola."[18] In addition, one of the Board members stated that the federal government insisted that "no discrimination of race or creed be made in their Aeronautics courses."[19] The Board appears to have felt caught in a vise: "It was the sense of the board that we should be on our guard at the University, and at the same time be very careful not to give offense. The Board felt that it would be the ruination of our University to admit colored students as long as the laws and customs of the South are what they are."[20]

It is possible that the law school sought to admit African Americans because enrollment was suffering greatly as a result of the war. It is also likely that most law faculty and students had concluded segregation was morally untenable and change desirable and inevitable. Vernon Miller was acting dean for most of the war years, while Connor served in the military. If Miller's views and actions at Loyola after the war in the late 1940s are any indication, it is likely that Miller supported the admission of African Americans to Loyola at the time. It is also likely that the pressure to admit African Americans came primarily from external forces like the NAACP.[21] Whatever the views and desires of the law school in 1942, the Board rejected any effort to admit African Americans at this time. And it is clear that the Jesuits, not the dean or faculty, controlled the answer to the question whether blacks would be admitted to the law school. Two Jesuits who joined Loyola in 1947 made the difference.

The Reverend Joseph H. Fichter, S.J., a professor of sociology, joined Loyola in 1947. From the start, Fichter aggressively sought to integrate Loyola. In fact, he planned for Loyola's integration prior to arriving at Loyola. In November 1947, Dean Miller responded to Father Fichter's inquiry as to whether the law school could admit blacks. Miller made it clear that state law posed no problem to Loyola's integration.[22] Loyola Board minutes for November 29, 1947, note an effort by Fichter to initiate a seminar for students from both Xavier and Loyola to discuss interracial problems. His dean made it clear to the Board that he had already "informed him that the negro students of Xavier could not be granted credit by Loyola University and further informed him that he would have to see the President of Loyola since the bringing of negro students to such a seminar involves the matter of administrative policy on the part of the university."[23] Fichter formed what would become the Southeastern Regional Interracial Commission (SERINCO), under the auspices of the National Federation of Catholic College Students, with students from various Catholic colleges to oppose segregation.[24]

The Reverend Louis J. Twomey, S.J., also joined Loyola in 1947 to head up its Institute of Industrial Relations. Loyola president, the Reverend Thomas J. Shields, S.J., appointed Twomey regent of the law school in March 1948.[25] Upon his appointment, Miller noted that Father Twomey "has impressed the student body with his enthusiasm and his insight to social problems."[26] Twomey proved to be a perfect fit for the law school. In that same year, members of SERINCO met with the archbishop of New Orleans, Joseph Francis Rummel, and Shields, Loyola's president, to urge the Church to eliminate segregation in the Catholic system, including integrating Loyola's school of law.[27] Anderson notes Shields's response: "Which one of you [black students] would apply for admission to the Loyola law school knowing that by your entrance into said school a vast majority of the students would depart from the school and go to Tulane or LSU law schools and thus you would take the responsibility of destroying the only Catholic law school in the entire South?"[28]

On the Loyola campus, the issue of race created tensions in 1949, the same year that Harry Alexander, a senior at Xavier and member of SERINCO, applied for admission to the law school. In March 1949, Loyola's Board discussed the response on campus to Inter-racial Day, held at Ursuline College in early March. The Board noted:

> Because of excessive and imprudent publicity for the Inter-racial Day, an unhealthy sentiment has been aroused among certain of our students towards the Negro race and thus those who would promote better race relations have actually caused them to suffer a setback here at Loyola.
>
> For some time past this question of inter-racial relations has caused increasing difficulties at Loyola both on the part of the faculty and the student body. Jesuit members of the faculty are not teaching the same doctrine in regard to race relations and two in particular are teaching diametrically opposite doctrines. This has never happened before at Loyola and cannot be tolerated now.
>
> With regard to the student body, some few favor abolition of segregation; the majority of the student body do not believe the present time is propitious for such a move. There have been well substantiated accusations that the extremists in the matter of racial relations have actually asked white girls, stenographers employed at Loyola University, to have

> dates with Negro men. Upon refusing, one girl was told: "Why not, aren't you a Christian?"[29]

The Board concluded, "This is not the time to agitate the abolition of segregation." There were to be no more posters on interracial matters, no Negro lecturers or speakers (except with the president's permission, "and these occasions should be few and far between"), and "doctrine taught in philosophy and social classes" was to "avoid questions of segregation . . . since experience has proved that better progress is made towards the abolition of segregation when segregation itself is not talked about."[30] The final edict was clear: no interracial social activities. Secretaries would not have to deal with the possibility of encountering a black man: "No Negroes are to be brought to the cafeteria on the campus of the university."

But at the law school a different spirit emerged. In February 1949, Miller worked with Fichter to establish the Sub-Committee on Race Relations Commission on Human Rights, under the auspices of the Catholic Committee of the South.[31] The Commission was a lay Catholic organization dedicated to eliminating "prejudice, intolerance, segregation, jim-crowism and kindred evils from within the framework of Catholic life in New Orleans."[32] Fichter led the Commission, and it worked primarily through integrated meetings, letter-writing campaigns, and public lectures and discussions.[33] Later, the Commission and Fichter were accused of being "communistic" by the Citizens' Council, a white organization dedicated to segregation and white supremacy.[34] In anticipation of an adverse reaction, the initial invitation by Miller promised invitees to the February 1949 meeting no publicity and a closed meeting.[35] Both Miller and Janet Mary Riley, law school librarian at the time, were active in the Commission's activities.

Fichter's efforts to integrate the institution focused on graduate programs, urging the institution to admit African Americans in 1949.[36] There were good reasons to pursue integration of the law school. In 1949, there were only three black lawyers practicing in Louisiana, or, as the *Times-Picayune* put it, "one to every 142,550 Negro citizens."[37]

For whatever reason, the Board minutes do not reflect further consideration by the Board of efforts to integrate the law school. If the matter came before them prior to 1952, it was not recorded in the minutes. The question became a matter to be pursued with the president and the head of the New Orleans Jesuit province.

Harry Alexander, a member of SERINCO and Xavier senior, applied for admission to the law school in 1949. It is likely that the law dean and faculty wanted to admit African Americans to the law school, but few documents concerning the Alexander application survive, and those that do primarily reflect the efforts by Fathers Fichter and Twomey to persuade the president and consultors to admit Alexander. Loyola rejected Alexander, but Georgetown accepted him.[38] Father Twomey, law school regent, had appealed to Georgetown's law school regent to admit Alexander: "As you realize under prevailing conditions it is not possible for us to consider his application. It is true that he gave arguments for his admission which we simply could not answer, and yet we are in the position of having to refuse Negro applicants."[39] Georgetown was happy to oblige.[40]

Thus far, efforts to integrate the law school had been unsuccessful. In 1950, however, Father Twomey enrolled black students in Loyola's Institute of Industrial Relations, a nondegree course of studies; Loyola admitted three African American nuns to a Saturday teacher-certification program; and one African American was admitted to its evening division.[41] Loyola had taken a step toward integration.

AT THE SUPREME COURT

In 1950, the Supreme Court handed down two decisions that made it clear that whatever alternatives states came up with to avoid admitting black students to white institutions, states had to provide an educational experience substantially equal to that of the white institutions, a standard difficult to attain given that states had for the most part ignored the needs of their black students. These rulings made it clear that at least for public institutions, integration was inevitable. In *Sweatt v. Painter,* the Court reversed a Texas Supreme Court ruling denying Herman Sweatt an order admitting him to the University of Texas Law School. The Texas Supreme Court had reasoned that Sweatt's equal protection rights were satisfied by his admission to the separate law school Texas had set up for blacks when Sweatt applied for admission to UT. The alternate law school was not accredited; in fact, it had just been set up in a way similar to that used in Louisiana to set up Southern. The Court made it clear: Mr. Sweatt had a full constitutional right to a legal education equivalent to that offered by the state to students of other races. The Court ordered Texas to admit him to the University of Texas Law School.[42]

Another case that same year, *McLaurin v. Oklahoma State Regents for Higher Education,* involved a challenge to the conditions that Oklahoma had imposed on an African American applicant to admit him to the graduate school at the University of Oklahoma. Mr. McLaurin had been admitted to the white institution, but he had to sit apart from white students in classes, the library, and the school cafeteria. The Court struck down the conditions and held he must be treated the same as students of other races.[43]

DESEGREGATION AND THE LAW SCHOOL ACCREDITING BODIES: THE ABA AND THE AALS

It was not until 1950 that the accrediting bodies of law schools began to address their members' racial policies. Ironically, it was the ABA's failure to take a progressive posture with regard to racial segregation that led the AALS to consider the question. The ABA had admitted blacks, albeit without realizing it, at the beginning of the twentieth century.[44] The organization allowed the inadvertently admitted black members to remain as members but excluded other blacks from membership. As a result, black lawyers founded the all-black National Bar Association.[45] In 1943, the ABA passed a resolution that "membership . . . is not dependent upon race, creed or color," but no black lawyers were admitted to membership until 1950.[46] At the 1950 annual meeting of the AALS, the AALS president, Columbia dean Karl N. Llewellyn, reported to the representatives of the member law schools that he had addressed the Board of Governors of the ABA that year concerning the denial of membership to individuals because of their race or color:

> I explained to the Board of Governors that the matter of possible discrimination against new members of their organization, based on color, was a matter which was giving rise to extremely unfortunate rumors in our organization, that those rumors were widespread, and that those rumors were believed, and that the matter of the whole color question was one which was reaching an intensity of worry in our organization such as had been reached in my time by no other issue, that in our organization questions of

> color had reached the point at which people were throwing around suspicions of bad faith without any sound foundation for them, and that when an organization got to the place where issues bit that deep, those things had better be attended to, and attended to seriously by any thoughtful organization for whom we were, essentially, the main recruiting body.
>
> I said further that it seemed to me that it was most unfortunate for any voluntary organization such as the American Bar Association to fall behind the lines of compulsion put forward by law, that it seemed to me that the position of leadership which such an organization could rightfully claim depended upon their ability to move far beyond what they could be made to do by law or what anybody could be made to do by law, in the furtherance of that line of decency and general approach to the dignity of man which was the foundation of the kind of law we live with. And I thanked them for their courtesy.[47]

Later at the meeting, the Yale Law School dean, Wesley A. Sturges, introduced what became known as the Yale Resolution. The resolution essentially conditioned AALS membership on a school's abolition of segregation on the basis of race and color: "No school which follows a policy of excluding or segregating qualified applicants or students on the basis of race or color shall be qualified to be admitted or to remain a member of the Association."[48]

Law school representatives discussed the Yale Resolution and introduced several amendments or substitutes. Indiana's proposed substitute stated that the AALS opposed segregation and believed that "it is the professional duty of all member schools to abolish any such practices at the earliest practicable time," and referred the Yale Resolution to a committee to report back at the 1951 annual meeting. The University of Southern California proposed an amendment to the substitute that broadened the question referred to the committee, but again deferred any action until the 1951 meeting. Extensive discussion indicated general acquiescence with the sentiments of the Yale Resolution but unwillingness to adopt a requirement that all member schools integrate. When the vote was taken, it was on whether to accept the substitute Indiana resolution, and a majority of schools including Yale University voted in favor of the substitution. Loyola was the only Louisiana law school to vote yes on the resolution. Immediately after the vote, LSU law faculty moved to table the motion, unsuccessfully. The Indiana resolution, declaring the policy of the AALS to be opposed to segregation and referring the Yale Resolution to a committee to report at the 1951 annual meeting, passed overwhelmingly, with Loyola again the only Louisiana law school voting in the affirmative.[49]

While the AALS committee considered whether the AALS would adopt a requirement that law school membership be contingent upon the abandonment of racial segregation and discrimination, black students eager for a legal education in Louisiana—a state with a strong African American population and few black lawyers—continued to press for admission to the state's flagship law school. In 1950, Roy S. Wilson applied to LSU Law School. When he was denied admission, he sued.[50] The case was assigned to a three-judge court made up of two Loyola Law alumni, the Honorable James Skelly Wright and the Honorable Herbert W. Christenberry, and the Honorable Wayne G. Borah on the U.S. Court of Appeals for the Fifth Circuit.[51] Judge Wright issued an order setting the hearing over whether the court should issue an injunction for September 25—a little over a week since the suit had been filed. Thurgood Marshall, then counsel for the National Association for the Advancement of Colored People, led Mr. Wilson's legal team, with A. P. Tureaud as Wilson's local counsel. At the hearing, Marshall argued that Southern Law School was inferior to LSU Law School and, thus, under the reasoning of the *Sweatt v. Painter* decision, the court was required to enjoin LSU Law School from denying Wilson admission solely because of his race.[52] LSU defended on the grounds that Southern was a better effort to provide blacks with a legal education, than the University of Texas Law School, struck down by the Supreme Court as not substantially equal to its school for whites. The ruling came down on October 7, 1950. In an opinion written by federal district court judge J. Skelly Wright, all three judges concluded that LSU had to admit qualified blacks to its law school.[53]

The reaction to Judge Wright's order in the Wilson case was strong. LSU vowed to appeal, but LSU Law School admitted Wilson.[54] State legislators asked for an emergency legislature session to allow for increased spending at Southern to "prevent the enrollment of Negroes in LSU," or if necessary to "pass legislation to close down the LSU law school."[55] Opinion was not unified, however. Ted F. Craft, chairman of the Interracial Commission at Loyola University, responded to a *Times-Picayune* editorial pointing out that "there is no Louisiana law which states that Negroes and whites over 18 years of age may not attend the same publicly-supported institution."[56] Wilson dropped out of

LSU's law school shortly after being admitted. Three other African Americans applied to LSU and were admitted. One dropped out, and the other two, Robert F. Collins and Ernest N. Morial, graduated in 1954. For the next ten years, no African Americans were admitted to LSU.[57]

Dean Miller left the law school in 1951 to become dean at another Jesuit law school, the University of San Francisco Law School. Antonio Papale took over as dean.

Richard D. Gumbel Jr. applied to Loyola's law school for admission on June 1, 1951. Gumbel was an Xavier graduate and a member of SERINCO.[58] Dean Papale wrote the letter denying Gumbel admission six days after the application, on June 7, 1951. According to Gumbel's appeal to Loyola president the Reverend Thomas Shields, Dean Papale stated in his denial letter that "I hasten to add that conditions for men in your position seem to be improving."[59] From this sentence, Gumbel surmised that "the reason for the rejection of my application was solely on the basis of racial discrimination."

Gumbel's appeal stressed the fact that increasingly "White Schools" were opening their doors to African Americans; that white students attending schools with African Americans had not registered "objections because of having to sit in the same class with the 'unwanted'"; and that in his case the decision was particularly harsh because "Loyola is the only place in the area where I might secure a Catholic Law education." Gumbel proceeded to explain the rationale for a decision that the legal academy often finds difficult to understand—Gumbel's preference for Loyola rather than Georgetown:

> As an alternative I have considered enrolling in the Georgetown University School of Law. However, this works many hardships upon me. For you see Father, I am a married man and the father of two sons, one five years of age and the other only two years of age. After serving more than five years in the Armed Forces of the United States during the last war, I was fortunate in acquiring a job which afforded me the opportunity to pursue an education at Xavier University. With the savings I was able to make while in the service of my country I now own my home. All of this I must forsake if I attend Georgetown. I must leave the place of my birth, my parents, my wife's parents, my home, and my community in order to get what can be secured here at home.

> True it can be said that many men have had to go far from home to get an education, but in all cases it has been voluntary. I, like many other men and women of my race, must leave home just because I am a Negro. I am sure that many able Negroes who could have and would have helped the community have been forced North for their education, and other communities have received all the benefits of their efforts.[60]

Shields was unmoved. Twomey, the law school regent, again appealed to Georgetown Law School, recommending Gumbel for admission. On June 15, 1951, Georgetown responded, asking for Mr. Gumbel's transcript.[61] He was admitted to Georgetown, and he, and eventually, his family, moved to Washington D.C., in order to allow him to pursue his legal studies.[62]

AN IMPASSIONED PLEA TO ROME

In September 1951, Twomey wrote to the Reverend Vincent McCormick, S.J., assistant to the Superior General of the Society of Jesus in Rome, commonly known as "Father General," for help integrating Loyola's law school. Twomey phrased his communication as a request for "advice and direction . . . rather than as a formal communication."[63] Twomey reminded McCormick that he had recommended several years back that the law school be permitted to accept African Americans, and thereafter that African Americans be admitted into all departments of the University. Twomey expressed his sentiments that the commitment to racial segregation rested on the theory of "white supremacy," and that he believed that younger southern Jesuits were critical of segregation. Twomey was convinced that the benefits of admitting blacks to the law school and Loyola as a whole "would far outweigh whatever loss Loyola would sustain."

Twomey's letter brought Father McCormick up to date on events that had transpired at the University since their initial meeting. Twomey described his efforts to persuade the New Orleans Province's consultors to allow the law school to admit Harry Alexander for the 1949–50 school year. His letter makes clear where the Loyola law faculty stood: "I assured Father Shields that the Law School faculty as well as the student body were prepared for such a departure in our admissions policy." Nonetheless, he had failed to convince the Jesuit leadership in New Orleans. Twomey expressed a desire at the time to write to the Jesuit Father General about the matter but concluded that such a letter would not be helpful. Subsequent events, however, had led Twomey to rethink the question, and he had decided not to write to the Father General direct, but instead to address his letter to his assistant, McCormick.

Twomey noted that since denying the law school permission to admit Alexander, Shields had consented to admitting an African American to Loyola's evening division, three African American nuns to Saturday classes, as well as to allow him to admit African Americans to Twomey's Institute of Industrial Relations. However, Shields had denied admission to Gumbel and other African American applicants to the law school, despite the fact that LSU had been forced to admit African Americans to their law school as a result of litigation. Twomey concluded: "Honestly, Father, I cannot understand this. Thus already the initiative, so very important in establishing leadership in interracial relations and in meriting the confidence of Negroes generally, has been taken away from us to a considerable degree."

Twomey went on to list the number of southern educational institutions that had admitted African Americans: "In face of this trend, which undoubtedly will soon be accelerated throughout the South, I am wondering how much longer must Loyola preserve its present admission policies." His impassioned plea urged action:

> The time for us to have become genuine pioneers in setting an example of dynamic leadership for Christ in race relations is passed. That opportunity will not return. But there is still time for Loyola and the New Orleans Province to recapture something of the initiative we have lost. We can yet bring to bear on these critical problems of human relations such well-conceived and well-executed applications of the eternal principles of Justice and Charity as to place Loyola and the New Orleans Province in the front ranks of those willing to fight for Christ without counting the cost.

Father McCormick responded, acknowledging the problem, urging patience, and suggesting that assistance would come, if eventually: "Don't lose courage, my dear Father; Rome moves slowly and at times is limited in its moves; but I do hope something will be done to make possible and encourage your truly Christ-like plans in this matter."[64]

In November 1951, Dean Papale notified Loyola's president that the AALS report would be sent to him and made it clear that the dean and law faculty would vote in favor of the recommendation of the AALS Special Committee on Racial Discrimination.[65] Once again, the accrediting law school bodies were instrumental in effecting change at the law school.

Twomey referenced the AALS report in his response to Father McCormick in December 1951, conveying that an AALS survey showed that "there are now sixteen Southern universities, public and private, which admit Negroes to their law schools."[66] He reported that, whenever Loyola students ask, "why didn't Loyola admit Negros," he fumbled around and tried "to save face for Loyola as best I can." Twomey also brought notice of the potential for "an attack on discrimination in the privately supported institutions, on the ground that tax exemption and other privileges they enjoy make these institutions subject to the same obligations as state universities as far as equality of treatment go." Twomey stressed what a calamity it would be for Loyola "to open its doors to Negros only after court action or even the threat of court action." Again, he urged action; the impediment he perceived was "the attitude of some of Ours [fellow Jesuits]. Once this difficulty can be eliminated or at least made negative, I am convinced that most of our students and alumni would accept and many would welcome forthright leadership from Loyola."

LOYOLA LAW AND ACTION AT THE AALS

At the 1951 annual meeting of the AALS, on December 28–30, the Special Committee came back with a measure that to some compromised the essential thrust of the Yale Resolution, and to others appeared a measured compromise to set the member schools on the road to eventual integration.[67] Again, parliamentary procedure made it difficult to engage in discussion of the actual merits of the resolutions. The committee proposed adoption of a resolution that provided:

1. Equality of opportunity in legal education without discrimination or segregation on the ground of race or color is beneficial to legal education, and will contribute to the improvement of the legal profession. It is in accordance with our democratic creed and would enhance our nation's influence in world affairs.

2. The Articles of Association are hereby amended by adding . . . as one of the Objectives which "the Association shall encourage its members to maintain" the following provision:

1-a. A student body selected without discrimination on the ground of race or color.[68]

The committee moved to adopt the second provision that amended the articles of the Association and required a two-thirds majority to pass. Yale urged its own original resolution as a substitute motion because it viewed the committee's resolution as "too little and that it already is too late."[69] Columbia then offered its own substitute, speaking against the Yale proposal because it was "too inflexible in that it compels schools either to adopt the policy . . . or to leave the association as of a date certain." Instead, Columbia proposed to condition membership on adherence to court orders and on adherence to the policy of affording "equality of opportunity in legal education without segregation on the ground of race or color" with extensions available to secure compliance.[70] The Yale and Columbia substitutes had been seconded, and when the floor was opened for debate, the first faculty to be heard from was from the Deep South—a young faculty member from Loyola.

Charles Driscoll, an assistant professor of law at Loyola in his second year of teaching,[71] rose to speak in support of the Yale Resolution:

> I should like to speak on behalf of the faculty of Loyola University of New Orleans in support of the Yale resolution. The Law School of Loyola University of the South in New Orleans wants to admit qualified Negro students. We believe we shall be able to do so only when non-discrimination becomes a flat requirement. Therefore, we want an opportunity to vote on the requirement. Therefore, we are uncomfortable at the prospect of being constrained by parliamentary tactics to vote for something less. Indeed, we were uncomfortable for the same reason a year ago in Chicago.
>
> The simple truth which has been stated here by previous speakers is that men and universities and communities act in response to pressure, that we are gathered here as men of good will to forge a new pressure and that when it is forged, it is going to be exerted, not upon ourselves, but upon others. These others may, in some few instances, be the individuals

who comprise a university's administration, but in the last analysis and in all instances, the others whom we seek to persuade are the individuals who comprise the university's community.

We seek to persuade them that an overwhelming majority of American law schools will no longer associate with a law school which continues to discriminate. Not today will this be so, but in two years. And not even in two years. If the Yale resolution is passed here today, the requirement will not become effective until January of 1954. It will not then be until September of that year . . . when new students seek admission to most of the nation's law schools, that a member school can be fairly said to have begun to build a record of "Failing to maintain a policy of non-discrimination." That comes to three years as a minimum—in some cases, even longer.

The real job of persuasion, the persuasion of the community, can be begun now by informing the community that in two or three or four years, it is going to require more than 10,000 books and four full-time teachers to make an American law school within the Association of American Law Schools. The objective proposed by the Special Committee cannot do that job. The objective, indeed, strikes us at home as something very much akin to a New Year's resolution—a resolution to resolve on next New Year's Day to resolve to quit stealing. The requirement offered by Yale University at least resolves right now to quit pretty soon! Thank you.[72]

Notwithstanding Driscoll's fervor, when the schools voted on the Yale Resolution, the motion lost overwhelmingly, 71 to 32, with Loyola New Orleans voting with the minority of schools. After much discussion and use (or misuse) of parliamentary procedure, a majority of schools voted to adopt the committee's proposal.[73] Loyola was the only school from Louisiana voting in favor of the proposal. Law schools would be encouraged, not required, to abandon segregation and provide equal opportunity to persons without regard to their race.

In January 1952, the New Orleans provincial appointed a committee to discuss thoroughly the matter of interracial relations and formulate province policy. Twomey was asked to serve.[74] As the committee pursued its work, another African American, an honor graduate of Xavier University, Norman Francis, applied to the law school. Father Twomey wrote again, this time to Loyola's president, Patrick Donnelly.[75] Twomey notified the president that he would be hearing from Dean Papale for permission to admit an applicant who "ordinarily we would not hesitate to accord . . . unqualified acceptance," but he could not do so "without prior clearance from higher authority" "for it happens that Norman Francis is a Negro." Twomey pleaded that Donnelly authorize Papale to admit Francis, urging some of the same arguments he had made to the assistant to the Father General: the increase in the number of southern law schools admitting blacks and the threat of litigation aimed at private institutions. Moreover, he quoted from the AALS report, "The experience of the Southern law schools which have recently admitted Negroes has been uniformly free of the difficulties forecast." He urged Father Donnelly to decide promptly: Francis was subject to the draft and he needed to know whether Loyola was going to admit him.

By August 1952, the decision to admit Norman Francis had been made. It was late, and the decision had taken years, two law school deans, several black applicants, and two ardent Jesuits urging action, but ultimately, the provincial authorized the admission of African Americans to the law school.[76] The law school admitted four African Americans: Norman Francis and Benjamin Johnson in the day, and Elliot Keyes and Pierre Charles in the night program.[77]

African Americans were admitted to the law school, but the road to full integration at Loyola had really just begun and would take much longer. A year later when asked to extend admission to African Americans in the dental school, the Board determined the experiment at the law school a success: "Four negroes had been admitted last year into the Law School with no untoward results."[78] However, the Board opted to inquire as to the views of the faculty of the dental school prior to extending the program. The dental school faculty, unlike the law school faculty, rejected integration at that time.[79] Loyola as a whole resisted integration until after the U.S. Supreme Court's decision in *Brown v. Board of Education* in 1954.[80]

Papale wrote to Robert Leflar at the University of Colorado on August 5, 1952, concerning the law school's admission of blacks. Papale's letter appears not to be available, but Leflar's response to Papale counseled to proceed quietly:

> The concensus [*sic*] of the school was that it is not desirable to try to adjust public opinion either in the community or on the campus to the new move in advance. It is better to let folks find out about it after it occurs, and in general they will not then have much to say about it unless they like it, in which case some people will tell you they like it and others will just get

> used to it. The less publicity that accompanies the event the better. The people who need to know about it will either be told in advance or will learn of it quickly.[81]

Leflar had conducted a survey of schools to integrate to find out about their experience. Other advice from Leflar included to talk to law student leaders and organizations in advance; to treat the black students exactly like other students; and to plan carefully for social events. Most law schools that had integrated "were surprised that no difficulties developed. Faculty and administrators feared the worst, then were pleasantly surprised. That was my own experience."

At the law school, the addition of Norman Francis and Benjamin Johnson to the class appears to have been for the most part welcomed and accepted by both students and faculty. Francis and Johnson joined a law school community that included Maurice "Moon" Landrieu, soon to emerge as one of the city's major political and defining leaders of the twentieth century, Pascal Calogero, Samuel Dalton, and Janet Mary Riley, all foes of segregation, and all to take on leadership roles in the city's legal community. As Father Twomey reported in a letter on October 30, 1952: "I have nothing but good things to report not only about the four themselves but about the manner in which they have been received by the student body. We are very much gratified by the whole situation. We now feel that the biggest obstacle of all has been overcome."[82] Later in the academic year, he noted: "I can say that we have experienced none of the grave repercussions that were predicted by some. As a matter of fact, it would be true to say that we have had no untoward incident to contend with as a result."[83]

At the school the student organizations became aligned on the basis of sentiments toward segregation: those students who favored integration joined the St. Thomas More Society, and those who favored segregation joined the Delta Theta Phi. Charles Driscoll left the Loyola faculty in 1953.

THE LAST OF THE REGENTS: A GREAT ADVOCATE OF HUMAN RIGHTS

The Board considered relinquishing regents in June 1955.[84] Jesuit schools throughout the country were abandoning the office due to the tendency of regents to interfere "with the academic administration of the Dean of the particular school."[85] Like Georgetown and other Jesuit institutions, Loyola opted to relieve Father Twomey of his duties as regent of the law school and replace regents with law school chaplains, whose duties would be to function as "a sounding board and a morale builder for students and faculty alike."[86] Ironically, Father Twomey had perhaps been the school's most successful and most appreciated regent. The Reverend Louis J. Hiegel, S.J., was named law school chaplain. Twomey continued to teach a course on the philosophy of law.

Twomey's success as regent may be due in part to the fact that he was too busy to play an excessively heavy hand at the law school. Primarily, he ran interference for the law school during the period of his regency. His heart was in the Institute of Industrial Relations at Loyola and worker rights. With some of that work, in particular in the context of the desegregation of the law school, his interests coincided with that of the law school, and he became an effective spokesperson with Loyola's president, Board, and the province consultors (the Jesuit advisory committee). Throughout, he spoke up for the needs of the law school, financial and otherwise, and defended the law school when it came under attack. The law school community was appreciative.

Twomey's view of the law school, and of Catholic law schools in general, appears to have been that their primary role was to infuse students with appreciation for natural law: "I am convinced that the development of such a philosophy of law is the greatest contribution that Catholic law schools can make. . . . [I]f a Catholic law school does not make this contribution, it has no good reason for existence. It is, therefore, the duty of any Jesuit associated with a law school to see to it that the natural law philosophy becomes the integrating principle in the whole curriculum."[87] Twomey was writing in 1953; already, natural law philosophy was being challenged in the legal world.

Father Twomey died on October 5, 1969. The law school's newspaper, the *Legal Rag,* marked his passing: "A Great Loss," the headline proclaimed, as it mourned the death of "a great advocate of human rights."[88]

THE CITY: PUBLIC SCHOOLS

Much in the life of James Skelly Wright evoked the sense of a man at ease with his talents and life, possessed of a keen intelligence and firm self-discipline but fitting in comfortably with his community. J. Skelly Wright was born in New Orleans on January 14, 1911, to a Scots-Irish, Catholic family with roots in

Louisiana politics. His mother, Margaret Agnes Skelly, was a ward leader, heavily involved in city politics, and sister of Joseph P. Skelly, who served as commissioner of public property for the City of New Orleans during the administration of Louis Maestri. His father, James Edward Wright, was an inspector for the Sewerage and Water Board. Wright grew up in the Irish Channel during the Depression, one of seven children in a family with little money to spare in a deeply segregated society. He attended white public schools including McDonough No. 7 for elementary school, and Warren Easton High School, segregated not just by race but by sex as well, from which he graduated in 1927. At Warren Easton he was selected by his classmates to receive a scholarship to calisthenics and gymnasium classes conducted by the New Orleans Elks in the summer of 1927.[89] He was also chosen to be the representative from Warren Easton to Boys Week, a weeklong opportunity provided by the mayor's office to allow boys from various high schools in the city to sample political life and "run" for political office. Skelly Wright ran for commission council.

He pursued a bachelor of philosophy degree at Loyola on a scholarship and, after graduating in 1931, taught at Fortier High School (where he was voted most popular teacher two years in a row) and taught history at Loyola as well. He attended Loyola's law school at night and graduated with a bachelor of laws in 1934. He continued to teach until he landed his first job as an attorney. Rene Viosca, then U.S. attorney for the Eastern District of Louisiana, hired the young man as an assistant U.S. attorney in August 1937. As an assistant U.S. attorney, Skelly Wright drew attention as the "Tom Dewey of New Orleans,"[90] aggressively going after organized crime and Huey P. Long machine leaders.[91]

When war broke out, he joined the Coast Guard, like many of his fellow Loyola law graduates. The first assignment had him on a submarine in the gulf. Soon after, the Coast Guard assigned him work on cases involving prosecutions of military personnel in the United Kingdom. He was assigned to serve in London, where he courted and married Helen Patton, secretary to the U.S. minister of economic warfare and daughter of Admiral Raymond Stanton Patton. Upon his return, he spent a brief time in New Orleans at the U.S. attorney's office and then took up private practice in Washington, D.C., where his biggest client was the Louisiana maker of PT boats and the "Higgins boats" (the LCVPs—landing craft, vehicle, personnel), Andrew Higgins.

During his time in D.C., he represented fellow Catholic Louisianan Willie Francis, a seventeen-year-old African American who had been sentenced to death for murder. Francis, a St. Martinville native, had been convicted of the murder of a white pharmacist on the basis of a confession. He had been appointed counsel at trial, and his attorneys failed to put on a defense and to appeal his conviction. The state scheduled the execution on May 3, 1946, but executioners botched the electrocution. As Gilbert King vividly describes in *The Execution of Willie Francis,* Francis endured two separate electric shocks on that day before state officials turned the current off from the electric chair holding Francis.[92] Francis's father asked local attorney Bertrand DeBlanc to take his son's case challenging the state's decision to send Francis to the electric chair a second time. DeBlanc filed a writ of habeas corpus and asked for a stay of the new scheduled execution date of May 6, 1946. The state agreed to a thirty-day stay to give the courts adequate time to consider the appeal. The Louisiana Supreme Court and the Louisiana Pardons Board denied Francis's appeal. A friend of DeBlanc's suggested he contact Skelly Wright for an appeal to the U.S. Supreme Court.

Wright filed a writ of certiorari on Francis's behalf, and the Supreme Court issued an immediate stay of execution. The Court's decision to deny the writ followed quickly on June 10. But on June 11, Skelly Wright heard from a clerk at the Supreme Court that they had made a mistake—the Court had granted the writ. Wright and DeBlanc based their appeal on the grounds that due process and the prohibition against cruel and unusual punishment in the Eighth Amendment and the double-jeopardy clause barred the State of Louisiana from subjecting Francis to the cruelty of a second execution. The problem for the legal argument was that the Court had rejected application of rights protected in the Bill of Rights to the states. The Supreme Court subsequently adopted Wright's position,[93] but he lost the case in 1947, five to four.[94] Louisiana executed Willie Francis on May 9, 1947. Helen Wright wrote in her memoirs, "Skelly felt so passionately that justice had not been served."[95]

Something had happened to Skelly Wright: "I was as southern as anybody else was around there. I saw what was going on down there. While I didn't embrace it, it didn't repel me." But the war changed that. "The Negro went to war like the white person did. He fought like the white person. We saw this, those of us who were in the service—we saw this."[96] The Christmas Eve of 1945 found him at the U.S. attorney's office annual Christmas party, watching another Christmas party at the Lighthouse for the Blind. He watched as the hosts led the blind whites to a large room in the front of the house, and the blind blacks to a room at the rear. He was incredulous at the sight: "When you go to bed at night you think of it. That was the beginning really."[97]

President Harry S. Truman appointed him U.S. attorney for the Eastern District in 1948, when he appointed Herbert Christenberry to the federal bench. Wright's appointment to the federal bench in 1949 made him one of the youngest judges on the bench at the time, and he and Christenberry, the only two judges on the federal district court in New Orleans, brought recognition to the Eastern District of Louisiana for its efficiency in administering justice.

While maintaining a crisp, moving docket in the Eastern District, which gave him time to spend summers helping to clear the docket of the Southern District of New York, Judge Wright became the name most prominently associated with desegregation efforts in the city and the state. Skelly Wright had been sworn in on the bench on October 16, 1949. Within months he faced a suit to desegregate LSU and a voting rights case involving Washington Parish efforts to frustrate black voters. He ordered the desegregation of LSU in 1950 and granted an injunction blocking Washington Parish from purging blacks from voter registration rolls in August of that same year. The order that generated a torrent of ill-will and animosity, however, was the order to come down in the case of *Bush v. Louisiana,* ordering the desegregation of the Orleans Parish public schools in 1956. Liva Baker has told the story of *Bush v. Louisiana* in *The Second Battle of New Orleans.*[98] The order came down February 15, 1956, Ash Wednesday, but penitence was not in evidence in the city of New Orleans.

Skelly Wright's only son, James S. Wright, still remembers the cross burning on their front yard. His son remembers the crank phone calls that he handled as a ten- and eleven-year-old. Although their home phone number had been changed, someone at the phone company gave their phone number to the white Citizens' Council, and the calls kept coming. The family became used to housing U.S. marshals and New Orleans police officers. The New Orleans community was unable to stand up to the face of white supremacy; the fight to desegregate the schools was ugly, ignorant, and, for many years, gave voice to the worst in human nature.[99]

Cases involving race discrimination challenges were assigned to three judges, as required by federal law, and most of the orders in those cases came down penned by Wright. Sitting alongside Wright was fellow Loyola graduate Herbert W. Christenberry. Christenberry was the older of the two, but their careers had overlapped at the U.S. attorney's office, where they had both served as assistant attorneys under Rene Viosca, and later on the bench. The third judge, Wayne G. Borah, served on the U.S. Court of Appeals for the Fifth Circuit.

By the time the *Bush* order came down, the Court had decided *Brown v. Board of Education I and II,* giving local jurisdictions time to implement desegregation "with all deliberate speed." Wright had indicated implementation would be gradual; nonetheless, the state legislature, under the leadership of Willie Rainach and Leander Perez, enacted a series of statutes in an attempt to nullify and frustrate the *Bush* order.

Joseph Francis Rummel, archbishop of the archdiocese of New Orleans, issued a pastoral letter later in the week declaring "racial segregation as such is morally wrong."

Judge Wright ordered the desegregation of City Park swimming pools in 1957, the streetcars and buses in 1958, public sporting events between black and white participants in 1958, and the public schools of East Baton Rouge and St. Helena Parishes in 1960. The Fifth Circuit Court of Appeals affirmed the *Bush* order in 1957; Rainach and Perez persuaded the legislature again to frustrate desegregation of public schools. But the final attack on desegregation came after Wright issued the order to begin desegregating schools in fall 1960. The Louisiana legislature again tried to prevent the schools from desegregating in what Judge Adrian Duplantier, another Loyola law alumni, described as "bedlam." Moon Landrieu, a young legislator from New Orleans and Loyola law graduate, "emerged a hero of the opposition during that turbulent legislative session."[100] Steadfastly, he opposed the numerous bills enacted by the legislature in a frenzied attempt to block Wright's desegregation order; just as steadfastly, Wright struck the bills down.

President John F. Kennedy appointed Wright to the U.S. Court of Appeals for the District of Columbia Circuit in 1962. Kennedy had considered Wright for an appointment to the U.S. Court of Appeals for the Fifth Circuit, Wright's home circuit, but political opposition made it impossible. Wright and his family took up residence in Washington, D.C., until his death in 1988. Throughout his years on the Eastern District, Wright taught Loyola law students the federal rules of civil procedure. Throughout his life in the law, Wright remained involved in the New Orleans legal community. He was a former president of the New Orleans Chapter of the Federal Bar Association, a member of the governors of the Louisiana State Bar Association, and a loyal Loyola alumnus. His ashes are buried at Arlington National Cemetery.

Both Wright and Christenberry taught law classes at Loyola throughout their tenure on the bench, including during the *Bush* years. Christenberry's son, Herbert Christenberry Jr., remembered attending his father's class at night. Judge Christenberry was concerned that other students not perceive any favoritism on his part toward his son and tended to be harder on him than on other students.

Christenberry withstood some of the same kind of attacks directed at Wright. Like Wright, he took the attacks in stride. But when the attacks were directed at the U.S. Supreme Court, he did not hesitate to speak out. At a meeting of the American Law Students Association he attended with Loyola's Dean Papale in New Orleans, Christenberry in his address to law students told them "it was 'outrageous for lawyers to impugn the judges of the supreme court.'"[101] He spoke both to the role of lawyers in the American system and the role of the Article III branch—the judiciary—in the American constitutional system. Lawyers, he said, are "bulwarks between tyranny and the freedom of the people." Judges are "not to be influenced by the voice of popular demand and passing prejudices, but to pronounce what the law is, and then submit their decisions to the impartial judgment of the people of the United States."[102] Christenberry served as chief judge of the Eastern District until his death in 1975. His portrait hangs in the law school library, a testament to his legacy to the school.

THE CITY: LUNCH COUNTERS

Lawyers are sometimes willing to wait or delay for strategic reasons in litigating rights. Some legal scholars criticized the U.S. Supreme Court for handing down *Brown v. Board of Education* instead of waiting for legislative action to undo segregation. Judge Wright, at times, felt hampered in the *Bush* case by what he perceived as a lack of aggressiveness, on the part of the plaintiffs, to move the litigation along. Courts, of course, cannot initiate reform—they decide cases brought either by individuals or by the state. But individuals often are not willing to sacrifice vindication of their rights to await reform at the legislative level, and local students in New Orleans in the fall of 1960 determined to secure their right to be served in establishments previously open only to whites, acted to secure those rights. Sit-ins had begun in Greensboro, North Carolina, where local stores opted to desegregate after five months of protests.

In New Orleans, where members of the local chapter of the Congress of Racial Equality (CORE) began their sit-ins, seven months after the Greensboro sit-ins, it was years before local stores abandoned segregation.[103]

On September 9, 1960, seven black and white college students entered a Woolworth store on Canal Street in New Orleans, sat down at its cafeteria counter, and waited to be served. The group "disrupted normal business operations for nearly five hours." The New Orleans district attorney told them to leave and then ordered police to arrest them. They were charged with criminal mischief and held until later that night. The next day, the superintendent of police issued a public statement condemning the protests and promising that police stood ready to enforce the laws of the city and state. Although there were no laws prohibiting restaurants and cafeterias from serving both whites and blacks, the city's mayor banned further sit-ins and picketing and informed the city's residents that he had directed the superintendent of police not to permit any additional sit-ins.[104] On September 17, 1960, four college students, three of them black and one of them white, entered the McCrory Five and Ten Cent Store, also on Canal Street, and asked to be served. They were arrested and charged with criminal mischief. Sydney Goldfinch, the Tulane white student, was charged with criminal anarchy, which carried a maximum prison sentence of ten years. The students sought assistance from the law firm of Lolis Elie.

Lolis Edward Elie was born on January 9, 1930, at home on Lowerline Street between Prytania and Perrier Streets with a doctor from Touro Infirmary in attendance. His father was Catholic and his mother a committed Baptist. He first attended McDonald 24 and in 1947 graduated from Gilbert Academy, a private school for African Americans located on St. Charles Avenue, across the street from the Jewish Community Center, the current site of De La Salle High School. He worked as a merchant seaman, and left New Orleans for New York City, where he experienced integration for the first time.

He joined the Army in 1951, and a world starkly different from that he had grown up in opened up for him. For the first time, Elie experienced equal footing with whites.[105] While in the Army in California, he met Frank D'Amico, an Italian American from New Orleans, with whom he became friends. Elie and D'Amico felt a kinship grounded in the treatment that Italians and Americans of Italian ancestry faced in New Orleans. Persons of Italian ancestry, like many other national origins including the Chinese and Japanese, were viewed in

New Orleans and other parts of the country, as inferior races, analogous to blacks. D'Amico suggested to Elie that he become a lawyer.

After Elie left the Army in 1953, he attended Howard University in the District of Columbia on the GI Bill. After a year at Howard, he decided to return to New Orleans and pursue the law. He spent two years at Dillard University to satisfy the minimum admission standards at Loyola Law School, the only law school in New Orleans open to blacks. Elie remembers reading in the *Louisiana Weekly* that Loyola was accepting African Americans and applied to Dean Papale.

Elie started at Loyola in 1956, the only African American in the first-year day class, joined by Nils R. Douglas in the evening division. The 1956 first-year class included Marcel Garsaud Jr., soon to join the law faculty at Loyola and eventually serve as dean. Also in the class was James Thomas Nelson, with whom he made friends. Tommy introduced him to John Nelson, his older brother known as "Jack," a Loyola law graduate at the time working for the district attorney, and Jack helped them with criminal law. Elie remembers going up to Jack's front door, something he was not used to doing—going up to a white person's front door. Elie got married after his first year of law school. He taught accounting and bookkeeping at the YMCA on Dryades Street, while attending law school.

Although there were few African Americans at the school, Elie enjoyed his time at the law school and felt comfortable as a student answering questions in class. He remembers with fondness Dean John McAulay, who taught him constitutional law and awarded him "Best Student in Constitutional Law," and Dean Papale, who taught him contracts, the subject he found most difficult in law school. Although there was little overt racism, one law faculty member in particular resisted the presence of African Americans at the law school.

When he graduated from Loyola in 1959, however, the cold, hard reality of life for an African American lawyer in New Orleans at that time became clear. No law firm gave him an interview. He hung up a shingle directly across the street from the YMCA on Dryades Street, at which he continued to teach accounting in the evening, and began to practice law with fellow Loyola law graduate Nils Douglas and another African American attorney, LSU graduate Robert Collins. When the Dryades Street establishments began their campaign to end segregation, they turned to Elie's firm to represent them. They provided free legal counsel for the Consumers' League of Greater New Orleans, an all-black organization dedicated to eliminating employment discrimination by New Orleans commercial establishments.

When the college students were arrested in the lunch counter sit-ins, they turned to Elie and Collins to represent them in their criminal case. Elie and Collins turned to Jack Nelson for help.

Lombard v. Louisiana involved four college students, Rudolph Joseph Lombard, a student at Xavier University; Cecil Winston Carter, a student at Dillard University; Oretha Maureen Castle, a student at Southern University; and Sidney Langston Goldfinch Jr., a student at Tulane University, all members of the local CORE chapter who sat down and asked for service at a whites-only lunch counter in a McCrory Five and Ten Cent Store in New Orleans.[106] Jack Nelson agreed to take the case and went on to argue it before the U.S. Supreme Court.[107] Nelson is recognized as the first white attorney not affiliated with a civil rights organization to represent African Americans in the South.[108] As the Court described it:

> The restaurant manager, believing that the "unusual circumstance" of Negroes sitting at the counter created an "emergency," asked petitioners to leave and, when they did not do so, ordered that the counter be closed. The restaurant manager then contacted the store manager and called the police. He frankly testified that the petitioners did not cause any disturbance, that they were orderly, and that he asked them to leave because they were Negroes. Presumably he asked the white petitioner to leave because he was in the company of Negroes.
>
> A number of police officers, including a captain and major of police, arrived at the store shortly after they were called. Three of the officers had a conference with the store manager. The store manager then went behind the counter, faced petitioners, and in a loud voice asked them to leave. He also testified that the petitioners were merely sitting quietly at the counter throughout these happenings. When petitioners remained seated, the police major spoke to petitioner Goldfinch, and asked him what they were doing there. Mr. Goldfinch replied that petitioners "were going to sit there until they were going to be served." When petitioners still declined to leave, they were arrested by the police, led out of the store, and taken away in a patrol wagon. They were later tried and convicted for violation of the Louisiana criminal mischief statute. This statute, in its application to this

> case, has all the elements of the usual trespass statute. Each petitioner was sentenced to serve 60 days in the Parish Prison and to pay a fine of $350. In default of payment of the fine, each was to serve 60 additional days in prison. On appeal to the Supreme Court of Louisiana the judgments of conviction were affirmed.[109]

Nelson challenged the convictions on the grounds that they violated the due process and equal protection clauses of the Fourteenth Amendment to the U.S. Constitution because they constituted discrimination on the basis of race. The Louisiana Supreme Court affirmed the convictions, reasoning that the constitutional protections did not apply to private actions, and since the statute being enforced, the criminal mischief statute, contained no reference to race, whatever racially discriminatory motive existed, existed only for private action beyond the reach of the Fourteenth Amendment.[110]

To help develop the argument that the police's arrest and the city's prosecution sufficed to establish state action, and, thus, a violation of the equal protection clause of the Fourteenth Amendment, Jack Nelson sought the assistance of fellow Loyola law graduate Janet Mary Riley, someone who had participated in early efforts at Loyola to secure broad-based community support for integration. Riley wrote the brief in *Lombard v. Louisiana.*[111] Initially, Riley thought the argument that the prosecution of the students itself sufficed to establish state action was not a particularly strong argument, but as she acknowledged, "we won the case."[112] The U.S. Supreme Court, without dissent, reversed the convictions:

> A State, or a city, may act as authoritatively through its executive as through its legislative body. See *Ex parte Virginia,* 100 U.S. 339, 347. As we interpret the New Orleans city officials' statements, they here determined that the city would not permit Negroes to seek desegregated service in restaurants. Consequently, the city must be treated exactly as if it had an ordinance prohibiting such conduct. We have just held in *Peterson* v. *City of Greenville, ante,* p. 244, that where an ordinance makes it unlawful for owners or managers of restaurants to seat whites and Negroes together, a conviction under the State's criminal processes employed in a way which enforces the discrimination mandated by that ordinance cannot stand. Equally the State cannot achieve the same result by an official command which has

> at least as much coercive effect as an ordinance. The official command here was to direct continuance of segregated service in restaurants, and to prohibit any conduct directed toward its discontinuance; it was not restricted solely to preserve the public peace in a nondiscriminatory fashion in a situation where violence was present or imminent by reason of public demonstrations. Therefore here, as in *Peterson,* these convictions, commanded as they were by the voice of the State directing segregated service at the restaurant, cannot stand.[113]

As it had with Judge J. Skelly Wright and Judge Herbert Christenberry, the New Orleans community ostracized Jack Nelson in retaliation for his role in integrating New Orleans institutions, in particular, Tulane University.

Nelson had been one of those in the New Orleans community to speak up in defense of desegregating New Orleans schools. The case he filed against Tulane University hinged on the same kind of argument that he had pursued in the *Lombard* case: that Tulane was a public institution and thus was prohibited by the equal protection clause from denying admission to blacks. The peculiar facts of Tulane's founding made this argument viable. Tulane had been founded as a public institution by public act of the legislature. One of Wright's last acts as judge on the Eastern District before leaving for the District of Columbia was to sign the order in the case against Tulane.[114] It was a short-lived success, as a matter of law, because Wright's successor reversed the order, but it didn't matter: the Tulane community had had its fill of segregation, and the University admitted blacks in 1964.

Nelson considered leaving New Orleans but decided to stay.[115] He served as director of Loyola's Law Clinic until his retirement in 1992. He died in 2006. Stuart H. Smith, a Loyola graduate (Class of 1986) honored Professor Nelson's memory by donating funds to establish the Jack Nelson Distinguished Professor of Law, currently held by clinical professor Luz Molina.

The Reverend Alfred Biever, S.J. Born in Belgium in 1859, he traveled to Grand Coteau, Louisiana, at seventeen to enter the novitiate at the Jesuit College. Biever founded Loyola University and Loyola's law school.

In 1914, its first year, the law school held classes at the College of the Immaculate Conception on the corner of Baronne and Common.

The law school moved to Marquette Hall on St. Charles Avenue in 1915, for its second term.

John St. Paul, founding dean of Loyola's law school, went on to serve as associate justice of the Louisiana Supreme Court. St. Paul's family donated his portrait to the law school; it hangs in the Louisiana Supreme Court Building.

Law school Class of 1921. Alice Agnes Allen joined a class of eleven young men in fall 1918. She was the first woman to graduate from Loyola's law school, coming in fourth in her class.

Thomas More Hall, an old refurbished residence at 6363 St. Charles Avenue, was the law school's home from 1942 until 1975. It was not air-conditioned, and law students and faculty often complained about lack of space, the heat, and mosquitoes.

James Skelly Wright earned a bachelor of philosophy degree at Loyola in 1931, taught history part-time at the University, and then returned to the law school at night and graduated with a bachelor of laws in 1934. President Truman appointed him to the federal bench in 1949, where he wrote the order desegregating Orleans Parish public schools in *Bush v. Louisiana*. President John F. Kennedy appointed him to the U.S. Court of Appeals for the District of Columbia Circuit in 1962.

Moon Landrieu was a student at the law school in 1952 when it admitted four African Americans, including Norman Francis and Ben Johnson in the day division. Later, as a young legislator from New Orleans, he opposed numerous bills enacted by the Louisiana legislature in a frenzied attempt to block desegregation of the city's public schools. He went on to serve as mayor of the city from 1970 to 1978.

Norman Francis (*bottom left*) and Ben Johnson (*top left*), and the day Class of 1952, the first class at the law school to enroll African Americans.

The Reverend Joseph H. Fichter, S.J., came to Loyola in 1947 as chair of the Loyola sociology department, determined to integrate the University. His efforts were successful at the law school but met with great resistance in the undergraduate and most of the other professional programs.

The Reverend Louis Twomey, S.J., law school regent from 1948 to 1956, helped lead the school to voluntarily admit African Americans in 1952. From Father Twomey's perspective, the change came far too late.

Norman C. Francis, the first African American to graduate from the law school and Loyola University. In 1968, Francis became president of Xavier University of Louisiana. Born in Lafayette, Louisiana, on March 20, 1931, he served as president of the American Association of Higher Education and the United Negro College Fund, and was chairman of the Carnegie Foundation for the Advancement of Teaching. He chaired the Louisiana Recovery Authority, the state agency in charge of administering recovery after Hurricanes Katrina and Rita devastated southeastern Louisiana. President George W. Bush awarded Francis the Presidential Medal of Freedom in 2006.

Janet Mary Riley, the first woman law professor at Loyola, and Jack Nelson (*standing*), appointed director of the law school's clinic in 1979, joined Ernest N. "Dutch" Morial, to be elected first African American mayor of New Orleans in 1978, and A. P. Tureaud, one of the city's most prominent African American attorneys, at the Sixth Annual Interracial Sunday in March 1954.

Marcel Garsaud, dean of the law school from 1971 to 1982.

Janet Mary Riley, the first full-time woman law professor at the law school and seventh in the nation, joined the law school faculty as an instructor in 1953, and as an assistant professor in 1956. Riley worked with Jack Nelson on the *Lombard v. Louisiana* case, defending students arrested for integrating cafeteria lunch counters. Riley helped convince the Louisiana legislature to repeal the "head and master" laws that gave husbands control over community property and to adopt instead the concept of equal management.

Jack Nelson, a 1950 Loyola Law graduate, was appointed director of the clinic and the Gillis Long Poverty Law Center in 1979. Influenced by Father Twomey, Nelson worked to integrate the city's institutions and represented students attempting to integrate lunch counters in the city in the *Lombard v, Louisiana* case in 1960.

Louis Westerfield, a Loyola Law graduate, was the first African American law professor to earn tenure at the law school. He returned to the law school to serve as dean from 1990 to 1994.

Brian Bromberger, the longest-serving dean in modern times, joined the law school in fall 2003. He had planned to retire at the end of academic year 2009–10, when, to the dismay of the law school community, he suffered a heart attack and passed away two months before his retirement.

When Hurricane Katrina rendered the city unlivable at the start of the fall 2005 term, the University of Houston Law Center generously allowed Loyola Law School to teach classes out of its Houston campus. Houston law dean Nancy B. Rapoport and Loyola law dean Brian Bromberger came to an agreement within days of the hurricane, and Loyola law classes resumed in October. The law school was the only Loyola college to teach classes throughout fall 2005.

The Reverend Lawrence Moore, S.J., dedicating the Stuart H. Smith Law Clinic, in 2011. Father Moore joined the law faculty in 1982 and served on the Loyola Board of Trustees from 1985 to 2011. He has served as associate dean for academic affairs since 2000 and will serve as interim dean in 2015–16.

Kathryn Venturatos Lorio, Leon Sarpy Distinguished Professor of Law, graduated from Loyola's law school in 1973 and joined the faculty in 1976. She is a past chair of the Section on Women in Legal Education of the Association of American Law Schools and is an elected member of the American Law Institute. She is the first woman to serve as associate dean for academic affairs and dean, serving as interim dean in 2010–11.

Former dean James M. Klebba (*far left*) accompanied by law graduates (*left to right*) Frederick J. Gisevius, Jr. (class of 1936), the Honorable Pascal F. Calogero, Jr. (class of 1954), and the Honorable Maurice Edwin ("Moon") Landrieu (class of 1954).

On October 24, 2014, Loyola's *Law Review* hosted a symposium celebrating the work of Judge James Skelly Wright, featuring many of his former law clerks on the United States Court of Appeals for the District of Columbia. The law school unveiled a bronze memorial to Judge Wright at the conclusion of the symposium, and fellow Loyola Law graduate the Honorable Moon Landrieu addressed the crowd, joined by Ruby Bridges Hall, one of four children to start integrating New Orleans public schools on November 14, 1960, memorialized in a Norman Rockwell painting; the Honorable Mary Ann Vial Lemmon, U.S.D.C. for the Eastern District of Louisiana; and the Honorable Kenneth Allen Polite Jr., U.S. attorney for the Eastern District of Louisiana.

The Honorable Carl E. Stewart, Chief Judge, U.S. Court of Appeals for the Fifth Circuit, earned his JD from Loyola in 1974. President William J. Clinton appointed Stewart on January 27, 1994. Stewart delivered the 2014 Centennial Commencement address.

5

GROWTH AND TRANSITION

A MEANINGFUL ROLE FOR WOMEN AND MINORITIES IN LAW AT A TIME OF DRAMATIC EXPANSION IN LAW SCHOOLS

> Despite the modest resurgence of the unapproved schools, the ABA and AALS had come close to achieving their goal of nationwide standardization by 1970. By 1950, three years of college became the norm, and by the 1960s four years of college.... A law student of 1970, thoroughly indoctrinated in the unyielding standards of his time, would probably have had difficulty believing that it was not until roughly 1950 that the number of lawyers who had been to college exceeded the number of those who had not....
>
> The law schools, however, ... were about to be enmeshed in the social ferment of the period. In 1963, women had comprised only 2.7 percent of the profession.... In 1969, blacks, although constituting about 12 percent of the national population, only accounted for 1 percent of the bar.... Despite a decade of civil rights, women's rights, and antipoverty agitation, the law schools had been little influenced by these developments in society.
>
> —ROBERT STEVENS, *Law School: Legal Education in America from the 1850s to the 1980s*

The Civil Rights Act of 1964 prohibited discrimination on the basis of sex, race, color, and national origin in the employment context, and the 1972 amendments to the act included Title IX expanding the prohibition on discrimination on the basis of sex to educational institutions.[1] The United States went from a world in which it was common to see "help wanted male" and "help wanted female" ads, to one in which those ads were unthinkable. But it took decades for meaningful change to occur both at the law school and in the country at large.[2]

At Loyola the changes in the law should not have made a difference: like most law schools in Louisiana, it had been admitting women almost from the start. At Tulane's law school, Bettie Runnels, the first woman admitted to practice law in Louisiana, was its first woman to graduate in 1898.[3] Clift Martin was the first woman to enroll in LSU's law school in 1913, and she graduated in 1916.[4] Despite the fact that the U.S. Supreme Court had upheld the power of the state to deny women a license to practice law in 1873,[5] by 1920 all states and many law schools, nonetheless, admitted women to law studies.[6] Their numbers remained dismal, nonetheless, until the 1970s. Nationwide, prior to 1972, women made up less than 10 percent of law school students.[7] Women probably were not encouraged to apply, and the application process at the time, at least at Loyola, often involved personal application to the dean, so it is almost impossible to determine who was denied admission. Throughout most of the twentieth century, the number of women in the law classes tended to be small, if they were present at all.

Some women at Loyola, like Anna J. Veters, a 1923 graduate, were highly successful. Veters was the first woman to serve as judge in Louisiana. In 1941, she was inducted as magistrate of juvenile court in New Orleans.[8] It must have been extraordinarily difficult for trailblazers like Alice Allen and Anna Veters to navigate the law program in the 1920s. There were no women on the faculty or apparently in any capacity at all. Loyola's College of Arts and Sciences did not begin to admit women until the 1950s, and although other professional programs admitted them as well, women must still have been a rarity on the campus.[9]

Early editions of the *Loyola Law Journal* offer a window through which to view their experience. They reflect considerable focus on issues relating to women, including articles on marriage, divorce, and abortion, at least one authored by a woman.[10] Humorous anecdotes or jokes centered on marriage, divorce, and women appear frequently throughout. The second volume of the *Journal* includes the continuation of an "anonymous" article on the property rights of married women through the ages. Immediately following the article is a brief note, something that appears to have been common for the law journal at this time. It is titled "The Female of the Species" and contains a commentary on the presence of women at the law school: "Now every Loyola Law Class has its lady lawyer, and Freshman and Junior have each a pair. There is imminent danger, too, that in each case she will prove the best man in the class. Sons of Adam, what if Miss Veters' achievement in 1919 were tripled in 1920."[11]

Genuine admiration for Veters's accomplishment upon her graduation comes through in the *Journal*'s commentary: "[T]his young lady was declared Bachelor of Laws, Magna Cum Laude, with the highest average of her class in the three year's course, outranking William Bell by a fraction."[12] But the comment also reveals apprehension over the possibility that more women might decide to attend law school and be equally or even more successful than Veters. The majority of the law class need not have worried. For the most part, few women applied and were admitted to law school at this time.

If women were scarce as students, they were even rarer in the faculty ranks.[13] At midcentury, out of an approximate 1,239 tenure-track law professors nationwide, only 5 were women, less than .5 percent,[14] none of them at Loyola. LSU Law School was the only Louisiana law school to hire a woman law professor in the first half of the century; in 1926, LSU hired Harriet Spiller Daggett as a law professor in the fall of the same year that she graduated from its law school.[15]

At Loyola, only the position of librarian was available to women, and it was through this position that Loyola hired its first full-time, tenure-track woman law professor.[16] When Solange Mille left her position as librarian in fall 1945 upon her marriage,[17] Janet Mary Riley replaced her in December 1945. In September 1947, Riley began to teach legal bibliography to both day and evening students. Encouraged by Dean Vernon Miller, she enrolled at the law school as a student on a part-time basis. When she was ready to graduate in 1952, Loyola offered her a contract to formally join the faculty but at a salary below what she had been making as law librarian. The librarian's contract was a twelve-month contract; as a faculty member she would be on a ten-month contract, leaving her summers free to pursue other projects. More importantly, as a librarian the highest rank open to her at the time was assistant professor; as a faculty member she could aspire to professor status.

Dean Antonio Papale may have been reluctant, as a new dean, to insist on Riley's hiring at the requested salary. Like many women law graduates throughout the majority of the twentieth century, legal employment did not come easy. When she received word of a position as an assistant law librarian at the University of Oklahoma law school that would pay far more than the salary she had been offered, she passed the letter on to Papale, who passed it on to the president at the time.[18] Riley continued to serve as librarian and to teach as an instructor until 1955, when she refused to sign another contract. She continued to work on a month-to-month arrangement, and in 1956 the University finally offered her a ten-month contract at the rank of assistant professor. That academic year, Riley joined the law faculty as an assistant professor.[19] She remained at Loyola for the rest of her professional life.

THE 1960S

Amid social and political upheaval on many university and law school campuses throughout the 1960s, Loyola's campus appears to have been for the most part quiet until the end of the decade. The decade had begun with desegregation of the city and the schools. Nineteen sixty-three witnessed the assassination of the country's first Catholic president, John Fitzgerald Kennedy, a devastating event for many Americans, but one received with eerie quiet on the Loyola campus. Nineteen sixty-five brought the assassination of Malcolm X, and 1968 the assassinations of Martin Luther King Jr. and Robert F. Kennedy. Frustration at the slow rate of change and anger over the escalating war in Vietnam prompted massive protests at the national Democratic convention. The protests that occurred on Loyola's campus in 1969 and 1970 may have involved law students and law faculty, but they do not appear to have revolved around the law school.[20] Apart from a protest mounted against a law professor over his too rigorous teaching style, and the departure of a number of law faculty in the late 1960s, the changes that were tearing Americans apart in other places occurred at Loyola with little disruption to the law school.[21]

In 1963, the law school had considered changing its curriculum to increase the number of required hours for the degree and ceased to offer courses in the common law to evening division students. At the time, Loyola's curriculum was similar to Tulane's—both law schools required approximately the same number of hours: 78. LSU, however, required an additional 12 hours for a total of 90 hours of course work in order to graduate, many of the courses required rather than elective. The Loyola law full-time faculty at this time numbered seven; adding a full additional year of required courses represented a substantial challenge without additional faculty resources.

The faculty had instituted common law courses in 1957 to encourage more out-of-state applicants, but the 1963 faculty wanted to expand the required curriculum and return focus to Louisiana law. The curriculum adopted mirrored that of LSU, with a heavy load of required courses to graduate. For the rest of the twentieth century and into the twenty-first, the law faculty struggled with a conflict initiated by a faculty of seven who committed the school to a curriculum that stressed Louisiana law and minimized the major developments of the legal world in the second half of the twentieth century.

A student entering Loyola law in 1963 faced a total of 78 credit hours to complete his law degree. His first-year courses consisted of contracts I, torts I, persons, introduction to law, constitutional law I, and criminal law in the fall; and contracts II, torts II, property, business associations I, constitutional law II, and criminal procedure in the spring. In the second and third years, the student was free to select from the offered courses.[22]

By contrast, a student entering Loyola law in 1964 faced required courses throughout her first and second years. The first year remained the same as for 1963, but in the second year, rather than select from the courses offered, law students were required to take legal accounting, successions, obligations, evidence, damages, moot court, and one elective in the fall, and in the spring, business associations II, donations, sales & leases, community property, income taxation, and an elective.

Students entering in 1965 faced a still more regimented and onerous schedule: not only the first and second years consisted of mostly required courses, but the third year as well. In the fall of their third year, students would take Louisiana procedure I, security rights, federal rules, commercial transactions, title examinations, and an elective; in the spring, Louisiana procedure II, jurisprudence, federal jurisdiction, conflict of laws, legal ethics, and whatever electives were left for the students to satisfy. Under this program of study, 76 of the 78 hours required for the law degree were required, leaving only 2 hours for possible electives (unless the student was willing to pay for extra hours for electives unnecessary for graduation).

Following the lead of other law schools to rename the bachelor of laws a juris doctor, Loyola began to offer the juris doctor in 1968 and offered to retroactively award a juris doctor to graduates who had earned the LLB degree between 1917 and 1967.

On the law faculty, Janet Riley became active in university affairs. Riley and Dennis Rousseau, also on the law faculty, helped to establish the University Senate and the University Rank and Tenure Committee, and to draft the *Fac-*

ulty Handbook. They, with other University faculty leaders, played prominent roles in the adoption of formal rank and tenure procedures and the principle of academic freedom.

The Loyola faculty senate was formed initially in 1964 at the urging of the Loyola Chapter of the American Association of University Professors (AAUP).[23] The University's attempt to dismiss an English professor in the mid-1960s made it clear that the University's rank and tenure policies were insufficient to protect faculty members. They did not provide faculty members with a method of appealing adverse employment decisions. The case also made it clear that the faculty senate and *Faculty Handbook* needed modification to become effective mechanisms for faculty to play a meaningful governance role in the University.[24] In 1968, the faculty senate promulgated its constitution and became formally known as the University Senate, and in 1969, the University Senate formed a University Rank and Tenure Committee to develop rank and tenure policies and to serve as the primary entity to process appeals from denials of tenure. The Senate also formed a Faculty Handbook Negotiating Committee to work with the University administration in ensuring a role for faculty governance in the institution and to secure faculty rights. The two committees worked on a policy statement on faculty rights, freedoms, and responsibilities that eventually became the new *Faculty Handbook*.[25] Dennis Rousseau served as the first chair of the University Senate, and Janet Mary Riley served as the first chair of the University Rank and Tenure Committee. Both held these positions for a number of years. Rousseau gave up his leadership of the Senate to assist the University president, and Riley went on to serve as chair of the Senate.

Change in the relationship between the faculty and the administration was facilitated when students began to protest. Both faculty and students participated in the protests, and to some degree it became difficult to separate protests directed at the war from protests directed at the way that the University responded to the protests themselves, particularly when it involved faculty. Loyola students urged the University to suspend classes in observance of the National Moratorium to end the Vietnam War on October 15, 1969. The University Senate voted to support the moratorium by a bare majority. The University declined to cancel classes and instead adopted an optional attendance policy. Many Loyola students and faculty demonstrated before City Hall in opposition to the war. In 1970, conflict over the University's denial of tenure to the professor in the English Department and the subsequent arrest of another professor of English for disturbing the peace and using obscene language in the course of a student march, spilled over to students and prompted more campus unrest.

Riley and Rousseau helped draft the 1973 *Loyola University Faculty Handbook,* first published in 1956 as a handbook for the faculty of the College of Arts and Sciences. The *Handbook* reflected a commitment to tenure, academic freedom, and institutional processes to protect and enhance academic integrity and growth. The 1973 *Handbook* introduced a form of sabbatical leave that was not guaranteed but for which faculty members could apply, and much stronger protection for academic freedom.[26] It opened its academic freedom section with a strong commitment to "the free and unhampered pursuit of truth and knowledge," alongside a similar commitment to the idea that such truth could be "discovered and understood."[27] Faculty was expected to "show respect for both Christian morality and Christian teaching," but "Loyola specifically warrants the right of every faculty member . . . the right to believe and to express that belief without fear of reprisal."[28] The 1981 revisions, effective in fall 1982, provided the basic framework for the current *Loyola University Faculty Handbook,* including the formation of the University Senate, the University Faculty Handbook Revision Committee, and a formal sabbatical leave policy that for the first time guaranteed to faculty a one-semester sabbatical leave at full salary or a two-semester sabbatical leave at two-thirds salary every seven years of continuous service at the University.[29]

In interviews, Riley later recalled the challenges facing a woman attempting to navigate terrain that had up to that time been reserved exclusively for men.[30] Despite her powerful leadership in negotiating the relationship between the faculty and the University, in law faculty meetings she felt unheard and ignored. Colleagues would overlook her contributions but laud the identical comment or idea if proposed by one of her male colleagues. In the classroom, male students did not hesitate to challenge her competency.[31] In these experiences she was not alone.

Law school publications, law student groups, and law school hiring practices give a sense of how the law school responded to the increasing presence of women and minorities. The law school published a student newspaper, the *Legal Rag,* in 1960. Early issues were mimeographed and distributed to students. The newspaper included the moot court problem, news about tuition increases and other law school matters, and news about the "Law Wives' Club," a club for the wives of law students that continued to exist into the 1970s. The May 1967 issue of the *Rag* noted a presentation of "Putting Hubby Through" diplomas to the wives of graduating seniors. Understandably, perhaps, the photograph of the class of 1967 photograph contains only one woman. The late 1960s issues of the *Rag* reflect concerns about the draft, the war, the bar, and the lack of a placement office. The 1968 *Rag* notes the failure of the student body to pass an honor code, due in large part to opposition by the first-year class.

In 1969, the paper began to be printed and to receive broader distribution. The January 1969 *Rag* noted an increase in the number of women at the law school: nineteen women were enrolled, eight of them first-years and an additional three as part-time students. According to the *Rag,* that was "the largest number of women ever previously admitted to any law school in the South."[32] The article noted that "five of the nineteen women are married, a positive indication that marriage and professional training can be successfully combined."[33]

The October 1969 *Rag* celebrated the opening of the law placement office and the appointment of the first director of admissions and placement for the law school, 1966 Loyola law graduate Katherine Schwab. The newspaper also welcomed three new professors to the law school: Frederick W. Swaim Jr., Keith Vetter, and Gerald D. Vinnard. Swaim, a native New Orleanian, had been teaching at the Detroit College of Law. He was a Tulane University law graduate with an LLM from the University of California at Berkeley. Swaim was also a member of the Louisiana bar. Vetter, a native Louisianan from Donaldsonville, had practiced with the U.S. Army, having earned his bachelor of arts and an LLB from Louisiana State University. Vinnard was a 1969 graduate of Harvard Law School with a bachelor of science degree from Fresno State College.

Student organizations reflected the societal changes of the 1960s and 1970s and became instrumental themselves in effecting change at the law school. Although Loyola's law school had integrated in 1952, the number of African Americans enrolled and to graduate remained small. The African American population in New Orleans was substantial, however, and black law students pushed the administration to initiate more aggressive recruitment of black students. In 1969, students established the A. P. Tureaud Chapter of the Black Law Student Association (BLSA), its mission to recruit and maintain the enrollment of qualified minority students. That same year the law school newspaper reported that in 1969, less than 1 percent of all lawyers in New

Orleans were black. Most of them were in private practice without partners. There was one all-black law firm in the city, Collins, Douglass and Elie, and black attorneys occupied a number of public and private professional positions. Only one black attorney, apparently, worked at an integrated law firm.[34] BLSA sponsored a moot court team in the National Frederick Douglass Moot Court Competition.[35]

Dean Papale retired in 1970, having presided over the law school for almost two decades. His last years as dean had proved rocky. Law faculty hires in the mid-1960s had been controversial, some of them making serious allegations that the law school facilities were unsustainable, that law graduates were receiving a "textbook" education, and sent off to become "legal practitioners."[36] A student letter to the editor at the law student newspaper in 1965 described the law building as being in deplorable condition and questioned why it was not being maintained properly.[37] Two of the new faculty had been placed in an office without air conditioning (Thomas More Hall was not air-conditioned), with no division or "privacy between themselves and among students and faculty members who wish to visit one or the other of them in the normal course of their duties." Dean Papale pleaded with Loyola president, the Reverend Homer R. Jolley, S.J., for an emergency budget request. Some of the new faculty left, and some were encouraged to leave. But the incident set off alarms among the alumni, and they did not hesitate to contact the Loyola president to express their concerns. Papale had also experienced a prolonged illness during this period.

Loyola appointed a search committee to replace Papale in 1968. Judge Ainsworth served as chair of the committee; Joseph Blasi, president of the Loyola Law Alumni, and Professors Jack Nelson, Marcel Garsaud, who had recently returned to the faculty with an LLM from Yale, Dennis Rousseau, and Leon Sarpy also served on the search committee.

The dean search yielded a number of candidates, all of them well briefed on Loyola's strengths and weaknesses. Judge Ainsworth stated to the faculty: "We heard a good deal about how far behind the Loyola School of Law was in salary structure." As with its predecessor, the committee determined that the best course of action was to select someone from the Loyola law faculty to serve as dean. Judge Ainsworth asked Garsaud and Rousseau, the two professors being considered for the deanship, to step down from the committee, and both agreed. "In the long history of the School of Law," Judge Ainsworth continued, "we have never had a Loyola man as Dean. . . . The man we chose is a graduate of Loyola and the holder of an advanced degree in Law from an outstanding University. He has had experience both in the practice and teaching of law. He has deep roots in New Orleans and a record of proven worth and loyalty to this University."[38] Ainsworth announced the candidate: law faculty member Marcel Garsaud.

THE 1970S

Garsaud, the first Loyola graduate to serve as dean of the law school, presided over a challenging period—a time of insufficient financial resources to adequately support the law school, and a time during which external and internal sources were pushing for change at a faster pace than could be delivered with limited resources. Legal education was changing. Loyola's effort to keep up with and, in some instances, lead change in the state was striking; that the resources to build on and maintain those initiatives were often lacking frustrated deans, students, and faculty. Garsaud led a faculty composed of twenty-four professors, only two of whom were women: Janet Riley and the law librarian, Caroline Heriot; all were white. The entering day class for 1970–71 consisted of 135 students, including 6 women, and an entering night class of 83 students, including 8 women. The school's student population had significantly grown; total enrollment for 1970–71 was 562.

New Orleans in 1970 made the top-twenty list of largest urban places in the U.S. Census that year: it came in at number nineteen, with a population of 593,471, a bit above the last city on the list, Phoenix, Arizona.[39] The city, however, was losing population; in 1960, the year in which New Orleans recorded its largest population, the Census Bureau recorded a population of 627,525. Of the population over age eighteen, 44.6 percent was reported as male. Of the city's population, 45.5 percent was recorded as "Negro and other races."[40]

Louisiana's total population in 1970 was a little over 3.6 million people. Two-thirds lived in urban areas, and the largest metropolitan area was New Orleans. According to the U.S. Census, approximately one-third of the state's population was "Negro and other races." The bulk of the state's population was native; approximately 140,000 individuals were foreign-born. Approximately 26.3 percent of the state's residents had incomes below the poverty level, but 53.2 percent of those were black. Fifty-one percent of those with incomes below the poverty level were female heads of family; 43.3 percent were sixty-five and over.[41]

Law schools throughout the country faced the challenge of increasing their enrollment of women and racial and ethnic minorities. For a law school in a Deep South state where African Americans constituted a significant proportion of the state's population, and a city in which they constituted almost half the population, enrolling significant numbers of African Americans emerged as a priority. In 1970, Loyola and the three other Louisiana law schools agreed to recruit minority students in the state and outside of the state. Loyola had been working with the Council on Legal Education Opportunity (CLEO)—an independent, nonprofit group founded by the ABA Fund for Justice and Education in 1968 to diversity the profession—to recruit black students. But Dean Papale (about to leave Loyola) thought Louisiana schools might be more successful in recruiting minority students working on their own. A 1973 article in the Loyola law student newspaper, the *Code,* noted the paucity of black lawyers and black law students in the United States and described the efforts of the Minority Recruitment Committee, a black law student group recognized by the Student Bar Association, to recruit minority law students throughout Louisiana to the law school. The article noted: "In 1970, statistics showed that in ten Southern states, 393 Black lawyers were available to serve a Black population of some nine million. At 17 major Southern law schools, the total number of Black freshman in 1972 came to less than 200."[42]

The *Legal Rag* became the *Code* in 1970. It was staffed and produced by law students, and the law dean generally had budgetary and censorship authority, although it is likely to have been exercised sparingly. In approving the law dean as the "publisher's representative," the University administrator with power to intervene in the publication and censor, then president the Reverend James C. Carter, S.J. made clear that he reserved the authority "to appoint someone other than the Dean of the College" to the position.[43] The new publication went out to alumni, radio stations, and other newspapers.

The *Code*'s first issue in 1970 opened with an interview of the new dean. Law students wanted to know about construction of the proposed new law building (Miller Hall would not open until 1973), bar passage (whether the new dean would introduce a policy of failing more seniors to improve bar passage), and the proposed law clinic. The student editorial board complained about incompetent instructors and the tenure system, which students felt protected incompetent faculty, and a lack of adequate classrooms.[44] "Some instructors have been here for as long as the law building itself has stood," the editorial complained, acknowledging that not all old professors were bad and that some were "very good teachers."

> But certain instructors have a habit of giving good grades to those who agree with him and walk three steps behind him in a bowed position. Then there are those instructors who don't even open the final exams to grade them and instead give a grade based upon the thickness of the paper returned by the student. This can be proven by the Teacher's failure to separate exam papers, which have been glued together with chewing gum. . . . You may never see your exam paper after grading due to its being misplaced or being left at the instructor's home.[45]

The issue noted that students for the first time at the law school had been asked to evaluate law faculty. Student participation, however, was poor, "and the tabulation of the few forms returned was meaningless."[46] Dean Garsaud began the move to establish formal teaching evaluations of law faculty perhaps in response to student complaints about teaching but also because the University as a whole began to use student evaluations of faculty as part of the rank and tenure process.

Nineteen seventy also welcomed three new professors: William Crowe, a graduate of LSU with an LLM from Northwestern University Law School; Thomas Puklin, a Northwestern University graduate with a JD from DePaul University; and Arthur Lemann, a graduate of Loyola with an LLM from George Washington University Law School, soon to head the newly established law clinic. In academic year 1971–72, the first African American law professor at the law school, Warren D. Bracy, joined the law faculty. Bracy left at the end of the academic year.

Black students felt the lack of African American law faculty most directly when they experienced problems on the law school campus. Faculty who had grown up in the deeply segregated and racist South found it difficult to understand the perspectives of young African American men and women students. During Garsaud's first year as dean, controversy arose over a student newspaper article on the anarchist movement that included a history of white-black relationships in the South and the United States and the rise of communism and anarchism in the twentieth century, in relation to the evacuation of one of the Loyola buildings over a bomb scare.[47] The pairing of these developments implicitly suggested that the "young American anarchist" movement had something to do with the Black Power movement; language in the article also suggested some sympathy for segregation in the post-*Brown* years: "The South was forced to capitulate a second time in one hundred years—the 'lost cause' lost once again."

Black students responded: "This article is racist and when published in *The Code,* it becomes offensive to Black People and should be offensive to all Students in Loyola's Law School."[48] Seven African American students signed the letter challenging the publication of the student article. The editors responded that black students were being "overly sensitive. . . . Mr. Vinet's article was his opinion and he had a right to express it."

The absence of black law faculty damaged white students as well. It helped to perpetuate bias and lack of confidence in black law students through its implicit suggestion that no African Americans were qualified to teach in law schools. The presence of African American professional faculty, like the presence of women professional faculty, made a difference. As Cynthia Epstein acknowledged, "Law professors are an honored elite in their profession and among the highest paid in the university."[49] The absence of nonwhite and women law professors on a law faculty spoke volumes to law students.

In 1970 the law school increased the total number of hours needed to graduate to 84 and made small changes to the required courses. In fall 1972, the school appears to have adopted the program that remained in place for the next few decades: first-years would take contracts I, torts I, civil procedure I, persons, criminal law, and legal bibliography in the fall; and contracts II or obligations, torts II, civil procedure II, property, introduction to the civil code, and administration of criminal justice I in the spring semester. The second-year curriculum included two semesters of constitutional law, successions, evidence, corporations, donations, sales and leases, income taxation, moot court; and the third year included two semesters of Louisiana procedure, security rights, federal rules, federal jurisdiction, and professional responsibility. In fall 1975, the total number of hours required to graduate again increased to 90, Loyola joining a very small number of law schools requiring far more hours for the law degree than those suggested by the ABA. Although the school offered electives in response to changes in society and the law, like environmental law first offered in academic year 1972-73, they tended to be offered intermittently and some, like consumer law and the problems of the elderly were eventually dropped from the curriculum. The heavy number of required hours made it difficult to offer a meaningful number of electives.

The law school had been largely unsuccessful in recruiting African Americans and other minorities. In academic year 1977–78, Loyola enrolled only seven blacks. BLSA complained that the school lacked an effective organized recruiting program for minority applicants, and felt the burden of recruiting minorities had been placed on student organizations.[50] The admissions director, Kathy Schwab, made it clear that the recruitment budget did not allow the law school sufficient funds to compete for minority students.

Women, on the other hand, were enrolling in greater numbers, and this development was threatening to the law school community in ways that the earlier women law students had not been. The ABA had noted a dramatic increase in the number of women law students and a substantial gain in minority enrollment in 1974. The *Code* noted concerns about the potential impact on employment.[51]

Notwithstanding the challenges of being the only woman on the faculty for almost two decades, Riley persevered and helped to change the course of Louisiana law to better realize equality for women in property and marriage laws. Riley wrote the first casebook on Louisiana community property law.[52] She served as head of the Louisiana Law Institute committee on the revision of Louisiana's community property laws. The committee was disbanded in 1977, but Riley's work yielded results.

Although Louisiana law recognized community property rights, in principle recognizing the rights of each spouse to property arising during a marital union, the state, through its "head and master" provisions, vested control over marital property in the husband, to the detriment of the wife, who often had no right to challenge a husband's financial decisions over marital property. Riley played an instrumental role in changing the law through her work on the *Corpus Christi Parish Credit Union v. Martin* case, in which she filed the amicus curiae brief for the League of Women Voters of Louisiana.[53] The case involved a challenge to the "head and master" provisions of the Louisiana Civil Code. The lower court held article 2404 of the Civil Code ("The husband is the head and master of the partnership or community of gains. . . .") unconstitutional. The Louisiana Supreme Court reversed the lower court and held that the "head and master" provision was constitutional. The court noted that holding article 2404 unconstitutional would necessitate a "complete examination of the constitutionality of the community property system."[54]

Riley turned her efforts to legislative reform, and in 1979, the Louisiana legislature adopted her "equal management" approach and repealed the head and master provisions.[55] The changes were to be effective on January 1, 1980. In the meantime, in 1979, in *Kirchberg v. Feenstra,* the United States Court of Appeals for the Fifth Circuit held Louisiana's head and master code provisions unconstitutional.[56]

Students pressured the law school to hire more women law faculty. The Association of Women Law Students (AWLS) was first organized in 1972, although the Student Bar Association (SBA) did not charter the organization until academic year 1973–74.[57] Women students urged the school to hire more women as faculty and to offer courses that explored the role of gender and gender discrimination in law. The AWLS persuaded the law school to offer a course in sex discrimination, to be offered for the first time at Loyola in fall 1974 by Lynne Stern. The employment discrimination course and sex discrimination seminar, first offered in academic year 1974–75, appear to have been the only course offerings to deal with the massive changes involving perspectives on race and gender in the law until the turn of the twenty-first century.

In 1974, the law school had welcomed four new law faculty: Lynne Stern, with a bachelor's degree from the University of Michigan and a law degree from Columbia University School of Law; Raphael Rabalais, with an undergraduate degree from Princeton University, a master's from Michigan State University, and his law degree from Harvard University; and Ira Bloom, a graduate of City College of New York with a law degree from Syracuse University. Stern had clerked for a federal judge, Bloom had worked as a trial and appellate attorney for the U.S. Department of Justice, and Rabalais had worked for the Housing Authority in Lansing, Michigan, prior to joining Loyola. Stern left after spring 1976 because she was pregnant.[58]

In fall 1975, the *Code*'s headline read "Barriers Lower for Women in Law." The article heralded the marked increase in the number of women in law school and concluded that on the whole, most of the time, women had felt welcome at the law school. Notwithstanding the good treatment, the author noted concerns expressed by women law students: "The main gripe concerned insensitive remarks made by teachers last year. While some women believe the remarks were misinterpreted, some are still fuming about the comment that 'rape should no longer be a serious crime now that women have the pill.' They believe physical degradation and personal humiliation are serious offenses, regardless of whether pregnancy results."[59] The student newspaper also elicited complaints: "Junior women also disliked an article in the Code last semester called 'Stella' claiming it stereotyped all women law students as losers who had come to Loyola as a 'last ditch effort to get a man.'" Other annoyances included the continuance of the "Law Wives' Club," and "teasing of married women that they didn't 'need to be here since they had husbands to support them.'" Women law graduates were likely to experience difficulty job-hunting, the article noted, as well as bias practicing before courts. The article also noted that "at least one student who sought a clerkship was asked if she could type and take dictation."[60]

Law students became adept at using humor and positive reinforcement to change behavior toward women. The *Code* featured a column titled "Living with Libby," along the lines of a "Dear Abby" column, except that Libby believed in passing the Equal Rights Amendment and resolutely gave advice that for the most part rejected gender stereotypes. The *Code* also reported on an award to be annually presented by the AWLS for the teacher who most improved his attitude toward women in law school. The winner of the award in 1976: Professor William Crowe.[61]

In its early years the AWLS sponsored a number of programs and conferences drawing attention to the problems that faced women in the world of law. In 1978, the AWLS organized a conference on "women and the law" at the law school. The conference was held on an annual basis for a number of years.[62] AWLS officers that year included Kim Gandy, who went on to head the National Organization for Women. The first conference featured Congresswoman Lindy Boggs as a keynote speaker, the first woman from Louisiana to be elected to the U.S. House of Representatives.[63] The program explored the *Corpus Christi Parish Credit Union v. Martin* case, in which a Louisiana court held that the head and master provision of the Louisiana Civil Code was unconstitutional under the equal protection clause of the Fourteenth Amendment.[64] This was Riley's case, and the AWLS put on a program featuring Riley and the attorney who represented the plaintiff in the case. Gandy continued to be active with AWLS as an alumnus. While working in the Orleans Parish district attorney's office, she returned to the law school for another AWLS program on domestic violence.[65] For a time, the AWLS issued a newsletter.[66]

In 1976, Kathryn Venturatos Lorio joined the law faculty when Lynne Stern departed. Lorio was a 1973 Loyola Law graduate. Lorio's family settled in New Orleans after leaving Smyrna and Greece in the early twentieth century. Her parents moved to pursue business opportunities, and she grew up in Pittsburgh, attending Pennsylvania public schools until the family returned to the New Orleans area in 1962. Lorio graduated as valedictorian from Ben Franklin High School, a member of the first class at Franklin to be integrated. She studied political science at Newcomb College, then the women's college at Tulane University, graduating in 1970 magna cum laude, a member of Phi Beta Kappa. Lorio decided to attend law school and chose Loyola instead of Tulane because of Loyola's scholarship offer. She started at the law school the same year Marcel Garsaud took over as dean, when the school was still housed at Thomas More Hall. There were nine women in her graduating class. Lorio made law review, where she served as casenote editor, and was chosen as a member of the national moot court team. Upon graduating in 1973, she joined local law firm Deutsch, Kerrigan and Stiles, and went to work for the only woman then at the firm (also the only woman partner), Marion Meyer Berkett. When Lorio joined the faculty in 1976, the teaching load was much heavier than is now common: Lorio taught three courses per semester. Her courses initially were successions and criminal law.[67]

Lorio was the first woman law faculty to continue to teach during and after a pregnancy, at a time when law schools in general and Loyola in particular did not provide maternity leave. At least two women faculty had left Loyola because of pregnancies, and while it is possible the departures reflected personal preferences, it is highly likely that the law school failed to accommodate the women's needs or encourage them to return to teaching after their pregnancies. Lorio's pregnancies obliged the academic calendar; her first child was born at the beginning of the summer, and the second was born also in May, and Lorio was scheduled to take a sabbatical leave the following year, giving her time to further develop her scholarship. It would be decades before the University adopted a maternity leave policy.

In its earlier years, Loyola had developed a practice of providing financial support to pursue graduate studies for Loyola law graduates who had accepted teaching positions at the school. By the time Lorio joined the faculty, however, the law school had ceased to provide that kind of support. Lorio's scholarship addressed issues of illegitimacy, concubinage, and alternative reproductive technologies. In particular, her later work explored the ethical and bioethical ramifications of assisted reproductive technologies, referencing Catholic doctrine as well as that of other religious traditions. Lorio went on to become the school's first endowed professor as the Leon Sarpy Endowed Professorship in Law.[68] Lorio was selected to serve as chair of the AALS Section of Women in Legal Education and was the first woman to serve as associate dean for academic affairs at the law school.[69] She was also the first woman to serve as interim dean.

Accompanying Lorio on the faculty were two young men: James Spoonhour, a Georgetown law graduate and a member of the law review at Georgetown who had gone into private practice in Florida; and William Walker, a graduate of Vanderbilt Law School and member of the *Vanderbilt Law Review,* also with private practice experience. Spoonhour left Loyola after one year to return to private practice. The year 1976 also marked the election of the first woman at the law school to be president of the Loyola Student Bar Association, Becky Macke.[70]

Win-Shin S. Chiang, sometimes referred to as Stella Chiang, also joined the law school in 1976 to replace law librarian Caroline C. Heriot. Heriot resigned to accept the head librarian's position at the College of William and Mary Law School.[71] Chiang had a law degree from the National Taiwan University and had earned a master's in library science from the University of Texas.

Professor Chiang pushed to have the law library improve its collection. In July 1978, she developed a proposal to establish a U.S. government publications depository collection in the law library, subsequently adopted by the University.[72] Chiang noted that although the collection "satisfied the ABA/AALS minimum size requirement of 60,000 volumes in 1976," it was "still largely insufficient to support the curriculum and particularly, the research needs of the faculty and students." At the current level of funding, she concluded it would take the library from fifteen to seventeen years to increase the collection to 200,000 volumes, the number she thought adequate. Her proposal was to obtain depository status to receive U.S. government publications. It would not only help develop the collection in international or comparative law materials, but also free up funds that would go to purchasing U.S. government publications for acquisition of other materials. The program would impose some burdens on the law library, but it would give the library government publications worth in excess of $81,000 per year. For availing itself of a benefit made freely available to libraries of accredited law schools upon request, Loyola law school would enhance its collection with an average of 5,000 additional volumes per year at no cost. The library would have to provide for the technical processing of these publications, which would entail adding two full-time permanent staff members, but Chiang made clear that the overall benefit to Loyola would far exceed the cost. Loyola approved her proposal, and the law school library became a depository in 1979.

In 1979, Professor Chiang developed a proposal to establish a Lexis computerized legal research system in the law library. The proposal discussed the changes that computerized legal research systems were bringing to law practice and legal education and recommended bringing the Lexis system to the law school. At the time, there were two computer legal research systems—Lexis and Westlaw. Lexis enjoyed a wider market than Westlaw, so Chiang recommended Loyola use Lexis: "The use of a CLR system in Loyola University Law School will provide many of its graduates with skills that will give them a competitive advantage in the job market; it will substantially increase the capability of the Law School to perform in-depth research; and it will markedly improve the reference capability of the Law Library to render service to the faculty and students of the law school."[73] Chiang asked for the system and for an additional reference librarian with a law degree to provide support for the system, and both requests were approved. By 1984, Loyola law school provided both Lexis and Westlaw systems.

Chiang instituted a series of law library exhibitions in 1979. That spring the library showcased an exhibition on women and the law, cosponsored with the AWLS and the Law School Division of the American Bar Association, as well as an exhibition on the history of the law school from 1914 to 1978.

Notwithstanding Chiang's efforts, by 1983, Loyola's law library collection lagged behind that of other Jesuit law schools (it came in tenth out of thirteen schools), and dead last of all the Louisiana schools including Southern.[74] A formal evaluation of the collection concurred that the law library lacked adequate funding, but the library itself emerged with for the most part stellar marks.[75] The evaluation was conducted by the librarian at the University of Minnesota Law Library and then president of the professional association of law librarians. She did not know Stella Chiang prior to the visit, and she was unstinting in her praise: "Director Stella Chiang is an organizational genius."[76]

In fall 1977, the law school hired Louis Westerfield, an African American law professor, the first to earn tenure at Loyola. Westerfield was a Mississippian of humble origins. He had grown up in the New Orleans housing projects, attended public schools, and graduated from Southern University in New Orleans. He started law school at Southern in Baton Rouge but transferred after a year to Loyola. He graduated from Loyola in 1974 and worked as a prosecutor in New Orleans for one year. He started his academic career at Southern Law School as an assistant professor, joining Loyola as a visiting professor after a year at Southern. In 1980, like most other Loyola graduates to join the law faculty, he left the law school to pursue an LLM from Columbia University Law School. Upon completion of the degree, he returned to Loyola, where he earned tenure in academic year 1982–83.

Alongside Westerfield, Michael Vitiello, a Swarthmore graduate with a law degree from the University of Pennsylvania, also joined the law faculty in 1977. The law faculty, however, still was overwhelmingly white and male. Law faculty hiring continued this trend into the twenty-first century. In this, it was similar to most American law schools.

Under Garsaud's leadership, the law school established a moot court board composed of law students in 1973. The board was placed in charge of coordinating the National Moot Court Program, the Philip C. Jessup International Moot Court Program, and the freshman Appellate Argument Seminar.[77] The seminar, a precursor to the moot court course in the second semester of the first year of law school, was restricted to eighteen students, all of whom had to be in the top 25 percent of second semester first-year students. Faculty member Brendan Brown served as advisor to the moot court board. The law school had been competing in national moot court competitions since fall 1954[78] and in the Philip C. Jessup International Competition since 1969. Law school success in both competitions came after the establishment of the Moot Court Board. Loyola law alumni donated Italian marble plaques to recognize the Loyola National Moot Court teams in 1973. The plaques recorded the team names since 1954, and the tradition continues today.

In 1974–75, Loyola law school students Patrick O'Keefe, Alexander F. X. Matulewicz, and Joseph A. Mengacci won the national championship in the National Moot Court Competition. O'Keefe, a native New Orleanian, won top oralist in the nation. Matulewicz came from Massachusetts, and Mengacci from Connecticut. In their final round, the team argued before Associate Justice William H. Rehnquist, U.S. Supreme Court; Cyrus Vance, then president of the New York City Bar Association; and Jack Greenberg of the NAACP Legal

Defense and Education Fund, among others. The Jessup team also met with success; it won its first regional championship that same year.

By 1974, the law school had instituted a system of anonymous grading. Student opinion on anonymous grading was split, but a majority favored the change.[79]

Under Dean Garsaud, the law school had expanded substantially: it began a law clinic; moved into a new building; turned the student newspaper into a more professional publication; began to hold its own graduation ceremonies, independent from the University; and made significant efforts to diversify the faculty and the student body. But the continual challenge of marshalling financial resources to sustain the efforts took its toll. Garsaud had tended the law school for over a decade; no dean to succeed him would sustain a deanship for that long a period until 2003, when Brian Bromberger became dean. The deans to follow Garsaud continued to experience difficulty navigating the relationship between the University and the law school, and mediating the conflicts within the law faculty, which seemed to exacerbate as time went on rather than be resolved.

Garsaud took a leave in 1981–82 and tendered his resignation in 1982. John McAulay served as acting dean while the law school undertook another dean search in 1982–83. Again, the search committee decided that hiring from inside the Loyola law faculty made the most sense because Loyola law faculty and dean salaries were substantially behind those of other schools. As their new dean, Loyola chose Thomas Sponsler, who had joined the Loyola faculty in 1968, had been promoted to associate in 1971, and professor in 1975. He held a juris doctor from the University of Toledo School of Law and an LLM from Yale University, and had received the "Best Teacher Award" ten times. He had been a visiting professor at the University of Mississippi, LSU, and Washington and Lee.

THE 1980S

By the 1980s, the repercussions of the societal changes brought about during the civil rights era began to be evident in law school admissions. The 1982 first-year class at Loyola was composed of 43 percent women, up from 38 percent in 1980, and up from approximately 30 percent in the years 1975–78.[80] Ethnic minorities for that same year made up 11 percent of the entering class, up from approximately 6–7 percent between 1975 and 1978, and up from "a distressingly low" 3 percent in 1977.[81]

The city of New Orleans dropped out of the top-20 metropolitan areas in the United States. It continued to lose population; African Americans, however, had become the majority group by almost 70,000. The city remained the largest metropolitan area in the state, with a population of over 1 million; Baton Rouge, the second-largest city in the state, recorded a population of only 350,754.[82] Statewide, the majority of the population was overwhelmingly white (2,915,310), approximately one-fourth black (1,238,472), with American Indians (12,841) and Vietnamese (10,853) forming the two next-largest racial and ethnic groups. More than 250,000 families survived on incomes below the poverty level: 8.3 percent of them white, 34.1 percent black, 19 percent American Indian, and 24.1 percent Asian.[83]

Despite the city's demographics, the law school had difficulty maintaining a diverse student body; the number of African Americans admitted remained low, and the school experienced a high attrition rate.[84] In 1984, under Dean Thomas Sponsler, the law school hired Glen L. Glenn, its first African American director of admissions. Glenn was a 1980 graduate of Ohio State University School of Law, where he worked as a recruiter for the undergraduate program. In fall 1986, Glenn brought in a bumper class of 278 students. The majority of the class consisted of men (175), but women comprised 37 percent of the class (103). The number of minorities in the class markedly increased, with 17 African Americans, 10 Hispanics, and 2 Asian students.

Diversifying the faculty continued to prove challenging. Cynthia Lepow, a graduate of Hunter College, with a law degree from Fordham University and a LLM in taxation from New York University, began teaching at the law school in academic year 1980-81. Richard A. Goins and Diane B. Pierce-Gonzalez, both African Americans, began teaching in academic year 1981–82. Goins, a graduate of Yale University and a 1975 graduate of Stanford School of Law, had been granted a fellowship to serve on the New Orleans Legal Aid Corporation (NOLAC) and had gone on to serve as its director. He joined the law faculty to fill in for James Klebba, who had accepted a visiting position at the University of Minnesota Law School. Klebba returned to Loyola, and Goins resigned from the faculty to return to private practice in 1984.

Diane Pierce-Gonzales, the first African American woman on the law faculty, started at a time when there were already four women on the law faculty:

Riley, Lorio, Chiang, the librarian, and Lepow. Pierce-Gonzales was a 1978 graduate of Harvard Law School, with a bachelor's degree from Hampshire College and a master's from the University of Hawaii, and a federal clerkship. Pierce-Gonzales left Loyola in 1986 to pursue an LLM at Columbia. Loyola was having difficulty retaining those African Americans it hired. Of those it hired, only one, Louis Westerfield earned tenure, the others departing for other schools or law practice.

William Nielson and David Normann, both white, also joined the law faculty in 1981–82. Nielson was a Loyola Law 1973 graduate, with an LLM in tax from New York University. He began teaching tax courses for the night program and eventually was asked to join the law faculty. Normann was a graduate of Tulane University and the Tulane University School of Law. Like Nielsen, Normann had taught as an adjunct at the law school for some years prior to being asked to join the full-time faculty. Of the four full-time faculty who joined the law school that year, only Nielson and Normann remained by 1984.

The Reverend Lawrence W. Moore, S.J., joined the faculty in 1982 after earning his law degree from the University of Missouri–Kansas City, where he was managing editor of the *UMKC Law Review*, and his master of laws degree from New York University. Moore had completed his undergraduate work at St. Louis University, where he earned his first master's degree in urban affairs. He earned a master of divinity from the Jesuit School of Theology at Berkeley in 1977. Moore, the only Jesuit to earn tenure on the law faculty at Loyola, went on to serve as associate dean of academic affairs under several deans. Moore served on the Loyola Board of Trustees from 1985 to 2011. Moore will serve as interim dean of the law school for a two-year term from fall 2015.

Dan Rosen, Henry Gabriel, Dian Arruebarrena, and Charles R. Penot Jr. were hired to start in academic year 1984–85. Rosen came to Loyola from a clerkship at the U.S. Court of Appeals for the Ninth Circuit; he had a law degree from Southern Methodist University and an LLM from Yale University. Gabriel had been clerking for the United States Court of Appeals for the Fifth Circuit and had a law degree from Gonzaga University School of Law and an LLM from the University of Pennsylvania. Arruebarrena was an LSU School of Law graduate, coming directly from the legal department at Shell Oil Company. Penot was a Loyola law 1982 graduate who had clerked for the Eastern District of Louisiana after graduating and went into private practice with New Orleans law firm Stone, Pigman, Walther, Wittman, & Hutchison. Penot left the law school after two years of teaching in spring 1986 to pursue an LLM, after which he returned to the faculty.

The law school instituted a program of Continuing Legal Education (CLE) in 1982, under the direction of Pamela Jackson, later Pamela Ebel, the law school's director of placement and CLE. CLE programming provided a small source of income to the law school, but the primary goal of the programs was to provide an avenue for practicing attorneys to acquire additional professional training.[85] Although the Louisiana bar at the time did not require CLE credits as a condition of bar membership, increasingly bar associations were requiring attorneys to earn CLE credits. The Louisiana bar made earning CLE credit mandatory in 1988.[86]

During the 1980s, the law school sought to enhance student life, not only by diversifying its faculty and student body but by offering law students opportunities to engage with national leaders of the legal profession. On November 10, 1984, Warren Burger, chief justice of the U.S. Supreme Court, delivered the inaugural lecture of the Judge Robert A. Ainsworth, Jr. Memorial Lecture Series.[87] Law students were not allowed to attend the lecture held at Nunemaker Hall, a venue of 420 seats all dedicated to invited guests. Instead, the lecture was telecast on closed-circuit television at the Danna Center.[88] Chief Justice Burger and Dean Sponsler met with the law students at the Danna Center after the lecture for a question-and-answer session.

Student organizations continued to blossom in the early 1980s. Loyola's chapter of the National Lawyers Guild (NLG) was established in 1982. The NLG is a national organization formed in the late 1930s with a commitment to human rights. Together with the Black Law Students Association, the NLG sponsored a conference on apartheid in 1983. In 1986, students formed the Spanish American Law Students Association (SALSA), now known as the Hispanic Law Student Association, to support and increase the Hispanic presence at the law school.

Another student organization, devoted to trial practice, the Association of Trial Lawyers of America J. Skelly Wright Chapter, was organized in fall 1982. The organization sponsored a mock trial competition to select a team to represent Loyola in regional and national competitions.

Since its founding, the law school had relied on students formed adjunct or part-time legal professionals to assist with the teaching of courses. In the modern era, law schools relied on adjuncts primarily for specialized or "boutique"-

type courses in which the practicing professional had special expertise. Most part-time adjuncts contributed their services without compensation. For a period of time until the late twentieth century, the University granted part-time, unsalaried law faculty tuition remission as a form of compensation. Beneficiaries of the policy were able to send their children to Loyola's law school free of charge.[89] Adjuncts tended to generate mixed student responses. Some adjuncts were too busy to really accommodate teaching; they missed too many classes or, as some students put it, "just read from the book." Some, however, became valued contributors to the law school experience and an integral part of the law school community.

Throughout, Loyola law graduate performance on the bar continued to be a source of concern to the law school because its graduates continued to come in third when compared to the other three schools operating in Louisiana: LSU, Tulane, and Southern. Thus, for example, in the July 1984 bar examination, LSU students earned a 91 percent pass rate, with 7.7 percent conditioning and 1.3 percent failing; Tulane students earned an 85.8 percent pass rate, with 9.7 percent conditioning and 4.5 percent failing; Loyola students earned a 72.5 percent pass rate, with 23.2 percent conditioning and 4.3 percent failing; and Southern, consistently ranked fourth in the state, yielded a 46 percent pass rate, with 23 percent conditioning and 31 percent failing. Students from out-of-state institutions taking the Louisiana bar earned a 69.8 percent pass rate that same year, with 23.2 percent conditioning and 6.9 percent failing.[90]

The 1984 bar results prompted challenges and concerns at the law school. The then dean's comments concerning the bar passage rate prompted more concern and a strong student response challenging his comments.[91] From the dean's perspective, most students who failed bar examinations failed because they did not study rigorously enough for the examination. Students responded to the article with a series of complaints and challenges to the school and the law faculty. The law school, in their view, should take more responsibility for ensuring they were prepared to take and pass the bar examination. Nevertheless, bar performance continued to place Loyola third among the Louisiana law schools, with students and faculty continuing to register concerns.[92]

Some faculty were uncomfortable with the heavy reliance on required courses, and students increasingly voiced concerns.[93] Both common law and civil law curricula at the law school were largely prescribed, giving students little room to take other courses of interest, or courses in specialized areas of law that were experiencing growth. The civil law curriculum featured more than 70 hours of required courses. During academic year 1985–86, Father Moore was among the professors urging the rest of his peers to consider reducing the number of required classes in the curricula. Moore's proposal was contingent on class standing: students with grade point averages of 3.0 and above or in the top 25 percent of their class should have more flexibility in deciding which courses to take, including the ability to mix civil and common law courses. Law faculty were not alone in urging change. Students had submitted a proposal allowing them to choose their own courses. Then Associate Dean James Klebba and curriculum committee chair "felt that neither proposal had a chance of being approved by the faculty,"[94] and he turned out to be correct.

One of the proposals mirrored the curriculum as it existed prior to the 1960s changes and a proposal considered over a decade later: reducing torts I and II, constitutional law I and II, and business organizations I and II from two-semester, multiple-hour courses to a single semester, four-hour course. In addition, civil law courses and donations would be combined and taught in a four-hour single-semester course, and the requirement that students take a course in jurisprudence would be eliminated. Although the faculty rejected the proposals, it approved adding a requirement that students take a course on poverty law, which resulted in an additional required course to the curriculum.

Adopted in academic year 1986–87, the course "Law and Poverty" was designed to introduce students "to the detrimental effects of poverty on society and poor people" and to offer "a critical examination of the legal system's response to the economic, social, and human problems of poverty, particularly in the fields of social security, welfare, unemployment and workmen's compensation." Adoption of the course requirement was controversial with the law faculty, with some opposed to any increase in the number of required hours, and others concerned that the course would be trying to teach something that could not be taught.[95] Others felt just as strongly that the course would "sensitize students to the problems of the poor" and "impart to the law school community that part of the privilege of being a lawyer is to help the poor."[96] The U.S. Supreme Court had rejected the idea that government was responsible for poverty and made it clear that except in criminal cases where individuals faced incarceration, governments were not required to address the needs created by poverty.[97] Nonetheless, a majority of the faculty voted in favor of adopting the course.

Law as a discipline was experiencing great change, in part as a result of movements in other disciplines including economics, mathematics (game theory), political science, and philosophy. The law and economics movement analyzed law and legal systems in terms of their relationship to economics.[98] In its simplest form, reflecting perhaps its greatest impact on law and legal systems, law and economics examined legal principles from the perspective of economic efficiency and costs and benefits; change made sense if the benefits outweighed costs.[99] Critical Legal Studies (CLS), critical race theory, and feminist legal theory challenged established legal theory and hierarchy including the hierarchy of law schools themselves.[100] CLS rejected formalism, objectivism, and determinacy in law. Critical race theory rejected neutrality and embraced storytelling as a way to develop theory and the role of race in the development of American law and legal institutions. Feminist legal theory identified the centrality of sex and gender in the development of American law and legal institutions. In 1973, Derrick Bell, the first tenured black professor at Harvard Law School and pioneer of critical race theory, published the first edition of *Race, Racism and American Law.* Duncan Kennedy self-published his polemic against the hierarchy inherent in legal education in 1983, and Roberto Mangabeira Unger described the development of the CLS movement that same year in *The Critical Legal Studies Movement,* based on Unger's talk at the Sixth Annual Conference on Critical Legal Studies at Harvard Law School in March 1982. Catharine MacKinnon laid the groundwork for recognition of sexual harassment as a legal wrong in *Sexual Harassment of Working Women* in 1979, and in 1988 she articulated a framework of feminist legal theory in her groundbreaking *Feminism Unmodified.*[101] Legal theory was changing, and law and legal institutions, while never wholeheartedly accepting of CLS, critical race theory, and feminist theory, inevitably were changed by them. As a general matter, Loyola faculty scholarship, like the curriculum, tended to avoid engaging consistently with the new theories. This may have been due to the lack of emphasis faculty placed on scholarship.

In 1986, the law school sought accreditation for a chapter of the Order of the Coif, a national legal honor society. Students who graduate in the top 10 percent of their class were eligible for membership if their school was a member of the organization. Both Tulane and LSU had chapters. Loyola's push to secure membership began at least by November 1981, when the proposal was made to the Law School Visiting Committee. The law school made public its application for a chapter of Coif in fall 1986, having appointed a committee to work on the application over the course of the year, and submitting it in August 1986.[102] The national office of the Order of the Coif rejected the law school's application, recommending instead that the law school strengthen its library and its "dedication to intellectual growth and scholarship."[103]

The law school shared the news with its student body in February 1987. Dean Sponsler and law librarian Stella Chiang attempted to explain to the students the school's failure to qualify. The law library collection was expanding, they noted, but it was not yet where it needed to be to support faculty research. Moreover, Sponsler noted, due to Loyola's programs providing courses in the day and at night, in the civil and the common law, the law faculty's emphasis had not been on scholarly research and publication. That was all changing, he promised.[104] Sobering, perhaps, was the fact that the law school had not realized in advance that its scholarly record was insufficient to initiate an application for Coif. An insufficient commitment to scholarship was to plague the school in future years.

Stella Chiang left Loyola the next year to take a position at Stanford. Edmund P. Edmonds replaced her in September 1988. Edmonds was the law librarian at William & Mary Law School and had earned his JD from the University of Toledo Law School, after completing a master in library science at the University of Maryland and an undergraduate degree at Notre Dame.

The relationship between Sponsler and the faculty in his last years as dean was tested over a dispute concerning the role of consulting and scholarship in law faculty hiring. The faculty had voted to deny tenure to an individual they believed had continued to practice while on the tenure track at the law school. The individual appealed to the dean, and the dean moved the Faculty Rank and Tenure Committee to reconsider its vote to deny the individual tenure.[105] The faculty refused to reconsider; Sponsler vetoed the faculty denial of tenure. From the perspective of the dean, many other tenured law faculty continued to practice; and the faculty member was a very strong and popular teacher, did a considerable amount of pro bono work, and did not engage in as much practice as many thought he did. The University Rank and Tenure Committee, the provost, and the president all concurred with the dean. Tenure was granted.

In 1987, Keith Vetter, instrumental in setting up the Loyola Law clinic, began to make plans for a summer study-abroad program in Mexico City, Mexico.[106] The school hoped to implement the program in summer 1988, building from an existing undergraduate program to Mexico operated by Maurice Brungardt. The program opened in summer 1989 in Cuernavaca, Mexico, and was deemed a success with 32 students enrolled in the program from Loyola and other law schools throughout the country.[107]

Throughout this period, Loyola featured a number of controversial speakers in tension with Catholic doctrine, including a lecture by Sarah Weddington, the attorney in *Roe v. Wade,* who addressed the abortion issue, first in 1975,[108] and again in 1987.[109] In 1988, the law school sponsored a symposium on privacy and featured Michael Hardwick, the individual who challenged the Georgia sodomy statute in the case of *Hardwick v. Bowers.*[110] During the 1980s, the law school enjoyed a degree of academic freedom and discourse very different from that of its early years. Its faculty's scholarship, for the most part, failed to engage with the storm of ideas challenging established orthodoxies at the national level.

In 1988 at the behest of Chief Justice Rehnquist, Congress funded death penalty resource centers in states that had the death penalty. Death penalty habeas corpus cases were clogging the federal courts, and the cases often resulted in a finding that the person condemned had not had competent representation. Chief Justice Rehnquist wanted to ensure that capital cases enjoyed competent representation at the trial and appellate level. The provost at the time, the Reverend George Lundy, S.J., PhD, learned about the program and asked Dean Sponsler whether the law school would be willing to apply to establish a death penalty resource center in Louisiana. Sponsler agreed, and the law school applied for and received the grant. For over a decade, the Loyola Death Penalty Resource Law Center thrived. The nationwide program lost its funding in 1999 during the budget battles between then president William J. Clinton and Congress.[111] The Death Penalty Resource Center, like the law school's clinic, emphasized aspects of the law school directed at engaging in the local community, something important to Sponsler, perhaps even more important than faculty scholarship. It was important, he and Lundy felt, to have law students "involved in meaningful experiences . . . anything that would bring the law school to the community and the community into the law school."

In 1989, after serving six years as dean, Sponsler resigned.[112] Loyola appointed James Klebba acting dean. Klebba had been serving as associate dean for academic affairs and enjoyed support from the dean and the faculty. Two women joined the law faculty that fall: Catherine Clarke and Madaline Herlong; Clarke as a tenure-track faculty member, and Herlong as a visitor. Clarke was a graduate of Catholic University's law school and was pursuing an LLM at Georgetown. Herlong had a law degree from the University of Virginia and an undergraduate degree from the College of William & Mary; she had been practicing at a local law firm.

Clarke instituted the street law program at Loyola, an outreach course developed at Georgetown University Law Center, taught by practitioners and law students to public high school students in Washington, D.C.[113] At Loyola, the course accommodated more than twenty law students teaching local public school students at Fortier High School and Phillips Junior High School regarding their legal rights and responsibilities, and practical legal problems. Loyola still offers the course, but the emphasis has moved away from public schools to private, parochial schools.

Even with the addition of Clarke to the tenure track, the Loyola law faculty continued to be predominantly male and white. Law students took a stand on diversity in spring 1990. The AWLS and SALSA cosponsored Faculty Diversification Day, urging the law school to diversify its student body and faculty.[114]

Kathryn Lorio chaired the search committee to replace Dean Sponsler. While the committee conducted its search, students voiced concerns about minority students at the law school, including a lack of minority faculty support, insufficient minority enrollment, and insufficient job placement efforts on behalf of minority students.[115] One of the candidates to come out of the search, chosen by the faculty and the University to lead the law school, was its first African American tenured law professor and now dean, Louis Westerfield. Westerfield had left the Loyola law faculty to serve as dean of the North Carolina Central University School of Law in 1986, a historically black institution.[116] Westerfield's return was greeted with optimism by many students and faculty; it signaled a commitment to diversity that some felt had been lacking.

THE EARLY 1990S

By 1991, the American Bar Association (ABA) had approved or accredited 176 law schools, 4 of them in Louisiana.[117] The Association of American Law Schools (AALS) had admitted 159 of them to membership, including 3 of the Louisiana law schools, Loyola, Tulane University School of Law, and the Louisiana State University Law School.

The total enrollment at the law school for 1990–91 was 786. The law school charged law students $410 per semester hour. First-year students carried 16 credit hours in the first semester and 15 in the second, so tuition annually would have been approximately $12,710[118] and $38,130 for the three-year course of study. The school awarded scholarship aid primarily on the basis of a student's academic achievements and test scores, but some funding was available for African American students in need of financial assistance.

That spring, 229 law students graduated. Loyola's bar passage rate for summer 1991 was approximately 65 percent; the statewide bar passage rate was 62 percent.[119] The median salary for attorneys joining law firms that year was approximately $40,000, with 40 percent of salaries in the $30,000 to $40,000 range and 6 percent in the $70,000 range, the median in big law firms.[120] A substantial number of law graduates, however, had difficulty finding employment, and some went directly into solo law practice (i.e., started a law practice on their own without having any practice experience). It was hard to determine exactly how many law graduates were going into solo law practice straight out of law school because neither the law schools nor the National Association for Legal Career Professionals (NALP) kept track. Approximately 20 percent of law graduates in Louisiana were unemployed after taking the bar. In 1995, the Louisiana Bar Foundation Conclave on Legal Education and Professional Development noted that solo practitioners in the state needed additional support and resources.[121] Nationwide, law school admissions offices in 1991 had no difficulty recruiting first-year classes; almost 100,000 applicants competed for approximately 40,000 seats.

In 1991, Loyola employed thirty tenure-track law faculty, including its dean, the director of the library, and the director of its clinic. The majority of the tenure-track faculty at the time was white and male; only one, the dean, was African American. Joining the faculty in 1991 were one African American and one Latina. An additional five of the thirty were women. The law school also employed four clinical faculty and two visiting clinical professors. Clinical faculty enjoyed long-term contracts but not tenure. Three of the four clinical faculty were women, and one was African American; one of the visiting clinical professors was a Latina. The law school employed six law library faculty, all of them women and one African American. Library faculty enjoyed tenure. As noted earlier, presiding over the law school was its first African American dean, Louis J. Westerfield, a graduate of the law school.

Loyola hired some law professors through what is known as the "meat market"—the annual gathering of prospective applicants to law faculties and law schools sponsored by the AALS. The meat market allows law school faculties to select prospective applicants to interview in fifteen- to thirty-minute time periods. On the basis of that interview and an applicant's resume, some would be invited to an interview on campus, which usually included a presentation to the law faculty. Many law professors are hired informally, not through the formal AALS interviewing process but through other, informal, ways.[122]

The AAUP reported the average law professor salary for academic year 1991–92 as $83,905 for full professors, $60,073 for associates and $56,569 for assistants.[123] Law professor salaries generally were considered to be higher than average for academic positions, but still substantially below what peers earned in private practice. The disparity between academic salaries and private practice income was most pronounced, as it still is, at senior levels. Most law faculty at Loyola had a practice background. That experience had not made a huge impact on the way law was presented to students, other than through the school's skills and clinical curriculum. Most of the skills classes were lecture-style classes, and the clinic served a relatively small proportion of the student body—less than one-fourth of the third-year class. Most professors used the case method and lecture, and most classes featured a class size of 60 to 100 students. Substantive courses were tested by a final examination, and there was very little opportunity for engaging with students through additional written exercises or through assignments that integrated the subject matter of the course with the form in which the subject matter actually might be dealt with in practice.

The state of the legal academy was in flux. Many law professors had never been admitted to a bar, many had never practiced law, and some found law practice abhorrent. Some law professors, at least at Loyola, spent considerable amounts of time engaged in the practice of law while holding a full-time, tenured position. There was some variance of opinion in the academy as to the need for faculty to engage in scholarship, the kind of scholarship that should be valued, and the need for law schools to support scholarship by providing sabbaticals and summer research stipends.

In 1992, the ABA published what became known as the MacCrate Report,[124] which provided an overview of the profession as a whole, as well as a "vision of the skills and values new lawyers should seek to acquire."[125] The

MacCrate Report was careful to spread the responsibility for training new lawyers among law schools, the bar, the courts, and the new lawyers themselves. Explicitly, however, it challenged law schools to do a better job of integrating the teaching of theory, doctrine, practice skills, and values to prepare graduates to enter the profession. It noted that nationwide a substantial number of lawyers were engaged in solo practice.[126] At the same time, the report noted the development of elite large law firms and the impact of large-firm practice on the profession, including intensive competitive practices in associate hiring and compensation.[127] The report also acknowledged the effects on the profession of the 1990–91 recession, classified by the Department of Labor as "mild,"[128] which slowed associate hiring of law graduates and laterals,[129] resulting in a temporary market glut of attorneys.[130] Some law firms were still expanding, but the expansion was outward, to new locations through branch offices and outside the United States. In response to the dramatic growth in law firms, law schools increased their class sizes and tailored their curricula to fit large law firm practice, and would-be lawyers viewed their success in their profession in reference to large law firm practice.[131]

MacCrate identified a set of lawyering skills and professional values that legal practitioners should have at various stages of their careers. Fundamental lawyering skills included problem solving, legal analysis and reasoning, legal research, factual investigation, communication, counseling, negotiation, litigation and alternative dispute-resolution procedures, organization and management of legal work, and recognizing and resolving ethical dilemmas. Fundamental values of the profession included competent representation, striving to promote justice, fairness and morality, striving to improve the profession, and professional self-development.[132] The report issued a call for action: "If a single public profession of shared learning, skills and professional values is to survive into the 21st century, the law schools together with the bar and the judiciary must all work for the perpetuation of core legal knowledge together with the fundamental lawyering skills and professional values that identify a distinct profession of law throughout the United States."[133]

Also in 1992, the Louisiana Supreme Court issued the Final Report of the Louisiana Task Force on Women in the Courts.[134] Loyola law graduate Chief Justice Pascal F. Calogero appointed the task force to determine whether the operation of the Louisiana judicial system resulted in inequality between men and women; "to assess the real or perceived effects of gender bias on courtroom interaction and the judicial decision-making process"; and "to educate the bench, bar and public about gender fairness."[135] The Honorable Miriam G. Waltzer, then a judge in the New Orleans criminal district court, chaired the task force, which held hearings, surveyed populations, and used other methods of collecting data to document the existence of gender bias in the Louisiana court and legal system, and to make recommendations to eradicate such bias where found. Louisiana's task force was part of a wave of gender bias task forces to identify and document gender bias in the state and federal legal systems.[136] The task forces sought to identify changes in the way the profession and court systems functioned to eliminate gender bias, as well as changes in the law. Louisiana's task force found substantial evidence of widespread gender bias in the courts, the bar, and law schools. Thus, the Louisiana Task Force's final reports included recommendations covering a wide range of areas, including ensuring women equal access to courts and ensuring that victims of domestic violence would have access to protective orders and that those orders would be enforced by law enforcement and district attorney offices, in the criminal justice system, and in the professional bar. The last part of the report dealt with law schools as part of the legal system. One of the findings of the report: "Some male professors . . . openly maintained that women are not suited to the practice of law or must be protected from its 'rough edges.'"[137] Neither the law school nor the law professor was identified by name, but some male law professors were still telling women law students that they "should be home raising . . . children and taking care of her husband."[138] Some thirty years after the Civil Rights Act of 1964 had prohibited discrimination on the basis of sex in employment, and the Equal Pay Act of 1963 prohibited sex-based wage discrimination between men and women who perform the same jobs, gender bias continued to pose serious challenges for law schools, still operating with tenured faculty, a majority of whom were male.

The report recommended that law schools incorporate coursework on professional ethics dealing with sexual stereotypes and gender bias both as attorneys and clients; and develop a system to report incidents of gender bias and recommended disciplining of professors or students who engaged in gender bias.[139]

The *Law School Bulletin* for 1992–93, published under the administration of the law school's first African American dean, Louis Westerfield, was the first to state the University's policy on nondiscrimination; it did not specifically address harassment but it made clear that the University and law school prohibited discrimination "on the basis of race, color, sex, creed, age, national origin or handicap . . . in accordance with federal regulations and guidelines."[140]

The changes in the profession presented a challenge for a law school like Loyola, operating with uncertain resources. Westerfield joined the law school as dean in fall 1990; he expressed his goals for the school in an interview published in the student newspaper in November 1990: improving the placement office; diversifying the faculty and student body, and becoming a member of Order of the Coif, something the past two administrations had attempted and failed to accomplish.[141] But first, he related, he wanted to make sure his faculty was on board. They were scheduled to have a retreat in the near future to discuss plans for the law school. The dean was committed to improving the placement office; providing more money for faculty scholarship by providing summer stipends to allow faculty to use summers to write; recruiting more minorities and women; and establishing a loan-forgiveness program at the school.

Westerfield's administration was hampered from the first by a lack of adequate resources,[142] by controversies over the clinic, and by his efforts to diversify the student body and the faculty, which, in the view of some faculty, valued diversity over academic credentials. Notwithstanding, in his short administration, Westerfield was able to substantially increase the diversity of the faculty and of the student body. By the time he left Loyola to take up the deanship at the University of Mississippi School of Law,[143] the Loyola law faculty had added three African American law professors and one Latina. In addition, the law school had hired another African American director of admissions, and minority recruitment was strong. The law school consistently began to attract meaningful numbers of minorities.[144] Under Westerfield's deanship, Loyola established its first loan-forgiveness program at the instigation of the Loyola Public Interest Law Group, which had been urging the school to adopt such a program since at least 1989.[145] In addition, Dean Westerfield established the practice of providing actual support for faculty scholarship by providing law faculty summer research grants.

In 1993, the law faculty established the *Poverty Law Journal,* now known as the *Journal of Public Interest Law.* The *Journal* was committed to addressing legal issues faced by the poor, children, the elderly, and those groups lacking voice in the political process. At the time, it was one of only two law journals in the country devoted to issues faced by the poor. In 2008, the *Journal* began a series of symposia on public interest law. The *Journal*'s first symposium explored criminal indigent defense. Subsequent symposia have explored predatory lending practices, education reform, state criminal regulation of noncitizens, and prosecutorial misconduct. In 1994, students founded the Asian Pacific American Law Students Association (APALSA) to increase recruiting of Asian American students and professors to Loyola.

Not all was well at the law school, however. Conflicts within the faculty were so severe that they were becoming evident in the classroom. A Student Bar Association October 25, 1993, report based on a law student survey formally requested that the law school prohibit professors from making disparaging remarks about other law faculty, members of the administration, or law students. The report found that "full time professors are hard to reach and even harder to meet to discuss academic problems" and requested that full-time professors post and maintain office hours. The student report requested a formal prohibition on faculty-student relationships and faculty harassment of students, and raised questions about bar content in the curriculum and the school's tolerance for intoxication.[146]

In 1994 Dean Westerfield resigned as dean of Loyola to accept the deanship at the University of Mississippi School of Law. The law school recognized his legacy by naming the professors who teach in the first-year legal research and writing program as Westerfield Fellows.[147]

6

LOYOLA'S CLINIC

TRAINING LAWYERS WITH A COMMITMENT TO SOCIAL JUSTICE

Loyola law initiated clinical education in academic year 1953–54, when upper-class students were given the opportunity "to assist in the handling of criminal and civil cases" in which the Legal Aid Bureau of New Orleans was authorized to act. However, the law school faculty had discussed instituting some form of a law clinic as early as fall of 1939.[1] This early effort came to naught when the director of the Associated Catholic Charities informed then dean James Connor that, "due to their limited scope of activity, they had very little need for such a service and so it would be impracticable to pursue the idea at this time."[2]

The law school's second attempt to initiate some form of clinical education was more successful. The "Legal Aid Program" instituted in 1953–54 placed students in the Bureau to work under the supervision of staff attorneys, interviewing clients, engaging in legal research, conducting investigations, and drafting pleadings.[3] Students did not receive academic credit for the work. The law school offered the program through academic year 1970–71.

In instituting some form of clinical work, Loyola joined a number of other law schools. By 1951, approximately twenty-eight law schools provided some kind of clinical experience for students, either by placement in a legal aid society, as at Loyola, in a law school clinic, or in public defender offices.[4]

The 1960s witnessed greater student demand for clinical education. The Ford Foundation made available funding for experimentation in clinical legal studies through the Council on Legal Education for Professional Responsibility (CLEPR), an entity begun under the auspices of the AALS. In 1966, New Orleans law schools, including Loyola, met with other organizations including the Legal Aid Bureau, to discuss a proposal for an agency in the city to provide legal services to the poor.[5]

Loyola's formal clinic was established in 1970–71 with financing from CLEPR. Marcel Garsaud, dean at the time, with Assistant Professors Bernard Keith Vetter and Thomas Sponsler, submitted a proposal to CLEPR for a grant to fund a civil and criminal clinical education program at the law school. The proposal noted Loyola's commitment to the "promotion of human and civil rights; to the education of the underemployed and unemployed; and to the alleviation of selected . . . problems" through the work of Father Louis Twomey's Institute of Human Relations, and Loyola's Inter-American Center, supported by the Agency for International Development, to provide leadership training seminars for individuals from Central and Latin American countries. The law school wanted to "move more vigorously into the areas of community service and clinical education."[6]

At the time the law school had an enrollment of 532 students (332 full-time day students and 200 part-time evening students). The proposal envisioned 20 senior full-time students participating in the clinical education program. They would receive 6 credit hours for a two-semester senior-year course. Students would choose from a criminal clinical education seminar or a civil clinical education seminar. They would be graded on the handling of the case or cases brought before a court, and they would be assigned to government agencies or public law firms to work under the supervision of an attorney.

The proposal requested funds for a period of two years, after which time Loyola would assume the full cost of operating the clinical program. Keith Vetter was designated acting project director in the original grant application.

While the proposal was pending with CLEPR, the law school, in conjunction with the three other law schools and the Louisiana State Bar Association, petitioned the Louisiana Supreme Court to change its rules to allow student practitioners to practice under the supervision of professors. The Louisiana State Bar Association initially opposed the petition,[7] but was persuaded to support it ultimately, perhaps due to the ABA's support of clinical education.[8] The law school's clinic initiative was supported by Louisiana Supreme Court Associate Justice Mack E. Barham, who, in an address to the Young Lawyers' Council of the Louisiana State Bar Association in May 1971, urged the bar to accept student lawyers to help serve the need for legal assistance by the indigent, and to help train new lawyers.[9]

The Louisiana Supreme Court granted the petition in 1971[10] by a slim majority,[11] and Loyola established the first program of clinical education in the state. Associate Justice Frank W. Summers wrote a dissent to the adoption of the rules cautioning that the order permitting students to engage in the limited practice of law would "adversely affect the already crowded programs of Louisiana's law schools and the ultimate qualification of lawyers." Taking time away from the "theoretical and academic study" of law was a bad idea, as law schools were "neither equipped nor designed to supervise law practice." Summers believed that an apprenticeship after law school in a law firm was the way to provide the kind of training a clinical legal program was seeking to provide. Clinic programs might be "subjected to influences which may be incompatible with the student's primary objective at law school," because they would be funded by external sources with different objectives perhaps than those of the legal education program.

Arthur A. "Buddy" Lemann III, assistant professor of law at Loyola and the first "Professor of Clinical Education and supervisor of the Loyola Law Clinic," defended clinical legal education as being the counterpart to medical education and emphasized "the valuable experience proffered students in a law clinic," and the additional benefit realized by providing free legal aid to the poor.[12]

Lemann was a 1964 graduate of Tulane University and a 1967 graduate of Loyola's law school, where he served on the *Loyola Law Review.* Upon graduating from Loyola, he pursued an LLM degree from George Washington University School of Law, having been granted a fellowship. Lemann practiced law before joining the Loyola law faculty in 1970. He taught for one year before being appointed director of the clinic.[13]

Loyola first offered clinical courses in academic year 1971–72. CLEPR awarded the law school a grant of $25,000 to assist in start-up funding for a clinical program.[14] The initial program consisted of a two-semester, six-hour course limited to 20 seniors, 10 each semester. The students were expected to devote eight to twelve hours a week in addition to the seminar. Initially, students were chosen on the basis of their class rank and their need for the program, based on the student's opportunity for employment after graduation. The original clinic, then, operated with a faculty member supervising and teaching 20 students—a high student-faculty ratio for a clinical program.

Even in its early stages, the clinic proved to be as controversial for the law faculty as it had been initially for the bar and the Louisiana Supreme Court. Buddy Lemann defended the clinic from attack by law faculty member Fred

Swaim in the April 1974 issue of the *Code*. Swaim thought the clinic and substantive courses incompatible; law students who learned the substantive law in class would sooner or later learn how to represent clients. Lemann responded that "the law school has an obligation to do its very best to turn out people who are qualified to practice law and who will not hurt any client through trial and error."[15] Rather than viewing them as incompatible, Lemann viewed them as mutually beneficial because clinical programs allowed students to explore law in a real-world context.

In 1974, the CLEPR granted Loyola additional funding in the amount of $7,500 for one year as partial support for a public-interest clinical program for senior citizens in partnership with the Louisiana Center for Public Interest, Inc. The University also agreed to provide partial support of the program, one of the conditions of the grant.

By March 1975, the law clinic had handled 438 civil cases and 400 criminal cases. Approximately 20 students per year were enrolled in the clinic in its first three years, with 30 students in its fourth year (including students serving as externs in the District Attorney's Office).[16] The clinic still featured only one law professor supervising law students, but additional students were supervised through the Orleans and Jefferson Parish District Attorney's Offices, which made it possible to have law students representing the State of Louisiana as prosecutors in criminal cases.[17] During these early years, the clinic partnered with Tulane's School of Social Work to provide clients with more services by referring to the School of Social Work those clients who might be in need of Tulane's services. In return, Tulane's School of Social Work would refer clients in need of legal services to the Loyola law clinic.

In 1975, when the CLEPR grant money ceased, the University entered into a contract with the Louisiana Commission on Legal Education and Clinical Services for additional funding.[18] These grants allowed for expansion of Loyola's clinical program by providing for an additional supervising attorney and secretarial assistance. In 1978, the U.S. Department of Health, Education, and Welfare granted additional funding to the law school to continue its clinical program.[19] That same year the law school budget included the law clinic. Since that time, clinical programs have been added as a result of additional external funding sources, and some have lapsed. Throughout, however, the law school continued to operate a strong clinical program. The clinic budget in fiscal year 1981 was $116,000; by 1986, it had almost doubled to $227,806.[20]

The work of the law clinic raised concerns in the New Orleans community, particularly when it represented a defendant accused of raping and killing a young woman. The clinic had been appointed to defend the young man, but some in the community were shocked that a Jesuit institution had undertaken the defense. Dean Garsaud sought to explain the clinic's role in representing indigent defendants in criminal and civil court: "We do not solicit cases and did not solicit this one. . . . As in innumerable other capital cases, the Clinic was appointed by a judge of Criminal District Court. . . . When the court makes such an appointment, it is our obligation to serve. We are then morally and legally bound to accord the defendant the best defense we are capable of providing regardless of what case is involved."[21]

In 1979, Loyola hired Loyola law graduate and civil rights attorney John "Jack" Nelson to head the clinic. Nelson came with thirty years of trial experience, having received national recognition for his work during the civil rights era.[22] The Reverend Michael Gallagher, S.J., a Jesuit with a law degree from Georgetown University, joined the clinic that same year. Gallagher supervised students at the clinic until 1981, when he left to pursue further graduate studies in divinity at Cambridge. He returned to the clinic in fall 1985.[23]

With federal funding through the U.S. Department of Education, the law clinic provided legal services for low-income Hispanics. Federal funding ceased in 1982, reflecting substantial cuts to education and social services that Ronald Reagan's administration instituted in the early 1980s. The New Orleans province of the Society of Jesus approved additional funding to extend the program through 1983.[24] The province grant was predicated on the law school and University agreeing to match the funding. The Reverend James Carter, S.J., approved the matched funds, and the program was continued through 1983. Loyola hired Luz Molina, a Tulane Law School graduate, as the attorney to provide legal services in conjunction with the program. Although the program was discontinued, Loyola's law clinic continued to offer legal assistance in immigration cases. Because it had the only immigration law clinic in the state until spring 2009,[25] Loyola accepted students from other law schools, like Tulane, who wished to gain expertise in immigration law.

A formal evaluation of the clinic by the Department of Education at Loyola resulted in findings that student morale at the clinic was "high, engagement in learning is optimal, complaints are few, commitment of faculty is outstanding, and, unlike other educational endeavors, there is a high degree of 'fit' among three important variables, expectations, program goals, and delivery of instruction."[26] The same report cautioned that staffing continued to pose a challenge given that clinical faculty served as attorneys, who actually represented clients, as well as teachers helping students to learn. Thus, the report recommended strengthening resources either by reducing enrolment in the clinic or adding more supervising attorneys. The report also noted that although faculty emphasized the social/ethical clinic goals, the program did not sufficiently foster or accomplish the realization of these goals. The report recommended that faculty explicitly address these issues with students. The third problem identified had to do with student evaluation and the difficulties inherent in evaluating students engaged in clinical legal education. Some recommendations were made to improve the evaluation process, including a recommendation to involve judges before whom students appeared in the evaluation.

In 1984, Loyola was one of nine law schools selected by the federal government to received funding; the clinic was awarded $90,000.[27] The purpose of the funding was to expand law school clinics to assist Legal Services Corporation–eligible clients and "educate law students to the problems of poor persons."[28] While there was a legitimate and justified use of clinical legal education in providing a practice and apprentice-like methodology to prepare law students for practice, the federal funding was primarily targeted at delivery of legal services to the poor: "These clinics will encourage future lawyers to become interested in the provision of legal services to poor persons, acting either as legal aid attorneys or through *pro bono* or reduced fee efforts as members of the private bar."[29] At Loyola, the funding was used to expand the clinical program by providing for an additional full-time supervising attorney, a part-time supervising attorney, and a secretary. The additional supervising attorneys would enable an additional fifteen students to take on cases in family, juvenile, consumer, and administrative law.

Enrolling in the law school clinic, however, was an arduous process. By the mid-1980s, law students interested in doing clinical work had to submit an application containing biographical information, explaining their reasons for wanting to work in the clinic and specifying whether they preferred to work in the law school's clinic or an outside placement. Applicants also had to submit a memorandum analyzing a hypothetical set of facts, something that students learned to do in law school. Then students had to undergo a personal interview with clinic staff. Students had to have a 2.0 grade average.

After consideration of all of these factors, clinic supervisors chose the students who they determined "need[ed] clinic education" and those who would "aid in maintaining the Clinic's high reputation for service in the community."[30] More students were interested in enrolling in the clinic than could be accommodated, and the application process helped eliminate potential candidates. This selection process differed from that used for most other courses. At Loyola, most courses were required; students had to enroll—there was no selection process. Certain activities were selective: membership on law review and moot court was primarily based on grade point average, but those activities were not part of the law school curriculum. Enrollment might be limited in courses like seminars, on the basis of numbers or prerequisites, and then on a first-come, first-served basis. The clinic, in these early years, was the first curricular program at the law school to limit participation on any basis other than the order in which students enrolled or prerequisites. Two factors were at work: the cost of clinical education and a sense that law clinics could be an alternative for students who could not participate in other activities like law review and moot court. The first was a common concern for all law schools; it may be that the second was a concern specific to Loyola.

Students enrolling in clinic in the mid-1980s could be placed in the general clinic, the Hispanic clinic, the grant program (i.e., family, juvenile, consumer, and administrative law cases), and the tax clinic, supervised by Loyola tax law professor William Neilson. Alternatively, they could pursue placement with the New Orleans Legal Assistance Corporation, the Orleans and Jefferson Parish District Attorneys' Offices, the New Orleans City Attorney's Office, the Louisiana Mental Health Advocacy Center, the Advocacy Center for the Elderly and Disabled, or the Internal Revenue Service.

Clinic students handled between five and twelve open cases under close supervision of clinic faculty. Students also wrote a series of reports for each of their cases, and two reflection papers each semester of clinic. They attended a classroom component exploring various aspects of lawyering, including trial technique and professional responsibility.[31]

One of the recurring issues in clinical legal education in general, and at Loyola as well, concerned the status of clinicians, supervising attorneys. Initially, the Loyola clinic was staffed by regular faculty. Teaching clinic was labor-intensive, however. Faculty had to accept representation of clients, train students, and supervise them in an active representation. Regular faculty were expected to teach and engage in scholarship. They were expensive to hire. Loyola maintained the director of the clinic as a regular tenured faculty position, but as the clinic expanded and the need for additional clinicians (supervising attorneys) increased, they were hired as supervising attorneys, often through temporary funding. This meant that they could be hired at a lower salary than regular faculty and had little or no structural role in setting academic policy at the school. They lacked the protections of the tenure system and could be more easily terminated for financial or other reasons.

Loyola was not the only law school facing the issue of faculty status for supervising attorneys.[32] Increasingly, clinicians protested what they considered their "second-class status." To address the problem, the ABA considered Proposed Standard 405(e) ABA Standards for Approval of Law Schools (1984).[33] The standard called for some form of protection for clinic faculty analogous to tenure, and application of standards of community service, scholarship, sabbaticals, and participation in law school governance. That June, Dean Thomas Sponsler informed the vice president for academic affairs that "there is bound to be an adverse reaction by the faculty."[34] Sponsler worried that then clinic director Jack Nelson's tenure bid would be adversely affected. Some law faculty continued to question the need for clinical education. Loyola's tenure-track faculty had just benefited from the establishment of a formal sabbatical program in 1981–82, specified in the new *Faculty Handbook*. Up until that time, the granting of research sabbaticals had been handled on an ad hoc basis, and the University's failure to provide sabbaticals for law faculty had been a criticism of prior ABA accreditation visits.[35] The proposed ABA standard meant that some benefits recently awarded to regular faculty would be available to clinical faculty.

Sponsler's worries about Nelson proved groundless, but his concern over continued relations between clinic and regular faculty proved prophetic. The law faculty granted Nelson tenure, and the law school adopted a form of long-term contracts for clinic faculty along the lines of what had been developed at some other law schools. Subsequently, separate provision was made for clinic faculty in the *Faculty Handbook*.[36] But the compromise engineered division between the law school and the clinic. The arrangement instituted an independent and separate process for the hiring and promotion of clinical faculty. In essence, it led to increasing alienation between the two faculties and between the clinical program and the rest of the law school curriculum.

THE GILLIS W. LONG POVERTY LAW CENTER

In 1985, Congress awarded the law school $4 million to establish and administer the Gillis W. Long Poverty Law Center in its new building on the Broadway campus.[37] A substantial portion of the grant, $3 million, established an endowment trust fund, the income to be used exclusively to fulfill the purposes of the grant. The remaining $1 million was to be available for facilities, equipment, and other costs incurred in establishing the clinical program. The Center honored a former and popular Louisiana state representative, Gillis W. Long. The grant was the result of efforts by Thomas Sponsler, the dean at the time; the University's Office of Institutional Advancement; President James Carter, S.J.; Louisiana senators, in particular Senator Bennett Johnston, and representatives to Congress. In the House of Representatives, then congresspersons John Breaux, Bob Livingston, Lindy Boggs, and Cathy Long (Gillis Long's widow, who had succeeded to her husband's seat), representing both political parties, rose to speak in favor of the legislation. Congressman Breaux, Democrat, noted:

> It is a rare opportunity indeed when we have occasion to honor one of our departed colleagues after having served this body and this institution and this country for a number of years... by approving a project which also serves... a real need, that being the poor of the United States of America....
>
> ... [T]he Government and the people of the United States... will get something very substantial and very tangible, and that is at least 160,000 legal service hours of work being contributed by the students and by the lawyers at the university working on programs that would benefit the poor not only of Louisiana but, of course, throughout the entire Nation.[38]

Congressman Livingston, Republican, supported the proposal despite the fact that it honored a Democrat:

> Although we were of different political and philosophical persuasions, both he and I, as former practicing attorneys, were aware of the need for the availability of adequate legal services for the less affluent as well as for those more fortunate....
>
> This amendment... will go a long way in assisting the needy and elderly by allowing law students and practitioners to provide quality legal services at no cost to the recipient.[39]

Dean Sponsler, the Center's first director, remembered its founding:

> Gillis Long was a very popular progressive Congressman from Louisiana. He was not a Loyola alum, but Congress was in a mind to honor him so Loyola president James Carter, the University Development Office and I, with the permission of his family, worked to produce a proposal that would be in keeping with his values and interests and steer funding to Loyola to help pay for the necessary renovations to the Dominican buildings and provide an endowment for the Clinic and other anti-poverty programs. As our proposal wended its way through Congress, the Chair of one of the crucial committees was an alumnus of Drake Law School in Iowa. He asked us if we would mind if Drake received a similar appropriation. We said no, of course, so both Loyola and Drake each received a four million dollar appropriation. Loyola invested the money wisely. Several years later I received a phone call from a Congressional staffer wondering if we would be willing to receive an additional two million dollars since they were going to give that much more to Drake to help them recover from their loss of the original appropriation. You can guess the answer. During this time we cultivated a good relationship with Drake's clinical program and visited back and forth.[40]

The congressional appropriation for the Center had as its purpose "to fund two University centers which will provide legal clinics to supplement the civil legal services of Legal Services Corporation grantees, demonstrate how such legal clinics can be operated to benefit both law students and recipients, and conduct continuing legal education courses and seminars to encourage and prepare practicing attorneys for pro bono services."[41] The grant conditioned the legal services to be funded only to recipients who qualified for services from Legal Services Corporation. The statute provided that the "endowment shall be held in a trust which dedicates the income exclusively to fulfilling the purposes above stated."[42]

Congress awarded this funding to the school during the presidency of Ronald Reagan. Although it was supportive of the award, the Reagan presidency had tried to eliminate the Legal Services Corporation, suggesting that perhaps it could be replaced by private attorneys undertaking pro bono cases and clinical legal education, perhaps staffed by volunteer private attorneys. Despite the administration's distaste for the Legal Services Corporation, Reagan signed the bills funding the grants.

When first established, the Center primarily funded the clinical program. The Center provided support for continuing legal education programs, programs on poverty law, and funding for student intern positions with organizations that provided legal services for the poor.

In a letter to U.S. Senator Mark Hatfield, then Loyola president James Carter thanked him for supporting the grant:

> We believe that the Gillis W. Long Poverty Law Center will serve both as the foundation for the expansion of the provision of legal services to the poor in Louisiana as well as an instructive example for other clinical legal education programs. . . . [W]e are developing plans to expand legal services to the poor by clinic students as well as initiating continuing legal education and poverty law workshop programs to rural areas outside of New Orleans.[43]

The commitment to providing legal services to the poor was consistent with Loyola's Jesuit character, as one of the attorneys at the Loyola clinic, also a Jesuit priest, stated in a memo to the dean concerning the new Center:

> The funding of the Gillis Long Poverty Law Center presents . . . an occasion of inestimable importance for the University as well as for the Law School. We are presented with the means to perform a significant service for disadvantaged and marginated people throughout Louisiana as well as expressing in ever more pronounced tones Loyola's beliefs . . . that professional education within the context of a Jesuit University is inextricably linked to service of the least advantaged groups in society.[44]

The fund allowed the law school to hire an additional supervising attorney to supervise students in adjudication procedures as well as to prepare them for their roles as student practitioners by conducting simulation exercises.[45] The fund was used to hire a legal secretary to support the clinic work.

The clinic already had a number of supervising attorneys and secretaries; what it and the law school did not have was a position dedicated to "computer, audiovisual systems coordinator for the law school and Gillis W. Long

Poverty Law Center," a position that would become increasingly important in the decades to come. The Gillis Long Poverty Law Center fund made possible the hiring of an information technology expert, who could assist the clinic in developing a case management system; provide advice, training, and technical assistance in the area of information technology (at the time described as "computers and audio-visual technology"); coordinate the purchase of hardware and software; and assist in the development of the continuing legal education programs to help legal services lawyers in delivering legal services to the poor.[46] The fund allowed the school to hire an individual to assist with skills training and continuing legal education, and a media librarian. In short, the Gillis Long Poverty Law Center grant substantially assisted the law school as a whole to respond to the increasing role of artificial intelligence and information technology systems in legal education and the legal profession as a whole.

The granting of the award prompted local ceremonial celebrations. The Legal Services Corporation presented the University with the $3 million endowment check at a reception, which it co-hosted with the National Institute for Trial Advocacy, at the AALS annual meeting on January 4, 1986. In addition, the University coordinated the institution ceremony of the Gillis W. Long Memorial Poverty Law Center to coincide with the dedication of the law school's move from Miller on the Loyola main campus, to the Broadway Campus on Pine Street. William H. Webster, director of the Federal Bureau of Investigation, delivered the inaugural address, the Ainsworth Lecture, on April 15, 1986.

PROFESSIONAL NONCLINICAL TRAINING: THE SKILLS CURRICULUM

The Gillis Long grant stimulated the development of short courses in professional skills, something that schools like Loyola had tended to emphasize throughout their existence, but that Loyola had been unable to successfully establish as part of the core legal curriculum. Law professor Gerry Rault had been working on a skills curriculum since 1982.[47] In 1985, the law faculty considered and for the most part embraced the concept of skills training. A law faculty committee led by David Normann, Gerry Rault, and Dennis Rousseau created the structure for the skills curriculum, and the law school offered the program for the first time in fall 1986. The professional skills that the program sought to develop were those identified by Roberta Ramo, a former chair of the ABA's Section on Economics of Law Practice: communication skills, writing skills, thinking to creative solutions, instilling a passion for the rights of a client, giving advice, cost/benefit analysis, learning financial management of a practice, understanding advanced technology, and instruction in ethics.[48] The committee decided to categorize skills on the basis of the kind of practice involved, and adopted four categories: trial practice, appellate practice, office management, and pro bono. The program required students to earn a minimum of 8 skills credits, with at least 2 credits in each category. The skills courses were taught for the most part by practitioners and were designed as short "mini-courses."

Some law faculty, like many in the legal academy, resisted the teaching of skills. From their perspective, students learned practice skills when they went out to practice or when they were hired and trained by law firms. One Loyola law faculty member is reputed to have asked in a faculty meeting, "What are we going to offer next: dress for success?" This may have been a typical view for many law school faculty at the time, but it was a view that was being steadfastly opposed by the bar and increasingly by other legal academics.

In 1987, students expressed concerns about the skills program. Students agreed the program was necessary but criticized the manner in which skills were taught. Some resisted additional requirements to the law school's already heavy academic requirements. Students complained about lack of feedback, lack of notice of written assignments, and confusion over what was actually going to be covered in a particular skills class.[49] They recommended requiring instructors to prepare a syllabus and course description; expansion of registration times; and more time in between classes to better accommodate their workload. Dean Thomas Sponsler responded in the *Code* and defended the program as "innovative, creative, and basically sound" but "still in an early stage of development." A faculty committee would review the program and decide what changes to recommend. Sponsler eventually gave supervision of the program to Pamela Ebel, the director of placement and continuing legal education at the time.

The 1990 report on the skills program noted continuing "concern and skepticism as to the educational value of the Skills Curriculum."[50] Students and law faculty evaluated the skills courses, although the practice of having law faculty evaluate the skills courses appears to have ceased at some point during the last decade of the twentieth century. Most of the skills courses throughout the latter part of the twentieth century and into the twenty-first were lecture-style courses in which students were not expected to role-play, practice, or demonstrate some level of proficiency in the skills. Conceptually the program's promise was to bridge the gap between law school courses and practice; as a practical matter, the program had difficulty in accomplishing this goal.

AT THE TURN OF THE TWENTIETH CENTURY AND INTO THE TWENTY-FIRST

In 1986, Jack Nelson led the clinic, with four supervising attorneys: Evangeline Abriel, Calvin Johnson, Michael Gallagher, S.J., and Patricia Regan. Johnson and Regan were Loyola law graduates. Johnson oversaw a program called Tel-Law designed to provide legal information through recorded messages on a phone line.[51] Johnson would go on to serve as judge on Orleans Parish Criminal District Court for many years, earning the respect and esteem of his peers and the community at large.[52] On his return to the clinic, Gallagher noted that students had much richer backgrounds than when he had first worked at the clinic in 1979, and the clinic handled a broader range of claims.[53]

By 1990, the law clinic funded a staff of one director who was also a member of the tenure-track law faculty, and five full-time clinical faculty members or staff attorneys. Although the *Handbook* provided for long-term clinical faculty contracts, the law clinic often relied on supervising attorneys, not on the clinical long-term contract track, to staff the clinic. The clinic at that time specialized in domestic, juvenile, consumer, immigration, administrative, and criminal law, and the law of the elderly. A 1990 Report to the Faculty on the Law Clinic stated that enrollment in the clinic had grown from 10 to 61 students. In order to accommodate more students in the clinical program, the law school would have to hire more clinical faculty or supervising attorneys.[54]

The clinic's docket consisted of 48 percent family law cases, including juvenile cases; 30 percent criminal cases; 10 percent immigration cases; and the remaining 12 percent a mixture of consumer, entitlement, employment, housing, public benefits, and other miscellaneous cases, with approximately 259 active cases during the year.

After leading the clinic for over a decade, Jack Nelson retired as director in 1991. Dean Louis Westerfield appointed William P. Quigley as interim director, and in spring 1992, he was selected to lead the clinic.[55] Quigley had moved to New Orleans to study for the Catholic priesthood at Notre Dame Seminary. Instead, he became interested in social work and ended up going to law school at Loyola. Upon his graduation in 1977, he worked for the New Orleans Legal Assistance Corporation, before taking the position of assistant city attorney during Mayor Dutch Morial's administration.[56] Subsequently, he entered private practice, where he enjoyed a strong reputation in the local legal community for his representation of civil rights cases. Quigley had joined the clinic faculty the year before.

The selection of the director of the clinic marked a conflict concerning faculty appointments. Some faculty wanted to hire faculty with strong academic credentials from more prestigious institutions with or without membership on law journals; some preferred hiring faculty from Louisiana law schools, including Loyola, as long as they had been members of a law review; some thought other factors, like practical experience and professional achievements, equally, perhaps even more material, particularly for clinic faculty. For some faculty, membership on law review was an unofficial requirement. This conflict affected not just the hiring of the director in 1992, but decisions over faculty appointments into the twenty-first century.

Similarly, the role of clinic staff attorneys and clinic faculty in setting law school policy on academic matters, including curriculum, continued to generate tension at the law school well into the twenty-first century. From the perspective of some tenure-track faculty who had to satisfy a seven-year scholarship, teaching, and service-intensive "trial" period, and a relatively rigorous tenure process to be admitted to the law faculty ranks, it seemed unfair to give clinical faculty, hired under the Loyola *Handbook* through a process that involved no regular law faculty input and participation, the same voting and decision-making rights that they felt they had "earned." Clinical faculty, on the other hand, felt they had earned their right to participate fully as part of the law school teaching community.

That under the Loyola system both faculties were hired through completely separate, independent, and unrelated processes fostered the tension. The tension caused the law school accreditation difficulties. In 1994–95, then Interim Dean Garsaud appointed a committee to study the status of clinic faculty in response to concerns raised in the 1994 ABA's site evaluation report.[57] Subsequently, in academic year 1997–98, the faculty meetings became open to clinic faculty and library faculty. But the matter of voting rights remained unsettled.

In 1997, at Quigley's request, the law faculty approved a change to the poverty law course requirement, making it possible for students to satisfy the requirement by doing community service.[58] Beginning in the 1998–99 academic year, students had the option of performing 50 hours of volunteer legal services for the indigent instead of taking the poverty law course. This requirement provided an alternative way for students to develop practical experience, in addition to instilling in students the importance of pro bono work in the professional life of an attorney.

Clinical education provoked controversy in Louisiana.[59] In 1998, the Louisiana Supreme Court adopted more restrictive rules governing student practice that limited clinical education in the state.[60] The rules were a response to the complaints of business groups, in particular those targeting the Tulane Environmental Law Clinic's work to challenge the construction of a plastics plant in St. James Parish in Louisiana by Shintech, Inc.[61] The proposed Rule XX included a prohibition on representation of community organizations affiliated with national organizations (like the Delta Chapter of the Sierra Club); required that at least 75 percent of the membership of an organization must qualify for legal assistance in order for the organization to be eligible for representation; stiffened the rules for determining whether an individual was eligible for legal assistance; imposed limits on solicitation of cases by clinics; imposed limits on providing legal information to potential clients; imposed limits on the ability of law students to practice before federal courts and agencies; and limited the ability of clinical law students to lobby or appear before the Louisiana legislature.[62]

Adoption of the rules prompted a threatened boycott by the AALS of the city of New Orleans for its annual conference, a protest by law professors,[63] a lawsuit,[64] and a run for justice of the Louisiana Supreme Court by Loyola clinic director Bill Quigley.[65] Quigley's bid for a seat on the court pitted him against another Loyola law graduate, Pascal Calogero, a longtime presence on the court. Calogero graduated from Loyola law in 1954, first in his class and president (the position now known as editor in chief) of the *Loyola Law Review.* Calogero had been elected to the Louisiana Supreme Court in 1972 and began serving on the court as an associate justice in 1973, and chief justice in 1990. Ultimately, Justice Calogero kept his seat on the court.[66] He was the longest-serving justice in the history of the Louisiana Supreme Court upon his retirement on December 31, 2008, having served for thirty-six years.

The Louisiana Supreme Court was persuaded to modify the rules in 1999 to ameliorate its most restrictive effects, but they continued to hamper the efforts of clinics to effectively represent the interests of poor Louisiana residents. The modified rules eliminated the restrictions on representation of community organizations affiliated with national organizations, eased the eligibility for legal assistance requirements, and eliminated the limits on providing legal information to groups and individuals.

As it faced subsequent accreditation reviews by the ABA, the law school continued to debate clinical faculty status and voting rights. At a 2003 faculty retreat, the law faculty took a nonbinding straw vote to unify the regular and clinical faculties. In April 2004, Dean Brian Bromberger appointed an ad hoc Committee on Faculty Unification to develop an implementation plan. Dane Ciolino chaired the committee, which included Bill Quigley, a member of both faculties; Pat Hugg, Ray Rabalais, Kathy Lorio, and Gerry Rault from the regular faculty; and Luz Molina, one of two clinic faculty at the time. In fall 2004, the committee brought a proposal to make all future long-term clinic hires ordinary faculty, to be hired through a similar process used to hire tenure-track faculty. The proposal applied the same tenure and promotion standards to clinical faculty as to tenure-track faculty. Loyola tenure and promotion standards at the time accepted work on legal briefs as sufficient scholarship, arguably, to satisfy tenure standards. Under the proposal everyone on the faculty would have enjoyed tenure.

The proposal failed because the tenure-track faculty refused to grandfather the two clinic faculty. They were encouraged to apply for clinical ordinary faculty positions, but they would be part of a nationwide search for the new faculty. Quigley and the clinic faculty strongly resisted the proposal. The compromise was to recommit the matter to the faculty unification committee.[67] When the matter was reconsidered at its October 2004 meeting, clinic faculty again strongly opposed the original proposal and emphasized that they were satisfied with their level of participation in governance. When faculty voiced concern over compliance with the ABA standards, Quigley stated that he felt the ABA would accept clinic faculty attending faculty meetings and being allowed to vote on committees as sufficient for their participation in faculty governance.[68] This compromise accepted at the time proved unsatisfactory in the long run. Efforts to develop a unified hiring process for members of both faculties have proved unsuccessful.

More recent efforts to curtail the work of clinics in the state, again primarily directed at Tulane's Environmental Law Clinic, involved legislative efforts to cut off public funding to clinics that sued governmental agencies, represented clients who sought monetary damages, or raised state constitutional claims.[69] Introduced into the Louisiana legislature in 2010, SB 549 would have prohibited law clinics at universities that accepted state funds from suing government agencies.[70] Although the intended target was Tulane's clinic, Loyola's clinics would have been similarly impacted.

Tulane and Loyola law deans at the time, Stephen Griffin and Brian Bromberger, sought to sway public opinion to oppose the legislation in an editorial in the *Times-Picayune,* cautioning that the bill would have disastrous effects by sharply curtailing access to law school clinics, if not eliminating clinical legal education from the state.[71] Public response to the proposed legislation stymied its passage.

In fall 2011, Stuart H. Smith, a Loyola law graduate, pledged $1.25 million to the law school. The funds were used to assist in renovations to a building on the law school to house the clinical and other law programs, and to honor one of Smith's former professors and the former director of the clinic, Jack Nelson. The clinic was renamed the Stuart H. Smith Law Clinic and Center for Social Justice, and a professorship at the law school was endowed in Jack Nelson's name. Law clinic professor Luz Molina is currently the Jack Nelson Distinguished Professor of Law.

The Gillis Long Poverty Law Center sponsors a summer internship program that provides stipends to students who spend their summers working in legal services offices and other providers of legal assistance; a loan repayment assistance program for graduates; the pro bono program, which places students in legal services officers to do pro bono work (as a way to satisfy the poverty law requirement); a distinguished lecture series; and public service awards.

The ABA's current standards require law schools to give instruction in "professional skills generally regarded as necessary for effective and responsible participation in the legal profession."[72] Moreover, law schools must offer "live-client or other real-life practice experiences, appropriately supervised and designed to encourage reflection by students on their experiences and on the values and responsibilities of the legal profession, and the development of one's ability to assess his or her performance and level of competence." Loyola meets this standard primarily through its clinical offering. Between 2001 and 2007, enrollment in the clinic ranged from 42 to 66 students. In more recent years, enrollment in the clinic has ranged from a low of 53 in spring 2012 to a high of 94 in fall 2011 and 2013.

Loyola's clinic continues to provide legal services directly to indigent clients. Students apply in the spring semester of their second year and generally must sign up for two semesters of clinic, although one-semester clinics are available in criminal defense, community justice, and prosecution. Under the supervision of a clinical professor or staff attorney, students may undertake representation of clients in criminal defense, workplace justice, immigration, technology and legal innovation, family law, landlord-tenant law, and community justice. Currently, clinical faculty enjoy their strongest numbers since the establishment of the clinic: nine clinical faculty, in addition to the tenured clinical director, staff the clinic. Consequently, the number of law students able to pursue clinic has expanded as well, with capacity for clinical participation at 100 students per semester per year.

Currently, the clinic accepts students on a first-come, first-served basis. In order to enroll in the clinic, students must have completed 60 credit hours or four semesters of law school. In addition, students must have taken professional responsibility, evidence, and four skills courses. The dean must certify that the student is eligible to be a Rule XX Student Practitioner, which includes a determination that the student is of good character. Also, the student may not be on academic probation, which means the student must have a grade point average of at least 2.0.

Students may request placement in a particular clinic, and clinic professors interview applicants midspring to ensure they understand the time commitment, minimize problems with their academic schedule during the semesters they take clinic, and help the student determine clinic placement. Students are required to sign a memorandum acknowledging that they understand the commitment required of them, including attending a mandatory orientation session in August of their clinic year. Students also may participate in the school's Volunteer Income Tax Assistance Program (VITA): a program developed in coordination with the Internal Revenue Service to provide free tax preparation assistance for people with low to moderate incomes.

Recently, the ABA adopted curricular standards requiring member law schools to complete "one or more experiential course(s) totaling at least six credit hours."[73] Experiential courses must be a "simulation course, a law clinic, or a field placement." Several law professors at the law school had developed and offered simulation-type courses prior to the ABA's adoption of the standards, and the addition of a new coordinator of skills and experiential learning to the law school in 2012 has renewed emphasis and focus on both the skills program and experiential courses. The skills program, in particular, was reconceptualized within the established structure to provide students the opportunity to practice skills, rather than just attend lectures. All students must take a skills course in client interviewing or counseling; negotiation; cultural competence and interpersonal skills; and law office management and professionalism. The additional skills credits may be satisfied through electives that are designed to follow one of five tracks: civil, criminal, transactional, social justice, and maritime. Although some skills courses continue to be lecture, many require students to complete practice exercises on which they receive feedback.

Several years after establishing the clinic, in 1976, then dean Garsaud spoke in favor of expanding the clinical program to provide a year of practical experience under the supervision of full-time faculty members.[74] At the time, however, he believed such a program would be too expensive to operate. He thought proposals to reduce the number of years of law school from three to two misguided: law was too complex, and the responsibility legal educators owed to students and the public required the three years. Decades later, a subsequent dean, John Makdisi, suggested an approach that sought to ensure adequate practical experience and the continuation of the three-year academic program. Makdisi wanted to institute a one-year apprenticeship program for all law students upon their graduation from the academic program. That proposal, however, did not draw sufficient support from the alumni in funding or the faculty to come into being. And the discussions as to whether law is better as a two-year or three-year program continue to engage the academic and professional legal communities.

7

A MEMORANDUM OF UNDERSTANDING

FORMALIZING THE RELATIONSHIP BETWEEN THE LAW SCHOOL AND THE UNIVERSITY

Loyola's law school was born as a school of access to Catholics, workers, and recent immigrants. Membership in the professional accrediting bodies did not change this, but it did materially change the character of the school, adding a full-time day program and a compensated, full-time academic faculty. Both of these developments necessitated greater financial expenditures by the University. Growth in the law school student population throughout the twentieth century fueled growth in the law school faculty and building.

Similarly, the relationship between the University and the law school changed as well, reflecting the law school's greater autonomy and independence from the University in terms of its operation. One of the central components to accreditation and membership in the American Bar Association (ABA) and the Association of American Law Schools (AALS) had been that the law school program be controlled by legal academics or professionals, rather than religious leaders, in the case of a religious institution like Loyola, or academics with no legal experience or training. The hiring of full-time, compensated, professional deans had a significant impact on the law school, and the ABA and AALS principles that the law deans have access to the presidents of their respective institutions ensured the law school a voice at the decision-making table. The office of Jesuit regent at Loyola, nonetheless, survived until the latter part of the century.

The University itself changed throughout the twentieth century, accepting a higher degree of involvement from lay academic and administrative leaders, in particular, in its Board of Trustees. The latter half of the century, moreover, witnessed a growth of formal faculty involvement in University decision making, with the establishment of the University Senate, the adoption of a faculty handbook, and an elaborate faculty committee structure designed to advise the president and other administrators on a variety of university policies and procedures.[1] Many law faculty, including Janet Mary Riley and Dennis L. Rousseau, played pivotal roles in these endeavors. The president of the institution maintained primary control over its operation, and all Loyola presidents to the present have been Jesuits.

The law school, in a sense, enjoyed life in two worlds—the world of law and the legal academy, increasingly professional, increasingly competitive, and increasingly attractive to students and faculty, and the world of the University, generally supportive but at times unaware and insensitive to the goals and needs of the law school. Throughout this period of time, the University asked its academic entities to complete three-year plans. The law school's plans reflected an effort to draw the attention of the University, echoed throughout the latter part of the twentieth century, and to secure sufficient funding to accomplish the law school objectives.[2]

Throughout most of the twentieth century, however, law school autonomy and control over its activities, in particular its financial resources, continued to be an issue. Although the latter part of the twentieth century witnessed greater deference to law school administrators and faculty over the conduct of law school affairs, financial control over the law school continued to reside with the central administration, traditionally composed of Jesuits with little or no formal legal training. Thus, when the law school sent a moot court team to compete in the National Moot Court competition in 1973–74, then law school dean Marcel Garsaud Jr. had to secure authorization from the president of the University to authorize and release funds in the amount of $1,703.08 to pay for the team to travel to New York to attend the competition.[3] The dean had little real autonomy or authority to make even relatively small decisions; as a practical matter, this also made it difficult for him to get things done since most decisions involving allocation of financial resources appear to have been routed through the president of the institution.

The law student newspaper, the *Code,* reported the student reaction to the financial relationship that students felt was responsible for the insufficient physical space at the law school and for an insufficient number of law faculty. "Law Strike Threatened," read the headline in the second issue of the 1970 *Code.*[4] The Reverend Michael F. Kennelly, S.J., then Loyola president, responded on the same page, acknowledging delays in the construction of the new building (Miller Hall) but noting that the delays had been resolved and construction would "soon be a reality."[5] Kennelly did not respond to the complaints concerning insufficient law faculty but requested "a reasonable, rational attitude." He stressed the service that the law school provided for the community as the only night law school in the state.

Law students expressed concerns again about the situation in 1973 through the Student Bar Association (SBA).[6] The provost of the university, the Reverend James C. Carter, S.J., soon to emerge as president of the institution, responded to the SBA in writing. As Father Carter explained in his letter, the University's budgeting practices were to "put the vast majority of its revenues into a general fund" and then "to support Loyola's programs and operations from the general fund as equitably as possible according to program need and institutional priorities."[7] Thus, as a practical matter, the University's practice ignored the amount of revenue generated by the law school in determining the amount of money the law school would be awarded in the budget to meet law school needs. This model might have worked in the early twentieth century, when law was an undergraduate discipline, but at a time when law was a competitive professional discipline available primarily to students with a bachelor's degree, this model ensured difficulties for the law school.

In his letter to the SBA, Father Carter reported the law school generated $917,970 in tuition revenue for academic year 1972–73 (not including any endowment or alumni contributions). Full-time law students paid $1,735 for the 1972–73 academic year, and part-time students paid $1,230. Carter reported that for that same year, the University had expended a total of $559,000 to the school of law for faculty and staff salaries and fringe benefits, scholarships, and supplies. He noted that this amount did not include "contingency appropriations" required to complete the third issue of the *Loyola Law Review* and to send the Loyola moot court team to the Philip Jessup International Law Moot Court regional competition. Thus, Father Carter concluded, the law school contributed $358,970 to the "general services provided by the entire university." Moreover, the University had recently financed the building of a new law school building (Miller Hall), which would cost the University annual debt service in an additional $150,000.

Carter emphasized, however, that "Loyola's primary budget philosophy is that academic operations are budgeted according to equity and need," not "cost analyses." Loyola valued the law school: "The Law School is an enterprise which the University takes seriously and intends to support at higher levels than in the past." Nonetheless, he stated, "[t]here is clear evidence that the Law School, as a total enterprise (including capital and operating budgets) is not supporting other schools in the University." He concluded with a warning:

> Years of study can be years which are very rewarding in a very personal sense. Time spent agonizing over imagined inequities is counter-productive for the individual and the University. If the efforts the University has made to improve the quality of legal education continue to be met with a spirit of distrust and criticism, it will be difficult for me to persuade others that the Law School is deserving of a higher level of support. I am deeply interested in working with the Law School faculty and student body in achieving the highest quality legal education consonant with Loyola's institutional goals. Suspicions and charges of injustice are not the sort of attitude which will inspire me to greater efforts in this enterprise.[8]

In 1972, the University agreed to adjust law faculty salaries. In addition, the University authorized two new law faculty positions for academic year 1972–73. The insufficiency of law faculty salaries had become obvious during the dean search for Dean Papale's replacement. In a memorandum to Father Carter, Dean Garsaud wrote: "Each and every candidate who was interviewed for the position stressed the fact that the salary structure was wholly inadequate and that no serious consideration could be given to taking the position unless certain commitments were made regarding substantial up-grading in faculty salaries."[9] He requested an additional $35,000 a year.

The average Loyola law faculty salary for 1971–72 was $16,500, the median, $15,750. By comparison, at LSU's law school, the average law faculty salary for the same year was $20,432 and the median, $20,200. Louisiana Supreme Court justices at the time made $37,500; law school faculty salaries were comparable to the $15,000 salary paid to the deputy clerks of the Louisiana Supreme Court and the state court of appeals. The dean was trying to get the institution to realize that competitive salaries were required to recruit accomplished law faculty. In the world of law, faculty were more like judges than clerks and deputy clerks of court; they were expected to have graduated near the top of their class and to have engaged in enterprises like law review and federal court clerkships. Faculty were expected to provide academic expertise and leadership to legislative and judicial reform efforts and to produce meaningful scholarship with the potential to impact the practice and the development of legal norms.

Kennelly authorized the additional $35,000 requested by Garsaud for two academic years,[10] but the problem of finances and adequate faculty compensation continued to pose a challenge for the institution that both Garsaud and Carter, soon to be appointed president of Loyola, strove to address in the years to come.[11]

Law school control over faculty hiring and faculty salaries remained elusive and subject to the discretion of university administrators. This point was communicated forcefully by the president to Dean Garsaud in a letter stating point-blank that hiring authority for law faculty rested with the president and Loyola's academic vice president. And, yes, the president was aware that this placed the final authority on individuals who had no law training and were not really in a position to evaluate the academic credentials of potential law faculty.[12]

Law school control over its student body appears to have been similarly circumscribed; in 1972–73, the law school was authorized to accept 180 new freshmen in order to improve the student to faculty ratio as well as the strength of the class.[13] In academic year 1972–73 the law school employed nineteen tenure-track faculty, including deans, the librarian, and the director of the clinic. The following year, however, the provost requested that the faculty increase admission to 210 full-time and 90 part-time incoming first-years. That number remained in place until academic year 1976–77, apparently with the consent of the law faculty. In fall 1976, the law faculty voted to return to an entering class of 180 full-time and 70 part-time first-year students for the 1977–78 academic year.[14]

In 1978, at the end of Garsaud's administration, the law faculty at an academic retreat adopted a number of resolutions. Even those that involved purely academic matters, such as the minimum grade-point average required for academic exclusion, as well as the academic entering credentials required for admission, appear to have been subject to approval by the academic vice president and president.[15] It is probably that, in most cases, approval of the academic vice president and president over purely academic policies was a formality.

The 1982 law school plan asked the University to change its goals statement to reflect more inclusion and consciousness of the law school, and prioritized the law school's own commitment to a values-oriented legal education dedicated to "serious examination of those conscious and unconscious assumptions of contemporary American civilization that tend to perpetuate societal inequities and institutional injustices."[16] The rest of the three-year plan, however, was dedicated to the need for more money for the law school budget, and although there were numerous items demanding greater expenditures for space, a skills program, the expansion of the clinic, audiovisual materials, and other library materials, the primary focus was the proposal to reduce the student/faculty ratio from 28.86 to 1 in 1981–82, to 25 to 1 by 1984–85.

The law school's student/faculty ratio had been noted as a problem by the 1979–81 ABA and AALS inspection, with the organizations suggesting that the goal was 25 students to 1 faculty member.[17] In academic year 1978–79, the student/faculty ratio was 38.83 to 1, but it had been slowly and steadily decreasing. The law school sought higher faculty salaries and stronger research support: the number-one item on the faculty wish list was summer research stipends. In addition, the plan sought equalization of teaching loads, a sabbatical program for faculty members, establishment of a formal program of faculty counseling for students, and enhancement of the library collection. To that end, the 1982 plan suggested maintaining the law school class size at 600 to 610 full-time students (to improve the student/faculty ratio), and increasing tuition to make up for the loss of revenue. The number of full-time students in 1978–79 had been 699; in 1979–80, 667 full-time students attended; in 1980–81, the number had dropped to 627; and in the 1981–82 academic year, the class had dropped to 606.

Law school tuition had been increasing as well: $3,800 in 1981–82, and $4,500 per year in 1982–83. Loyola's president announced the increase in tuition of an additional $700 for 1982–83 to the student body in a February 1982 letter. In explaining the increase, the president identified a number of factors including the need to address the student/faculty ratio; the need to increase funding for the law library and installation and maintenance of the Lexis system; the addition of new positions like the writing skills specialist and a recruiter; and higher faculty salaries, "which must be competitive to insure quality."[18]

Law students again complained to the administration when the school announced the increase in tuition in 1982–83. The Loyola University chapter of the National Lawyers Guild wrote to Carter on April 7, 1982, to express concern over the tuition increase.[19] The president's response was short and to the point: it was too late to discuss a tuition increase; the increase was going to law faculty salaries; and "Loyola's students are asked to pay for only about fifty per cent of the cost of their education." Financial aid was available, and students who needed assistance should "avail themselves of our rather extensive financial aid program," which for the most part consisted, as it does now, of student loans.[20]

Garsaud's administration was marked by a continual struggle to secure adequate funding for the law school and a battle to identify the portion of law tuition revenues properly assigned as indirect costs to the law school. In 1981 Loyola agreed to grant him leave for academic year 1981–82 to pursue practice during the period of the leave.[21] At the conclusion of the leave he would decide whether to resign or return. Unable to come to an agreement with the University upon the conclusion of the leave, he resigned.

This remarkable leader was the last dean to preside over the law school for any length of time until later in the twenty-first century. He inspired uncommon loyalty in both faculty and students throughout his tenure at Loyola. Subsequent leaders of the law school found it difficult to inspire trust and collaboration in the faculty. The extent to which the lack of cohesiveness between faculty and administration stymied the development of the law school into a stronger institution is difficult to gauge. Garsaud's departure, however, signaled challenges to come.

The 1982 faculty plan for the law school noted his retirement and asked the University to commit to a substantial salary increase for his successor. The institution again decided to hire in-house.

Thomas Sponsler, the incoming dean and a member of the law faculty since 1968, identified the general goals for the law school upon his accepting the position:

> 1. Improved academic performance . . . by faculty and students; 2. The identification of some area of specialization that could permit the Law School to attain a stronger reputation outside Louisiana; 3. Greater emphasis upon the social responsibility of lawyers and sensitivity to ethical problems encountered by lawyers; 4. Greater cooperation with the integration of the Law School into the University as a whole; 5. Some accommodation of Law School admissions decision to University-Community relationship;

6. My own personal participation as greatly as possible in activities that will attract public attention.[22]

The goals suggested that primary authority for financial decisions, including setting of law school class size and faculty hiring and salaries would remain with the University. More problematic, the memo suggested that the problems Marcel Garsaud had identified a decade earlier continued to plague the law school: Sponsler noted that Loyola "agreed to support an effort to 'close the gap' between law faculty salaries at Loyola and those at Tulane and L.S.U." This would be accomplished, if necessary, by "raising law school tuition and dedicating that increase to law faculty salaries." Moreover, Loyola granted the new dean "reasonable leeway to solicit funds for the restricted use in the Law School in consultation with the University Development Office."[23]

In addition to concerns over recruitment and retention of competitive law faculty and bar passage rates, the law school continued to struggle with space issues. All of these issues involved funding and resources, and none perhaps was as challenging as finding a home for the law school that would accommodate the full range of law school needs, including adequate space for classrooms, clinical education, faculty and staff offices, and rooms available for student use.

After its opening at the College of the Immaculate Conception on Baronne Street, the law school had spent most of its early years in Marquette Hall. Gaining accreditation meant a move to Bobet Hall until 1942, when it moved to Thomas More Hall, a converted residence on St. Charles Avenue that served as the law school's home until it moved into the Branch Knox Miller Building in 1974.[24] The Miller Building was made possible by a gift from Alice Josephine Miller in honor of her father, attorney Branch Knox Miller. The Honorable Earl Warren, chief justice of the United States Supreme Court, delivered the address at the dedication of the Miller Building. Miller proved a lifeline to the law school; students who attended law school in Thomas More Hall remember it as a firetrap without air conditioning, basically a minimally renovated old house with insufficient classroom space to accommodate all law school classes.

Although Miller Hall was built specifically to house the law school, by the early 1980s the law school had outgrown the building. In a 1984 memorandum to Loyola president Reverend James C. Carter, S.J., the law school noted that the law clinic had been relocated to a house adjacent to Miller Hall; portions of the library had been used for the moot court board; there was a need for more faculty office space, storage space, and staff positions; there were inadequate restroom facilities for the school's enrollment; and classrooms were too few and too small.[25] The University was contemplating another move for the law school, this time away from the main University campus, to the former Dominican College campus on Broadway Street, St. Charles Avenue, and Pine Street, which Loyola had acquired. After extensive planning and negotiations, the law school agreed to move to the Broadway campus.

In justifying the law program's need for the new Broadway campus, which still houses the law school today, Sponsler noted the changes in the legal academy that in 1984 placed new requirements for law school buildings: a decrease in the law applicant pool, which required that law schools step up recruitment efforts; an increase in the number of elective and skills courses at the law school; the increase in student organizations with a need for additional space; the need for a placement office to help students find employment after graduation; the development of the law school as a provider of continuing legal education; and increased emphasis on and demand for clinical courses.[26]

The possibility of change in Loyola's general budgeting practices came from Father Carter. At the invitation of Carter, in November 1991, the dean at the time, Louis Westerfield, appointed an ad hoc committee to look into "whether it would be in the best interests of Loyola Law School to enter into an arrangement with the University that would provide for budget independence based on a formula such as that now in effect at the University of San Francisco."[27]

That arrangement involved a formal agreement reserving to the law school a percentage of its law school revenues with a view to putting the school on a "more or less autonomous financial basis." This kind of arrangement was in place not just at the University of San Francisco (USF), a Jesuit institution, but also at a number of other law schools. The University would "take" a percentage of law school revenues, which in theory compensated the University for providing infrastructure not reflected in the law school budget costs.

Westerfield's administration had been hobbled from the start by budget restrictions and a University-wide budget freeze. Although three faculty positions had been authorized to help the school diversify its faculty, other aspects of the law school were hit with severe budget cuts. Even the law school's newspaper, soon to go out of existence, had to ask alumni to send in mailing costs in order to receive the *Code.*[28]

The law school had instituted a placement office in 1969, and the office first hired a full-time director for 1991–92.[29] Given the growth in the student population, however, additional resources were needed to adequately provide placement services for graduating law students.

In addition, the law school faced substantial challenges in keeping up with developments in instructional resources and information technology. Law schools had to keep up with the practice, and practitioners had to keep up with the technology. The days when law students could learn to research using bound volumes were quickly being relegated to the past, and even basic document screening by attorneys was something that would shortly be done through computer programs. Don Woodman, the law school's director of instructional resources, noted that the main campus and law school were not aligned as to computer and information technology needs. Thus, it was difficult for the undergraduate institution to provide adequately for law school needs.[30] His report identified a critical shortage of manpower to meet the needs of the law school community as well as inadequate funding to meet those needs.

The ad hoc committee's report noted that the ABA had suggested that universities could reasonably keep 15 percent of a law school's revenues, but that anything more than 20 percent "raises a presumption that the university is not allowing the law school a fair share of the resources that it generates." Based on the arrangement at USF, the report proposed that the law school retain 80 percent of its revenues, with 18 percent for the University, and 2 percent to be devoted to a "Reserve Fund" for the benefit of the law school to cover future revenue shortfalls.

The report concluded that the law school would benefit from the arrangement. Using only budget expenditures treated as direct budget expenditures by the ABA, which included faculty and staff salaries and fringe benefits, the operating budget, including the law library book budget, financial aid, and actual law school revenues over a period of eight years, the committee compared actual budget revenues and expenses during those years to budget revenues and expenses using the proposed formula. The results of the comparison made clear that prior to 1989, the University had retained much less than 20 percent of law school revenues for general expenses.[31] In 1989, however, the percentage of law school revenues devoted to University general expenses had starkly risen to 29 percent for the 1989–90 academic year, and since that time the percentage of law school revenues diverted to University general expenses had stayed above the 20 percent mark. The reason for the disparity appears to have been the returns from the University's endowment. In years when the University's endowment returns flourished, everyone at the University benefited, including the law school. In years when the returns did not do as well, a greater proportion of law school revenues were diverted for general expenses. Thus, the committee concluded that adopting a formal agreement to keep 80 percent of law school revenues for law school budget expenditures would benefit the law school. In addition, the law school would presumably exercise discretion as to how to apportion those expenditures.

In preparing the final report, the ad hoc committee considered similar systems in place at Georgetown, Tulane, Fordham, and Lewis and Clark. The report was presented to the dean, the law school Visiting Committee, and the provost and senior vice president for academic affairs.[32] The final report contained a proposed draft agreement.

These discussions laid the groundwork for the negotiation of a memorandum of understanding between the law school and the University that ensured that the majority of law school revenues would go toward the law school and ensured that the portion of law school revenues reserved to the University would be within the average range for law schools nationwide. Before an agreement could be concluded, however, Westerfield left Loyola to become dean at the University of Mississippi School of Law.

Marcel Garsaud had been invited back to the law school in 1993 as a visiting professor, and Father Carter appointed Garsaud interim dean when Westerfield left in 1994. In late fall 1994, the faculty voted to extend the offer of one of two open tenured faculty positions to Garsaud and he accepted. The law faculty chose Mitchell F. Crusto, a native New Orleanian with a master of arts from Oxford University, a JD from Yale Law School, and bachelor of arts degrees from Oxford and Yale, for the other faculty position. Crusto, an African American and currently Henry F. Bonura, Jr. Distinguished Professor of Law, joined the law faculty after a varied practice including stints in government and the corporate world.

Garsaud served as interim dean for two years when the initial search for a new dean failed. During his first year as dean, the University agreed to provide the law school with a development officer. In addition, the University agreed to allow law alumni gifts to go to the law school, unless the donor expressed a wish not to contribute to the law school.

The first dean search committee consisted of faculty members Dian Arruebarrena, Ed Edmonds, Blaine LeCesne, M. Isabel Medina, Ray Rabalais, and Keith Vetter. Professor Arruebarrena served as chair of the committee but the committee's work was affected by the resignation of Father Carter as president of the institution. The University proceeded with the search for a new dean at the same time that it engaged in a search for a new president. That search concluded in January 1995, when Loyola's Board of Trustees selected the Reverend Bernard J. Knoth, S.J., the institution's new president. Father Knoth's inauguration took place on October 28, 1995.

The dean's search committee identified five external candidates for the position of dean, but none of the candidates received sufficient faculty support to yield an actual candidate for the position.[33] Although this search failure created tensions both at the law school and the University, the provost appointed Garsaud as interim dean for a second year, and the law faculty selected a new search committee.

As a result of the failed search, however, the provost formalized the protocol for the dean search, which provided for input from law faculty, law alumni, and law students and for participation by each of these entities including law library faculty and law clinic faculty. The next search committee consisted of Professors Arruebarrena, David Gruning, Bobby Harges, James Klebba, Blaine LeCesne, and Kathryn Lorio. This time, the search committee—chaired by David Gruning working closely with Judge Adrian Duplantier of the U.S. District Court for the Eastern District of Louisiana, chair of the law school's Visiting Committee and a fervent supporter of the law school—generated the requisite three names.[34]

The candidate chosen by the University administration had been highly ranked by the faculty: John Makdisi, a former dean of the University of Tulsa College of Law from 1991 to 1994 with a solid academic pedigree and track record of rigorous scholarship. Makdisi was a graduate of Harvard College with a law degree from the University of Pennsylvania, and the highest academic degree in law from Harvard, one that few law professors possess, an SJD. Moreover, his Catholic and religious identity made him equally attractive to the University administration. Makdisi's commitment to his faith was sincere and deep, and his deanship brought the school's Catholic identity to the forefront.

Makdisi appealed to those in the faculty who sought the elusive chapter of the Order of the Coif and wanted the law school to make a firmer commitment to scholarly work; he appealed as well to those who viewed the law and the law school as a mechanism through which to achieve social justice because of his adherence to Catholic values. Neither group realized that achieving either goal would require substantial change at the law school.

The recurring challenge for the law school had been its financial relationship to the University. That relationship was formalized under Dean Makdisi, who successfully negotiated a memorandum of understanding between the law school and the university. The memorandum ensured that the majority of law school revenues would go to the law school and that the portion of law school revenues reserved to the University would be within the average range for law schools nationwide. The agreement, initially negotiated at the time of his acceptance of the deanship at the law school and finally formalized in 1998, provided that the law school make a fixed payment of $2.45 million to the University over the next four fiscal years, from 1999 through 2002. The law school would retain all other revenues to cover law school budget expenses.[35] The fixed payment was designed to cover the indirect costs the University provided for the law school, including infrastructure support like that provided by the physical plant, campus security, financial aid services, technology support and services, major equipment purchases, and renovations. But at the law school, not all infrastructure support was provided by the University; increasingly, in order to keep up with the profession and other law schools, the law school had to pay for computer hardware and software out of its own budget rather than rely on University-wide expenditures.

The memorandum did not formally change financial decision-making processes. In fact, it expressly provided that it was not meant to change procedures or "the present structure of authority or control over these funds." But both Dean Westerfield and Dean Makdisi had been successful at convincing the University administration that change at the law school was necessary if the law school were going to maintain and improve its current standing among law schools. Father Bernard Knoth, the new president, and Dr. David Danahar, the provost and academic vice president, conveyed strong support for Makdisi's efforts to strengthen the school.

The initial memorandum again noted the "ultimate purpose of achieving Order of the Coif in accordance with the Academic Plan." The memorandum was formally approved by the law faculty and signed by the dean, president, provost, and senior vice president of academic affairs and chief financial officer for the institution. It tied law school revenues to the law school budget and gave the dean and the law school the opportunity to plan for its academic needs, with the support of a budgeting structure that could now, to a great extent, be relied on. Moreover, although the memorandum did not expressly grant authority to the dean to authorize spending in reliance on his budget, as a practical matter, the dean's position in authorizing spending increased. He might still have had to make a trip between campuses to convince the administration, but he did it from a position of strength, always able to show that his budget accommodated the spending. Financially, things at the law school began to turn around for the benefit of the students and the faculty. The memorandum did not grant the law school power to determine its tuition and the size of the class to be admitted, but the dean had secured agreement to reduce the size of the class in future years, and at that point in time University faculty actively participated in discussion of tuition increases. Faculty participation in those decisions ensured that tuition increases would receive serious consideration before being adopted.

Loyola was much like the city of its birth—a paradoxical mix of sophistication and provincialism with a natural tendency to resist change, particularly change initiated by newcomers with few or no roots in the city. The law school admired Makdisi and what he stood for—the promise of change and the strength to bring it to fruition. But the idea of change may be more appealing than its reality, and when Makdisi sought to realize that change, some in the faculty resisted. While Makdisi began the process of change that was ultimately to lead to a stronger law school at Loyola, he was himself not there to see it come about.

Makdisi was on the cusp of a wave of change transforming the legal academy. Many law schools, not just Loyola, were in the process of determining the extent to which law faculties needed to publish, the role of clinical legal education in law schools, the need to diversify what were still overwhelmingly white and male law faculties, and the need to ensure that students from racial and ethnic minorities had the opportunity to join the legal profession. The pressures of law practice were causing many to turn to teaching instead of law practice. This in turn swelled the ranks of candidates seeking teaching positions at a time when law schools were trying to undo the decades of racial and gender segregation in their own ranks. The push for faculty publication in part was driven by the tremendous competition for law faculty positions. It took a while before most law schools began to accept the idea that law faculty were expected to produce scholarship at a fairly consistent level, and that this expectation applied to its most senior members, not just the junior faculty intent on establishing their right to tenure.

At Loyola, law faculty had engaged in scholarship, but their work was sporadic and tended to focus on local efforts. Some faculty did not produce any scholarship. Some had developed substantial law practices on the side that kept them from devoting their time and resources fully to law school endeavors including research and publication. Makdisi strongly encouraged faculty scholarship and publication, facilitating the law school's transition to a school that valued scholarship because of its positive benefits to better teaching, to faculty-student engagement, and to the development of legal norms. The emphasis on scholarship, however, cost the dean support among some faculty used to less demanding expectations. A campus-wide push to enforce limits on the amount of time that full-time tenured faculty could devote to outside practice also caused tensions among law faculty.[36]

Makdisi, although a strong supporter of academic freedom, emphasized the school's Catholic nature and encouraged more formal acknowledgment of the role that religion played in law and legal education. He believed firmly in affirmative action to increase diversity with regard to race and economically disadvantaged applicants but wanted to improve the entering credentials of the class substantially.[37] During his tenure, the law school adopted an alternative admissions program designed to consider students with weak entering credentials on the basis of actual performance in a law school course. The program was initiated in 1997.[38]

In the 1990s, the Association of American Law Schools adopted regulations requiring law schools to ensure that their internal operations and career services prohibited discrimination on the basis of sexual orientation.[39] At the time, the law school's nondiscrimination policy explicitly addressed race, color, religion, sex, national origin, age, handicap, or marital status, but not sexual orientation. The AALS deemed the school's policy insufficient in 1997–98, on the grounds that the internal policies did not prohibit discrimination on the basis of sexual orientation; the career services nondiscrimination pledge required of employers did not include sexual orientation; and the school allowed the military to recruit without taking ameliorative steps to note the disparity between the military's policy on sexual orientation and the law school's nondiscrimination policy.[40] The law school complied and changed its internal policy to include sexual orientation, but with regard to the military and employers, the school refused to accede on the grounds that the Catholic Church distinguished between status and conduct, as did the military and probably employers, and, thus, that the school was justified in its treatment of sexual orientation.[41] While the law school welcomed gay and lesbians as students, it failed to provide explicit support for them on campus; many felt forced to hide their sexual identity and preference.

In fall 1998, the law school considered a variety of measures to improve bar performance, in response to a drop in bar performance below the statewide average. Generally, Loyola's pass rate had been well above the statewide average, but in the summer of 1995 the statewide average pass rate dropped well below what it had been for the past decade. Louisiana's statewide average pass rate from 1989 to 1994 had ranged from a low of 59 percent for the summer bar in July 1990 to a high of 70 percent in July 1994. In July 1995, however, the Louisiana statewide average pass rate dropped to a low of 53 percent. That year, Loyola's bar passage rate was 55 percent. The pass rate improved in 1996, with Loyola's rate equal to the statewide average at 67 percent, but in the next two years, Loyola's bar passage rate dropped below the statewide average.[42]

The law faculty considered adopting mandatory classes for at-risk students to prepare them for the bar; requiring students in the bottom third of the class to take a bar review–type course; instituting an upper-level writing course to focus on bar exam–type problems; having faculty who teach bar courses cover the major areas tested on the bar; adopting stricter enforcement of mandatory attendance rules; ensuring that students know in advance what courses were "bar" courses; team teaching; revising grading curves; more writing opportunities for students, and other measures. Most of these measures were adopted a decade later, in 2008, as the law school remained dissatisfied with its students' performance in the bar. In addition, the faculty and administration made a concerted effort to talk to the Louisiana Supreme Court Committee on Bar Admissions, and to bar examiners, to ensure that the bar process was fair and worked to identify competent practitioners.

Loyola students' performance on the bar improved in the next few years. Although the school still came in third, for the most part, among Louisiana schools, its students were performing at or above the statewide average. The statewide average increased as well, perhaps because of litigation challenging the Louisiana bar examination process or complaints about the Louisiana bar. Despite its weak educational system and relatively small population, Louisiana has had, at various times, one of the hardest bars in the country.

In addition, Makdisi's strong support for the clinic similarly inspired criticism. At this point in time, the only persons who participated in faculty meetings were regular faculty: tenure-track or tenured faculty, which included the dean. Makdisi proposed to invite the clinic faculty to law faculty meetings, which some in the faculty strongly resisted. He also asked the faculty to consider the curricular reforms that had been brought before it in the 1980s and early 1990s to reduce the total number of required hours for law students. The faculty agreed to some changes to the curriculum, in particular to reduce the number of hours required in constitutional law from 6 to 4, but shied away from massive change. In 1999, the law faculty agreed to reduce the overall number of required hours, particularly in the common law curriculum. Faced with a very similar proposal to that fielded in 1986, law faculty teaching constitutional law and business organizations agreed to reduce the number of hours in those courses, and offer them as single-semester, 4-credit-hour courses. Faculty who supported the change viewed it as necessary to allow the law school to compete for students with other law schools. The majority of other law schools taught most of the courses as one-semester, 4-credit-hour courses. The move continued to be controversial among the faculty, with some feeling that a requirement-heavy curriculum was necessary to equip law students to do well on the bar. Those in favor of reducing required hours pointed to the apparent lack of correlation between the number of required hours, including in Louisiana law courses, and the bar passage rate, noting that the law school had been fairly consistent in bar passage rates, regardless of required courses. This controversy over the curriculum contributed to the deterioration of the relationship between Makdisi and the faculty.

Makdisi's efforts to improve teaching performance also created tensions. The issue came to a head over the hiring of additional faculty, and Makdisi resigned, soon to take another deanship at St. Thomas University School of Law. Makdisi may have taken on too many battles at one time. His legacy, however, proved invaluable to the law school. He had made it possible for the law school to establish itself on sound financial footing and secured sufficient independence for it to develop itself as a stronger institution than it had been. He had also established the basis for the recognition that scholarship was an integral part of serving on the law faculty.

Makdisi's resignation was itself a traumatic event for the law school. Among some of the faculty he had been a visionary leader; among alumni he had been popular as well. His departure left tensions unalloyed and heightened. It would be years before the school would hire another dean. Longtime faculty member James Marshall Klebba was called upon to preside over the law school for four years.

Initially, the provost appointed Klebba to a two-year term to accommodate preparations for an ABA accreditation site visit scheduled for spring 2001. Klebba faced a fractious faculty, split on a number of issues including proposed new faculty by-laws designed to restrict decanal authority, authorship of the site accreditation report, faculty scholarship and publication, faculty engaging in outside practice, clinical education, clinic faculty voting rights, affirmative action, and admission standards. Some in the faculty distrusted the University administration despite its willingness to work with former dean Makdisi in restructuring the financial relationship between the law school and the University and in allowing a reduction in class size to allow the law school to better meet the instructional needs of its students. A dean search committee appointed in 2001 resulted in a failed search. Klebba's term was extended, and the school embarked on a second dean search. Klebba was recognized for his contributions to the law school with the title of "dean" during his last year in the position.

During this period, law librarian Ed Edmonds left to join the faculty of the University of St. Thomas School of Law in Minneapolis, Minnesota, and the law school selected P. Michael Whipple to join the law faculty and serve as director of the law library. Whipple had served as director of the law library at the University of Puerto Rico for ten years prior to joining the Loyola law faculty. His law degree was from the University of Iowa, and his master of laws degree from the University of Denver. Whipple served as professor and director of the law library until his retirement in 2013. Under his leadership the law library enhanced its collection, enjoying better financial support under the new arrangement between the University and the law school, and reflecting the increased class sizes made possible by additional faculty hires and a strong law applicant pool. Notwithstanding, the library continued to lag significantly below the average for all accredited law schools.

Despite faculty disputes, the school prospered under Klebba's leadership. The faculty adopted standards and criteria for annual evaluation of faculty performance in teaching, scholarship, and service.[43] The law school adopted formal by-laws that provided for an established committee structure and appointment process that gave both faculty and the dean a role in staffing the various committees. The school's direct expenditures per student, however, continued to lag below the average for law schools.

Klebba was a strong fundraiser for the school and supported faculty willing to explore areas and issues being addressed nationally, including environmental law, gender law issues, and domestic violence. Klebba was instrumental in securing funding for the law school's first and only endowed chair, the Gauthier–St. Martin Eminent Scholar and Chair in Environmental Law, as well as a number of professorships.

The funding for the endowed chair came from two of the law school's graduates: Wendell H. Gauthier and Michael X. St. Martin. Gauthier, a 1970 graduate of Loyola law's night program, successfully litigated on behalf of individuals injured by silicone breast implants and tobacco products.[44] Gauthier was considered one of the country's top trial attorneys, responsible for developing the strategy that tobacco companies had known about and exploited nicotine's addictive potential, ultimately successful in establishing the industry's liability.[45] In spring 2003, Wendell Gauthier's family and fellow Loyola law graduate Michael X. St. Martin, class of 1967, donated sufficient money to allow the Louisiana Board of Regents to award the school of law its first and only endowed chair. In fall 2004, the school's first Wendell H. Gauthier–Michael X. St. Martin Eminent Scholar Chair in Environmental Law, Robert R. M. Verchick, began his first year at Loyola.[46] Verchick earned his law degree at Harvard and his bachelor's at Stanford. He had practiced before joining the faculty at the University of Missouri–Kansas City School of Law.

Klebba also secured funding from Mary Kay, Inc., to host a three-day, interdisciplinary conference on integrating responses to domestic violence,[47] and he was supportive of more active faculty engagement with the national legal academy. To that end, the school hosted a conference for professors of immigration law in May 2002.

To address the deficiencies in faculty scholarship noted by the ABA accreditation team, the law school, with University approval, instituted a faculty publication incentive grant. To the extent that some law faculty turned to practice to supplement salaries they viewed as insufficient and out of step with national averages, the incentive grants were designed to reward faculty productivity and to an extent reduce the incentive for outside practice. Some faculty viewed the expectation of faculty scholarship and publication as an inextricable part of their responsibilities as faculty; they viewed scholarship as necessary to their remaining effective classroom teachers. The incentive grants were available only for a few years, until the demands of the law school and University budgets made them unfeasible.

The University also approved the hiring of several new law faculty. In 2002, the law school hired three entry-level candidates, two local individuals and one out-of-state candidate selected through the AALS process, and an established international scholar, Dominique M. Custos. Three of the four new faculty greatly strengthened the school's civil law program.

Dominique M. Custos, now Judge John D. Wessel Distinguished Professor of Law, earned her doctoral degree summa cum laude from Pantheon-Sorbonne University in Paris in 1989, after graduating as valedictorian of her public law master's degree class from the same university. After working at the Pantheon-Sorbonne as a teaching and research fellow, she joined the faculty at the University of the (French) Antilles & Guiana, and in 1994, upon successful completion of the highly competitive "Agregation de Droit Public," was appointed full professor to the University of Caen in France. She was a Fulbright Visiting Scholar at Columbia University in 1997–98, joining the Loyola faculty in 2002. Her areas of expertise included communications and administrative comparative law and European Union law.

Robert A. Garda Jr., a Duke University School of Law 1994 graduate with an undergraduate degree from Duke as well, had turned to teaching after working for a law firm for almost ten years, making partner in 2001. Garda, now the Fanny Edith Winn Distinguished Professor of Law at the law school, taught education law and contract law.

John A. Lovett was practicing with the New Orleans law firm Liskow and Lewis when he was selected by Loyola to join its civil law faculty. Lovett had graduated from Haverford College in 1988 and had earned a master of fine arts from Indiana University in 1991, before turning to the study of law at Tulane Law School, where his father had served on the law faculty. Lovett, now the De Van D. Daggett, Jr. Distinguished Professor of Law, had clerked for a federal district court and the United States Court of Appeals for the Fifth Circuit prior to joining Liskow and Lewis.

Monica Wallace had graduated from Loyola Law in 1998, first in her class. She had clerked for the U.S. Fifth Circuit Court of Appeals, like Lovett, and for the federal district court in the Southern District of California before joining a New Orleans law firm. Wallace had developed expertise in civil law courses, particularly those dealing with family law.

The new faculty hires helped to establish and secure the expectation that faculty would engage in scholarship and publication, like the publication incentives grant. The legacy of these hires was to prove much stronger than that of the incentives grant.

During his tenure as dean, Klebba, with the support of then University president Bernard Knoth, successfully navigated a negative community response to a nationally renowned speaker invited to the campus. Loyola law alumni Kim Gandy had been elected president of the National Organization for Women, and she was invited to speak to the law school community on March 29, 2001, on judicial nominations. Anti-abortion activists from outside the New Orleans community generated substantial protest against Gandy's talk, including death threats against the president of the institution. Both Knoth and Klebba stood by the invitation to Gandy and the professor who had issued the invitation to Gandy, and the speech was well supported and received by the University community.

But the nation had changed. The community reception to Gandy in March 2002 was starkly different to the reception offered Sarah Weddington in 1975 and again in 1987, and Michael Hardwick in 1987. A visit by U.S. Supreme Court Associate Justice Ruth Bader Ginsburg earlier in the spring semester, in February 2002, to deliver the annual Judge Robert A. Ainsworth, Jr., Memorial Lecture on "Four Louisiana Giants in the Law," similarly generated an anti-abortion protest. The threats and protests that flowed from the Gandy visit were unprecedented, but they made clear that the University's commitment to academic freedom was strong and wholehearted.

Klebba began his service as interim dean in summer 1999. At that time, no one would have anticipated that the next dean at the law school would be Jewish and hail from Australia.

8

TRANSCENDING DISASTER

The hurricane caught everyone by surprise, and most New Orleanians who left, left thinking they would return in at most a few days. Like the city, neither the University nor the law school had plans in place for what to do in case of a severe, lengthy disruption to New Orleans. No one had really planned for the aftermath of a severe disaster, natural or man-made, that would leave a city uninhabitable for a substantial period of time.

Fall 2005 law classes began earlier than the undergraduate colleges, as regularly scheduled, in the third week of August. The law school's entering class consisted of a total 280 students, 69 of them in the evening program, higher than the 271 new first-year students enrolled in fall 2004. Total enrollment at the end of the first week of classes was 818 students, a little bit higher than the 813 students enrolled in fall 2004.

When the storm hit, the law school was under the leadership of Brian Bromberger, and at the helm of the University, the Reverend Kevin William Wildes, S.J., PhD. A spry sixty-five, Bromberger had just finished his second year as dean, and the law school seemed to be headed in a strong direction.[1] Bromberger had been serving as associate dean for academic affairs at the University of North Carolina at Chapel Hill before joining the law school as dean in fall 2003.

THE NEW LAW DEAN

Bromberger had a unique background. He was born in the rural hamlet of Bunyip in the Australian state of Victoria. His father, Sam Bromberger, was the sole teacher in an even tinier nearby hamlet. Both his parents had immigrated to Melbourne from England as teenagers. Bromberger was the youngest of their three sons; the first died while still a toddler. The Brombergers brought up their children in a traditional Jewish home.

Bromberger loved living in the Australian bush, but at the end of World War II, when he was six, the family returned to Melbourne, where his father served as principal of the first Jewish day school in Australia. Upon finishing high school, Bromberger completed mandatory national service and began boxing. He later became Australian amateur featherweight champion, and fought on television under an assumed name to prevent his mother finding out about it.

Law had always interested Bromberger, but his father, whom he greatly respected, had a prejudice against lawyers. Bromberger did not want to follow his brother into medicine, so when he began university studies he settled on dentistry. This he hated, and he dropped out, losing his scholarship. He then became a television technician. When he was twenty-one, his father died suddenly. His death caused considerable emotional and financial distress to his family, but it freed Bromberger to pursue law school studies. In order to do so, he took advantage of a government-funded teacher-training program that enabled suitable candidates to teach part-time while studying to become teachers. While studying law at the University of Melbourne, Bromberger taught history and math at a gritty inner-city high school. He also coached the football team, coming to the attention of one of the major league teams, Fitzroy (now the Brisbane Lions), who hired him to coach their training team, which helped him pay for law school.

Bromberger earned his bachelor of arts/law degree with honors from Melbourne University, and a teaching certificate from Melbourne Teacher's College. He taught briefly at the new law school at Monash University, also in Melbourne, Victoria, before pursuing a master of laws at the University of Pennsylvania. He was a visiting professor at a number of law schools including the College of William and Mary and Syracuse University. In 1973, he returned home with his young family after being offered a position as senior lecturer at a new law school at the University of New South Wales in Sydney. There he developed a new course, law and medicine, which became his specialty. While at the University of New South Wales, he served as junior counsel for 150 patients of a psychiatrist whose unorthodox treatments came before a Royal Commission. In 1992, he and Janet Fife-Yeomans wrote a biography of the psychiatrist, *Deep Sleep: Harry Bailey and the Scandal of Chelmsford,* that was on the Australian best-selling list.

In 1995, he returned to the United States, to the University of North Carolina at Chapel Hill faculty, where he remained until accepting the deanship at Loyola. He was the first non-Catholic dean chosen to lead the law school. An observant Jew, he became a member of the local conservative congregation, Shir Chadash. Like John Makdisi before him, his adherence to his faith informed his character and leadership of the law school and facilitated his relationship to the Jesuits leading the institution.

Of slight stature, irrepressible energy, and general good humor, Bromberger solved one of the problems facing the law school in his first year as dean: a shortage of space. With a growing student body, additional faculty, and a clinical program that provided practical training to many more students than when it had started, the law school was again starved for space. Its existing facility, essentially unchanged since its opening in the late 1980s, needed renovation. Dean Bromberger secured funding in large part from Anne Gauthier, widow of law graduate Wendell H. Gauthier, and persuaded the University as well as the neighborhood, normally threatened by any kind of expansion plans, to allow the school to proceed with renovations to the existing building, and a four-story extension of 16,000 square feet that would provide additional classrooms and office space to be known as the Wendell H. and Anne B. Gauthier Family Wing.

Bromberger also proved adept with long-standing issues that had proved the downfall of prior deans including curricular reform, faculty scholarship, the clinic, and extensive practice commitments by regular faculty. Although Bromberger's deanship was to face one of the most challenging times in the school's history, over the course of time Bromberger led the school through one of its most successful periods for students and faculty alike.

BEFORE THE STORM

The Reverend Kevin Wm. Wildes, S.J., PhD, had been appointed president of the university in 2004.[2] His first convocation address to faculty and staff announced the development of a new University-wide strategic plan to better "educate the whole student and to benefit the larger community" and "to help move our University to a greater level of national recognition." He joined the community in celebrating renewal—the start of a new academic year. He closed the convocation:

> Later this week we will welcome new students who will also renew us. But in our renewal, we also have dreams about the future. Dreaming is hard work. It involves freeing our imaginations from what is to what can be. The University Community has been involved in the work of dreaming. Now begins the work of making those dreams come true. At this moment of renewal and planning I am reminded with the words of Henry David Thoreau with which I will end: "If you have built castles in the air, your work need not be lost: that is where they should be. Now put foundations under them.[3]

As promised, later that year, the president established a University Strategic Task Force to develop a new strategic plan for the University.

Fall 2004 witnessed the opening of another evening part-time law program in the state. Southern University Law Center obtained the approval of the American Bar Association (ABA) in summer 2004 to operate a part-time evening school.[4] Loyola now faced competition for local students interested in pursuing a legal education. Since Loyola's admission standards tended to be substantially higher than Southern's, the impact might be minimal, but it was no longer the only law school in Louisiana offering a part-time program at night.

At the end of Wildes's first year, in spring 2005, the law school honored the family of 1954 law graduate and noted politician Moon Landrieu at its May graduation. The institution gave the Landrieu family an honorary degree. Moon Landrieu had been a student at the law school when it admitted Norman Francis and other African Americans. He had married Verna Satterlee, a fellow Loyola graduate, the year he graduated from the law school. They had raised nine children, several of them (or their spouses) graduates of Loyola. Mary Landrieu had gone on to serve in the U.S. Senate, and although not a Loyola graduate, she had been supportive of the institution. Mitch Landrieu, at the time lieutenant governor of the state, was, like his father, a law school graduate. The school decided to honor the family. The only cloud in the sky that May was the New Orleans archdiocese's objections to the decision to honor the Landrieu family because of the younger Landrieus' support for reproductive rights. But the event went as planned with the Honorable Moon

Landrieu delivering the commencement address.[5] At the same ceremony, the school gave an honorary doctorate to Janet Mary Riley, the law school's first woman professor.

The second year of Wildes's presidency, 2005, witnessed a bumper entering class of undergraduate first-years—with 972 students, it was the largest entering undergraduate class in Loyola's history.[6] Total enrollment on the undergraduate campus that fall was 3,750. Total enrollment for the University including the law school was 5,644. The University started classes a week later than the law school so undergraduates began to arrive on campus as law students entered their second week of classes.

THE STORM

Law faculty and students left school that Friday not expecting anything unusual for the weekend and the coming week. By early evening, however, news of the storm making its way across Florida drew the attention of New Orleans residents as forecasters suggested the storm might energize once it hit the Gulf and aim for Florida's panhandle.[7] Later that night, forecasters predicted landfall in the New Orleans area, and by the next morning, New Orleanians were torn between immediately departing and waiting to see if the storm veered off, as often happened, or lost intensity.[8] Louisiana's governor, Kathleen Blanco, declared a state of emergency for Louisiana late Friday, but New Orleans mayor Ray Nagin delayed issuing a mandatory evacuation order for the city until Sunday morning.[9] Many metropolitan area residents left on Saturday. Many more followed on Sunday. Most spent hours on the road stuck in traffic—trips that normally took five or six hours took double that time.

Loyola's dean headed for Houston. Loyola's president remained at the campus in New Orleans. Neither the law school nor the University had instituted a method through which administrators, faculty, or students could communicate with each other if the University's website and e-mail system failed. The law school did not maintain a list of alternative e-mails or personal cell phone numbers through which faculty might be reached. No one had thought to establish a phone tree similar to what parents of children in elementary schools use to communicate throughout a community when something happens.

The storm made its second landfall on the morning of Monday, August 29, east of New Orleans along the Louisiana and Mississippi border, as a strong

Category 3 hurricane on the Saffir-Simpson Hurricane Scale, with a storm surge of 25 feet on the Mississippi coast. It lost intensity as it made its way inland, causing some damage and flooding, but the city, once again, on Monday morning appeared to have been spared the storm's worst. Slowly, news began trickling in of severe flooding at various points in the city along the levee system linked to Lake Pontchartrain and the intracoastal canal. Levees had given way at various points, and the water in some places had rushed in with sufficient force to sweep away homes and people, or had risen so quickly that some had been unable to reach high ground before being overcome by the water.[10] By Tuesday, those who had evacuated knew the city had sustained a catastrophic blow. Grimly, they watched television news as the water rose in the city and thousands who had stayed waited for assistance. On Saturday, September 3, 2005, the U.S. Army's Eighty-Second Airborne Division deployed in the New Orleans area. On September 6, the city implemented a mandatory evacuation of all of its residents, and prohibited those already evacuated to return. Reentry would not begin until late September.

For a time, it felt as if the city might not survive. The immediate damage was daunting. Eighty percent of the city flooded.[11] The city's population (approximately 484,674 people) was displaced. At least 986 Louisiana residents were dead, 40 percent by drowning. Seventy percent of occupied dwellings in the city were damaged. Total damages were estimated at $135 billion.[12] Those who had left the city questioned whether to return.

At Loyola, the storm caused little damage, compared to that sustained by other educational institutions in New Orleans, but the law school sustained wind damage that caused flooding in upper-floor faculty offices. By the time some law faculty returned to their offices for materials, stacks of books, papers, and files were covered in mold. Even that minimal amount of damage, however, proved costly. The University claimed $4.8 million in damages, $3 million covered by insurance, with $1.8 million constituting the deductible, and a revenue shortfall of $25 million, due to the loss of projected tuition revenue. Ultimately, the shortfall for 2005–6 came to approximately $5 million.[13]

The storm's strongest immediate impact on the law school was the disruption of its e-mail and web servers and the dispersal of faculty and students. While trivial when compared to the enormity of devastation to portions of the city and the loss of life, the lack of e-mail and Loyola web access left students and faculty unable to communicate. Neither dean nor faculty could post messages to the law school community. The storm sharply reduced cell phone service to New Orleans area codes, rendering another major avenue of communication unavailable. Like all area institutions and residents, the law school faced a dispersed population that it could not contact easily. Loyola was unable to restore web page and e-mail service until over a week after the hurricane struck on September 8, 2005. By that time, the law school had planned and announced that it would offer a good portion of its fall semester out of the University of Houston Law Center.

THE LAW SCHOOL IN HOUSTON

Bromberger arrived in Houston after a long drive on Sunday and watched in dismay as events unfolded in the city. Within days he and his spouse planned a return to his native Australia to wait until the city became habitable again. Barbara Wilson, Bromberger's executive assistant, evacuated to Houston as well and contacted Bromberger upon her arrival the Monday the hurricane struck. She remembers his initial reaction to the catastrophe.

> Two days after our initial contact, Dean Bromberger called to tell me he and Carolyn had been transfixed by the television reports of the devastation in New Orleans. He felt because of the enormity of the destruction that we would not be able to return to New Orleans in the immediate future, and the law school's fall program seemed in jeopardy. He explained that they had decided to return to Australia, and, in fact, Carolyn was at the airport purchasing the tickets.[14]

With the help of faculty and students who managed to get in touch with each other through non-Loyola e-mail addresses, and in particular a blog set up by Eric Muller at the University of North Carolina at Chapel Hill School of Law, slowly law faculty and students began to communicate about the challenges ahead. But the first few days were chaotic for all, with very little information available to anyone, and faculty not in a position to make promises to students as to what to expect.

Bromberger's decision to return to Australia did not last long. A telephone conversation with Rob Verchick, the law school's environmental chair, helped persuade the dean to reconsider. When the University of Houston Law Center offered to allow the law school to operate out of the Law Center, Bromberger met on August 31, barely two days after the hurricane struck New Orleans, with Houston's then dean, Nancy Rapoport, and associate deans Sondra Tennessee and Seth Chandler, to discuss the feasibility of operating Loyola Law School during the fall semester out of Houston. Soon after the meeting, word spread among the faculty about the possibility of offering courses through Houston. Some faculty who had evacuated elsewhere headed toward the Houston area. Loyola law faculty and staff who had evacuated to Houston, including Bobby Harges, John Lovett, Rob Verchick, the Reverend Lawrence Moore, S.J., and Barbara Wilson, joined Bromberger to plan the Loyola at Houston program.

Brian Huddleston, senior reference librarian and professor, described the University of Houston Law Center's decision to help out the Louisiana law schools in an article published in the *Journal of Legal Education.*[15] Houston had experienced flooding as a result of tropical storm Allison in 2001, which had caused extensive damage to its facility. Other law schools had assisted; the Houston deans decided to help the two New Orleans law schools, Loyola and Tulane, by offering to host a satellite program staffed by the New Orleans schools' law faculty. Chandler was conscious of the potential impact that losing an entire first-year class would have on a law school's viability. Chandler set out to contact Loyola and Tulane in the early part of the week, an almost physical impossibility.

Chandler was able to make contact with Bromberger on Wednesday, August 31. Gail Agrawal, then dean of the University of North Carolina School of Law, had tracked down Bromberger at the Houston Hilton. Agrawal had forwarded Bromberger's contact information to the ABA Deans LISTSERV, making it possible for Chandler to contact him. Tulane's law dean, Larry Ponoroff, had evacuated to Houston as well but had decided to move on to Chicago to join family. The ABA and the Association of American Law Schools (AALS) communicated with both deans to work out a formal policy as to displaced students for the semester. Tulane passed on the Houston offer, but Loyola seized it with zeal and gratitude. The law school committed to offering a full first-year course of studies, as well as core courses to second- and third-years.

The formal policy ultimately adopted by the ABA and AALS for displaced students allowed New Orleans law school students to visit at other schools for the fall semester, conditioned upon the students' paying Loyola and Tulane tuition for that semester. Students who visited at schools with higher tuition than Loyola's benefited from the arrangement, but students who visited at schools with lower tuition criticized the arrangement. Subsequently, Loyola reimbursed students for the difference in tuition rates.

After securing approval from Wildes, Bromberger formally communicated the plans to students through Eric Muller's *Loyola–New Orleans Law School Post-Hurricane Blog* in the early days after the hurricane, the primary means of communication for the Loyola law community. On Monday, September 5, 2005, the dean wrote:

> This letter is to reassure all of you about our plans for the fall and to further let you know that we intend to be as flexible and understanding as possible.
>
> We have all suffered serious losses and an emotionally draining dislocation. With that in mind, we have done our best to put together the following program to accommodate you all. I am determined to ensure that all students graduate in time and complete a degree course of the highest caliber.
>
> For those students who wish to attend another law school this fall, we have arrived at a policy agreed to by Dean Ponoroff of Tulane Law, the leadership of the American Association of Law Schools, and me. Under this policy, any student enrolled at Loyola Law School may be accepted as a "transient/visiting" student for the fall semester. Acceptance to another school for the fall is conditioned upon the student's financial good standing, that is, meeting all financial obligations to Loyola Law for the fall semester. All current student scholarships will remain in effect.
>
> For those wishing to remain at Loyola Law during the fall semester, we will be providing the following program based at the campus of the University of Houston Law Center in Texas:
>
> 1. A full, comprehensive 1L semester program for civil and common law students. These courses will be taught by regular full-time faculty of Loyola Law School.
> 2. Many upper-class courses—also taught by regular full-time faculty of Loyola Law School—will include: Evidence, Trusts and Estates, Constitutional Law, Federal Income Tax, Successions, Family Law, Persons, Environmental Law, Secured Transactions, Education Law, Poverty

Law, and other courses to be finalized in the next few days. The faculty is also willing to offer self-designed independent study options. Current restrictions on the number of independent study courses will be waived for students who take an independent study option for this fall.

3. We anticipate that classes will be offered both during the regular work week and on the weekends.
4. Although we are not in the position to provide housing for students, we have been assured that the University of Houston and its law students are willing to help locate affordable accommodations, which may include limited dormitory space or (on mutual agreement) the sharing of accommodations with Houston Law Center students.
5. We will be establishing an office for career services at the University of Houston Law Center.

Please keep well and don't panic. Compared to the problems currently being endured by thousands still in New Orleans, ours pale into insignificance.

Most New Orleans residents at the Superdome and the Convention Center had been airlifted or transported out of the city by Monday, September 5. But the graphic images on television screens and newspaper headlines conflicted starkly with the attempt by institutions like law schools to take up work where they had left off. This caused its own kind of stress and tension as faculty and students, some of whom had lost everything, struggled to continue life and work as usual. Bromberger's promise of available housing in the Houston area was tested as displaced New Orleanians sought temporary refuge in one of the major metropolitan areas closest to New Orleans.

Father Moore, associate dean for academic affairs and ex officio Philip and Eugenie Brooks Distinguished Professor of Law, faced the challenge of deciding which courses to offer and how best to schedule them to ensure the requisite number of hours. Moore had served as associate dean for academic affairs since the turn of the twentieth century, first appointed by interim dean Jim Klebba, in the years after Dean Makdisi's resignation, throughout Klebba's deanship and into Bromberger's deanship.

Moore had evacuated to Grand Coteau, where Loyola's founding president, Albert Biever, had completed his novitiate, and made his way to Houston at

Bromberger's request, in the days after Katrina, when the Houston program became a possibility. Father Moore constructed a schedule of courses and lined up faculty to teach them, often discussing plans with faculty miles away from Houston but eager to teach and to help the school hold its students. The schedule had been a challenge to construct; Moore had to work around the times and days made available to Loyola for classes. The challenge to Houston was grand—it had agreed essentially to host two separate and independent law programs in the same physical facility for the fall semester. Father Moore managed to make the schedule work.

Houston made available to Loyola Law primarily evening and Friday–Saturday hours for law classes. This meant that most classes were offered twice a week, many with one class during the week and another on Friday or Saturday, a schedule that, while challenging, made it possible to accommodate students and faculty traveling from New Orleans to Houston for classes, a journey generally completed in five hours. More challenging were evening classes scheduled from 6:00 to 9:40 p.m.

Law classes began at the University of Houston Law center on Monday, October 3, 2005. The significance of the date went unremarked. Minds were far away from the law school's founding, if any one on that Monday in October had remembered or even known that the law school had first begun classes on a first Monday in October in 1914. The law school had to postpone restarting classes when Hurricane Rita threatened the Houston area in late September. Like Katrina, Rita was a Category 5 hurricane in the Gulf of Mexico; by the time Rita struck land on September 24, 2005, at the Louisiana and Texas border, it had weakened to a Category 3. With Katrina fresh in everyone's mind, Rita prompted one of the largest evacuations in U.S. history.

The majority of Loyola law faculty—twenty-seven—taught in the program, with 317 students in attendance. Five of the faculty were Westerfield Fellows, selected by the law school to teach first-years legal research, writing, and advocacy skills. Westerfield Fellows were modeled after programs developed at other law schools, designed to provide individuals interested in law teaching an opportunity to develop as scholars and law teachers in an entry-level but temporary position. Through this program, the law school could afford its students strong entry-level teachers and provide those candidates a two-year period within which to develop as scholars in a law faculty. The program had worked well for both ends—most Westerfields were successful at finding permanent employment on a law faculty after conclusion of their term, and students benefited from a strong legal research and writing program that prior to the Westerfields had been staffed by law students under the supervision of two tenured law faculty, Patrick R. Hugg and Mary G. Algero.

In Houston, at least one of the Westerfields, Craig Senn, agreed to teach a required course, something not normally allowed without formal faculty approval.[16] Senn earned his law degree with honors from the University of North Carolina at Chapel Hill School of Law, where he served as articles editor for the *North Carolina Journal of International Law and Commercial Regulation.* He earned his bachelor's degree from the University of Georgia. He was selected as a Westerfield Fellow after a short labor and employment practice. He proved a popular choice. Although he accepted a faculty position at another law school upon finishing his term as a Westerfield Fellow, he joined the tenure-track faculty at Loyola in 2009.

The remaining twenty-one regular law faculty consisted of eighteen tenured and three tenure-track faculty. The three tenure-track faculty, Robert Garda, John Lovett and Monica Wallace, were beginning their third year on the tenure track when Katrina hit. Upon joining the faculty in 2002, Rob Garda had purchased a home in the Lakeview community in New Orleans, a community that had not existed at the time of the law school's founding in 1914, but that had throughout the twentieth century grown into an affluent, family-friendly community close to Lake Ponchartrain, the publicly funded University of New Orleans, and the city's nationally recognized public high school, Benjamin Franklin High School. Garda, a Utah native, lost his home to the floodwaters. He traveled from Utah to teach in the Houston program.

John Lovett moved to Houston after Katrina hit, and assisted Dean Bromberger in setting up the Houston program. Lovett's sister lived in Houston and was happy to provide a gathering place for Bromberger, Lovett, and others to plan the program. Lovett taught property, both common and civil law, to more than 200 students in Houston—the school's entire first-year class.

Monica Wallace, like Garda, lived in the Lakeview area and lost her home. All three had just been promoted to associate professor. Wallace was pregnant, and Bromberger granted her a leave during the fall semester.[17]

Other faculty were released from teaching for the semester, like the undergraduate faculty, and the undergraduate faculty subsequently made up the missed fall semester by teaching two spring semesters, with no additional compensation. The majority of law faculty either took up life in Houston or commuted every week to teach. Some, like Lovett, arranged temporary housing in Houston while commuting when possible back to New Orleans to repair homes damaged either by flooding or by wind and rain. Some, like Ray Rabalais, Jim Klebba, and Keith Vetter, flew or drove by car from the New Orleans area to Houston every week. Their residences in New Orleans had escaped the worst of the damage. Rabalais remembers getting accustomed to country music—the stretch of highway between Houston and New Orleans had been impacted sharply not just by Katrina, but by Rita. For some time after Katrina, few gas stations were available on the highway in the Louisiana portion of the New Orleans to Houston route. Klebba and Vetter flew the route, instead. Many law students drove into Houston on a weekly basis as well. Others, like Garda and Mitch Crusto, traveled from other states to Houston every week. Crusto had evacuated to St. Louis, Missouri, and he flew into Houston to teach his courses.

The law clinic faculty continued to operate in a number of locations. Bill Quigley set up the Katrina Clinic in Houston with the assistance of clinic staff attorneys, to assist evacuees with various issues, in particular, housing. Stephen Singer assisted the New Orleans Public Defender's Office and was released from his teaching obligations so that he could devote his efforts full-time to reestablishing that office, totally devastated by Katrina. Singer, a 1988 graduate of Harvard Law School with a BA degree in history and a BS degree in finance from the University of Illinois, Urbana-Champaign, had joined the clinic after working with the Public Defender Service in Washington, D.C., and teaching at the University of Wyoming College of Law. In the months to come, the school's clinical professors and staff attorneys would initiate a variety of legal services to emerge out of the Katrina crisis including worker clinics, immigrant legal services, and services to help residents return to New Orleans.[18]

AFTERMATH

In November, Father Wildes sent an e-mail to the University faculty and staff asking all nonfaculty employees to return to work by November 28. If unable to return, employees would begin using accumulated leave, eventually being placed on unpaid leave. Employees who failed to return by January 2, 2006, would be terminated. The president's e-mail acknowledged that some employees might not be in a position to return, as well as that some would decide to remain wherever they had taken up residence in the days after the hurricane when it became clear that a substantial part of the housing stock in the city had been destroyed and that returning would be a trying, long-term process. As a practical matter, the University had already asked certain employees to return and had obtained trailers to provide temporary housing for employees.[19]

While the University campus was shut down, the law school continued to teach classes in Houston. For both law faculty and students, the Houston program was both comforting and challenging—comforting in that the shared purpose of focusing on intellectual pursuits brought relief from the worries and travails arising from the devastation of the city; challenging in that for many the constant traveling while trying to deal with housing and other issues, including deciding whether to return to New Orleans for the long term, proved grueling.

The city's devastation did not just create a housing crisis; it created a health-care crisis, an educational crisis (most city public schools had indicated they would not reopen for the spring), and an environmental crisis, with many residents concerned at the health effects of having much of the city's geographical areas under the toxic soup left for weeks by Katrina. The city's sewage and water system as well as its electrical grid were severely disrupted, and many of its roads destroyed. Residents of the city deciding whether to return had to evaluate the risks to children and the ability of the city to rebuild its infrastructure. Residents had been left unnerved by the failure of the various levels of government to respond quickly to the ravages caused by the hurricane and the failure of the levee system. The city's officials did not appear to be responding effectively to its aftermath; trust in institutional processes, private and public, seemed naïve. Understandably, perhaps, some professionals, in particular, physicians and health-care providers, chose not to return.

The failure of the New Orleans public school system to quickly reestablish itself stimulated the rise of the charter school movement in the city. Schools that previously had been part of the Orleans Parish Public School System, like Benjamin Franklin High School and Lusher Elementary School, reinstituted themselves as charters through the leadership of parents, principals, and teachers. Both schools opened their doors to their students for spring 2006, and in the years to come the New Orleans area would become a laboratory for educational and charter school reform movements.

Both the law school and University held registration prior to the Thanksgiving break. In spring 2006, 208 first-year law students registered at Loyola. Most of them were day students; Loyola lost the majority of evening students from the 2005 entering class. Only 18 evening students out of the original 69 returned to Loyola. Total enrollment at the law school that spring was 693, a loss of 125 students from the original 818. At the undergraduate level, 802 first-years and 2,080 others returned, a loss of 868 students from the original 3,750. The law school had lost 15 percent of its class and the University had lost 23 percent, a substantial loss to the law school but a potentially crippling loss to the University.

After Thanksgiving, Dean Bromberger notified faculty and staff that the provost had announced across-the-board budget cuts to all colleges including the law school—the personnel budget had to be cut 15 percent and the operations budget by 20 percent. Dean Bromberger decided to come up with a budget that provided the necessary money from the law school's budget, $1.6 million, to be realized as a result of the cuts, "without costing anybody their job."[20] The provost approved Bromberger's offer. As a result, no one at the law school was terminated, although some staff elected not to return.

The news that came from the University in December, however, was grim; the headline in the *Times Picayune* sobering: "Loyola Plans to Lay off Dozens—About 4,000 Students Expected Next Semester."[21] Twenty-eight staff had been terminated, and an additional forty-eight positions were not to be filled. Some of the positions not to be filled included law staff who had been unable to or decided not to return to New Orleans.

That spring, Loyola faced an uncertain future. The reality that following fall augured promise. In fall 2006, the law school enrolled 303 entering students, 58 in the evening class. The entering credentials of the class dropped a bit, but stayed within the range for past classes. Seventy-two students from the first-year class did not return. Total enrollment at the law school in fall 2006 was 799 students. The University as a whole was not so fortunate: enrollment dropped by 16 percent with the entering class dropping almost by half, to 527. The University faced a deficit of $12.9 million for 2005–6 and of $12 million, if no budget cuts, for 2006–7.

It may be that the law school's continued operation throughout 2005–6 helped it draw in that 2006 entering class. It may be that the difference between undergraduate and professional programs, the former relying on younger students, explained the substantial differential. It may be, as the University subsequently explained, that the undergraduate campus was exercising care in preserving the academic credentials of its undergraduate class, whereas the law school had been willing to offer a place to more students to ensure that it would have a viable first-year class.

But the uncertainty felt in the spring led the institution to charge ahead with an academic reorganization that caused it to terminate academic programs and tenured faculty. In addition to the president's task force, the University's Standing Council for Academic Planning (SCAP), a faculty committee chaired by the provost and vice president for academic affairs, came up with criteria in spring 2006 to evaluate programs to determine which might be cut. The University presented the criteria to the University Senate for approval, and the Senate deliberated over the criteria and appointed a subcommittee to review them. Some senators expressed concern that the criteria did not include rationales or guidelines for discontinuing tenured positions, that the criteria lacked information about weighing and ranking the criteria, their relation to mission, and a methodology for comparing program expenses. Some senators were concerned that the University had not yet made available the data supporting the application of the criteria to particular programs and about the speed with which the University was moving in developing and implementing the plan.[22] On April 5, 2006, SCAP issued a report, nonetheless, articulating the criteria to be used to determine whether to discontinue, consolidate, or suspend programs. Five days later, on April 10, President Wildes released the blueprint for a reorganization of the institution titled *Pathways: Toward Our Second Century*. The University made available some of the data relied on to determine whether to discontinue programs on the provost's website.

Pathways surprised the New Orleans community. It set off a firestorm in the University community. Loyola was discontinuing programs in communications and education that had been considered highly successful. Its teaching certificate program was considered the leading teacher certification program in the city, perhaps in the state; its communication majors similarly were highly respected in the community. Also discontinued were majors in computer science, computer information systems, and communication information systems, all areas that while expensive to provide, seemed key to a twenty-first-century education. Seventeen tenured faculty, at least eleven of them with records of long service to the institution, were terminated.

Both SCAP and the Senate filed formal protests with Loyola's board of trustees.[23] SCAP reviewed the data and the *Pathways* recommendations and concluded that the data were insufficient to support the recommendations. It urged a complete reevaluation of the programs. While acknowledging the need to reorganize and eliminate or cut back programs, SCAP thought it vital that whatever changes were made be based on complete and reliably analyzed data, with articulated rationales justifying the changes. In April, the College of Arts and Sciences, one of the colleges to be disbanded and reorganized, and the University Senate voted "no confidence" in the process that produced *Pathways.*[24] Later in May, both voted "no confidence" in the provost's office. Despite the strong faculty criticism and resistance to the plan, Loyola's board of trustees adopted the plan on May 19, 2005. Later in June, termination letters went out to the seventeen faculty eliminated as part of *Pathways.* Ultimately, eight faculty challenged their termination in court; all cases eventually settled.[25] The University Rank and Tenure Committee vindicated those professors who filed internal appeals through the *University Faculty Handbook* process.

Pathways led the Association of American University Professors (AAUP) to censure Loyola, finding that the institution had failed to observe its own guidelines and procedures in discontinuing programs and terminating tenured faculty.[26] The provost and chief financial officer of the institution affiliated with *Pathways* resigned in 2008. After the litigation over the terminations settled, the president traveled to Washington to meet with the AAUP. Conversations between the AAUP, the president, and the University Senate yielded two additional conditions for the removal of censure: "reaffirmation that the university's stated provisions regarding its faculty [the *Faculty Handbook*] are contractually binding and official adoption of newly formulated provisions regarding faculty governance."[27] The president agreed to both conditions, and by letter reaffirmed the principle that the *Handbook* carried contractual force; the Board of Trustees in May 2011 adopted the *Handbook* provisions on faculty governance, and the AAUP agreed to remove the University from its censure list.[28]

The law school, for the most part, had been spared. *Pathways* had abolished some of its joint graduate programs, but those programs had not generated a significant number of students. Its primary impact at the law school was a change of name. The School of Law became the College of Law.

Katrina's long-term impact at the law school, however, was greater. The school admitted larger than usual classes, encouraged by the needs of the undergraduate campus. In return, the University authorized Dean Bromberger to hire additional new law faculty, some for openings created by retirements, but also new positions.

In the past, law faculty hiring had been sporadic. Once on the faculty, individuals, many with roots in New Orleans, tended to stay. The law school tended to go years without a new faculty hire, something that did not help it keep up with developments in legal education. The Westerfield Fellows program had helped by bringing a steady stream of recent law graduates into the faculty, but the Fellows were temporary, at most two-year positions.

But during the post-Katrina years, Dean Bromberger persuaded the University to allow him to hire nine new tenure-track faculty and five new clinical faculty. The new tenure-track faculty were eager to publish, something that the school needed not only as a way for law faculty to stay abreast of changes in the law and keep class material fresh for students but to continue to remain competitive in recruiting students. Increasingly, a law school's reputation among other law schools depended to a considerable extent on the scholarship produced by its faculty.

Loyola's bar passage rate continued to place the school third among Louisiana law schools, and the school continued to direct considerable resources to improving its students' performance on the bar. Louisiana embarked on a review of its bar examination in 2001, through the Louisiana Supreme Court Committee on Bar Admissions (COBA), a committee appointed by the Louisiana Supreme Court to administer and grade the Louisiana bar examination.[29] COBA's review was prompted perhaps by litigation and by mounting criticism of its methodology and lack of an effective appeals process for applicants. Critics voiced concern about the validity of the test, the validity of grading metrics, and fairness to applicants. Louisiana tested all subjects, even federal subjects for which most states used the Multistate Bar Examination, an objective test prepared and administered by the National Conference of Bar Examiners (NCBE). Although the Multi-State Bar Examination had itself been the subject of criticism at the national level, it seemed a more defensible way to test for admission to the bar than the Louisiana process.

The Louisiana bar examination consists of nine examinations: most of them, five, test Louisiana law (Louisiana property law; Louisiana law on estates [successions, donations, and trusts]; Louisiana contract law; Louisiana Code of Civil Procedure, which although modeled after the federal rules of procedure is tested separately; and Louisiana tort law). Two other examinations test a mix of Louisiana and other law, business entities and negotiable instruments and the criminal law test, which tests Louisiana criminal law, together with constitutional criminal procedure and evidence. Two of the examinations test purely federal law: constitutional law and federal jurisdiction and procedure. COBA appoints practitioners to make up the tests and to grade them. The process is not fully transparent, and there are no merit-based criteria to determine who should qualify to compose tests and who should qualify as a grader. While the tests are released after they are administered, the model answers are never released, leading some to doubt the validity of the answers and thus of the grading process itself. The examination, at least as structured during the first decade of the twenty-first century, could not be subjected to established methods and criteria to determine whether tests were valid, reliable, and consistent over the long term.

By 2008, COBA announced proposed changes to the Louisiana bar examination. COBA's proposed changes included elimination of test-takers' ability to "condition" the exam, which allowed those who had passed a number of exams but failed too many to pass the examination as a whole, to retake only those portions they had failed. Instead, the examination would use "compensatory grading," which would require test-takers to achieve one score, computed by combining the scores of all of the individual portions of the examination. COBA also indicated it would weigh the Louisiana law portions of the examination more heavily than the federal; would use more objective questions, like those used in the Multi-State; and would use paid consultants to develop those questions.

In response to the proposed changes, the law school held a faculty retreat in 2008 to discuss curricular reform and bar examination preparation. Among other things, the law faculty agreed to recommend to the dean and the University the hiring of a director of academic support to develop a program for students whose first-year performance placed them in the bottom 25 percent of the class. The law faculty also instituted two formal courses to assist law students whose performance in law school indicated they were at risk for failing the bar examination upon graduating from law school: a principle of legal analysis course (intended to help weak-performing students in the first year) and a consolidated legal analysis course (intended to prepare students to pass the bar). The University approved the hiring of a new director; neither the dean nor the faculty pushed to have this position be a member of the tenure-track faculty.

In 2007, the law school instituted a master's of law degree designed for international students, with a first degree in law (LLB or its equivalent) from a law school outside the United States or Canada. From 2007 to 2013, twenty-four students completed the LLM. They came from all over the world, including Venezuela, Serbia, Puerto Rico, Haiti, Germany, Pakistan, Peru, the United Kingdom, Russia, and the Ukraine.

Bromberger's administration was marked by growth—both in terms of the size of the student body, the law faculty, and the school itself. After Katrina, Bromberger had persuaded the University to allow him to purchase a building across the street from the law school, with access to the next street, Broadway. With additional funds provided by law alumnus Stuart Smith, who purchased naming rights to the clinic building, the law campus now consisted of two buildings, one primarily devoted to the law clinic and career placement, and the other devoted to the rest of the administrative offices and regular law classes.

The law school seemed on a roll. Some faculty expressed concern about the size of the law school classes and the lack of emphasis on improving the academic strength of the class. Some hesitated at the number of law faculty being hired, thinking that it might make sense to stagger the hiring a bit, particularly if it would mean that the law school could admit a smaller entering class. But those voices went unheard amid what seemed to be a runaway train of success.

In fall 2009, Dean Bromberger announced his retirement. In the past year, he had undergone heart surgery. His recovery went well, and he returned to the law school, but after much thought and reflection, he decided to retire at the end of the spring semester and return with his family to his native Australia. That spring, the University formed a search committee to conduct a dean search, and the law school planned for Dean Bromberger's retirement. At his retirement dinner, law faculty presented him with a watch and a set of golf clubs. It was hard to envision such a vibrant person in retirement, and some faculty suspected that his heart was not in it. Others could see him attacking retirement with the same zest and energy he had brought to his deanship.

On May 27, 2010, the unthinkable happened—Brian Bromberger suffered a massive heart attack and passed away two months before his retirement. It was a tragedy for his family and for the law school. Kathryn Venturatos Lorio stepped into the void as interim dean for the next academic year and steered the school steady, while the search committee worked to identify someone to lead the law school in the coming years—years that were to prove perhaps the most challenging in the law school's existence.

CONCLUSION

In 1995, the Louisiana Bar Foundation responded to the MacCrate Report by organizing a conference of judges, professors, and practitioners chaired by one of Loyola's alumni, faculty, and then interim dean, Marcel Garsaud Jr. In his opening remarks, Dean Garsaud referred back to a 1978 speech in which he had discussed legal education's role as an academic institution and as a professional school: "I begin with the proposition that the entire profession has the responsibility for the education of a lawyer. The primary responsibility of preparing a lawyer in the academic context falls upon the law school. The education of a lawyer in lawyering or in the practice of law is really a responsibility of the bar."[1]

Garsaud went on to acknowledge a change in his own thinking, his realization that a law school's role as a member of the academic community "simply isn't enough in our profession today,"[2] and echoed the call of the MacCrate Report for the profession as a whole to address the shortcomings identified in the report. In their discussions, conclave members also discussed concerns that there were "too many lawyers" and that law schools were admitting too many students;[3] concerns as to the impact of limiting admissions on women and minorities; concerns about lawyer competence and the need for skills courses, internships, and apprenticeships, usually envisioned as something that would take place after law school and after passing the bar;[4] concerns about the degree to which law school revenues were diverted by universities to subsidize other university departments;[5] and what one participant described as "a crisis in placement"—insufficient jobs for all of the law graduates in Louisiana.[6]

Much that concerned Garsaud in 1995 are concerns for law schools today, including Loyola. Law schools today, as often in the past, face declining enrollment, reduced job opportunities for law graduates, stagnant salaries, and greater competition for law students. Law schools like Loyola have worked hard to improve their academic program and to keep abreast of the changes in the profession as a result, in part, of technology. The legal academy remains primarily male and white. Much remains to be done, but much has changed. In academic year 2009–10, precipitated by incidents involving bias against gay and lesbian students, some law students worked to establish a chapter of Lambda Law Alliance at the law school. With the support of faculty and the Student Bar Association, by 2011, Loyola law students could openly participate in a student organization designed to support gay, lesbian, bisexual, transgender, and intersexed law students. Lambda Law Alliance changed the dynamics at the law school for all students and made clear the law school's and University's support for LGBT students.

In 2011, Loyola selected Maria Pabón López as its new dean. López became the first woman law dean at Loyola and in Louisiana. López, a native of Puerto Rico, had a bachelor of arts in religion from Princeton University and a juris doctor from the University of Pennsylvania. After law school she practiced law in Philadelphia, Puerto Rico, and Texas, including as an assistant U.S. attorney in San Juan and in legal aid in Texas. In 1999, she joined the faculty at the University of Missouri School of Law in Columbia as a lecturer, before joining the tenure-track faculty at the Indiana University Robert H. McKinney School of Law in Indianapolis in 2002, where she was promoted to professor of law in 2008. She came to Loyola with little administrative experience but great enthusiasm and a commitment to public service.

Loyola's law student population ranged from 700 to 820. In academic year 2012–13, a total of 736 students enrolled at the law school. The College of Law's 2012 graduating class was one of its largest at 270.

The law school's 2011–12 entering class continues to reflect some diversity. The 2011–12 class consisted of 242 students, 200 of them in the day division and 42 in the evening. At least 63 of those students contributed to the school's racial and ethnic diversity. Total enrollment at the law school for academic year 2011–12 was 820 students, 689 in the day division and 131 in the evening. Of those 820 students, 131 identified themselves as persons of color. Overall, the law school's population is almost even when examined by reference to sex: in academic year 2011–12, Loyola's class consisted of 407 men and 406 women. For the past three decades the number of men in the first-year class has been about the same as the number of women.

The law school faculty has grown substantially since 1991, and it is a far more diverse faculty in 2013 than it was in 1991. The College of Law began academic year 2012–13 with a faculty composed of 39 tenured or tenure-track faculty. Approximately 40 percent of the tenure-track faculty (15) are women; 6, 15 percent, self-identify as black or African American; 3 self-identify as Hispanic or Latino, and 1 as Asian. A substantial number of the tenure-track faculty (not yet tenured), 15 percent, are women and/or persons of color. The clinical faculty are now composed of 9 full-time faculty: 6 are women, 2 self-identify as Hispanic, 1 as African American, and 1 as Asian. Law library faculty experienced the least growth in numbers: there are 7 library faculty. It is a more diverse faculty, but it is a far larger faculty. Law faculty salaries remain below the average for law professors nation-wide at the professor level, although more recent law hires enjoyed salaries either at or above the average nation-wide.

In 2011, law school graduates experienced a substantial decrease in employment opportunities and salary. NALP statistics are based on self-reporting; that is, they report what law schools report, which is in turn based on what students self-report. Their statistics for the class of 2011 recorded a substantial drop in law firm employment and acknowledged a rise in the number of graduates entering part-time or temporary employment and solo practice.[7] The NALP reported declines in mean and median starting salaries for graduates joining law firms and for graduates overall.[8] The ABA reported the mean wage for attorneys in the New Orleans area per year at $106,910.[9] For much of Louisiana, however, the average attorney salary was from $40,820 to $85,000. This mean is based on associate, government attorney, and corporate salaries and does not include equity partners or solo practitioner income or unemployed graduates. In the words of Marcel Garsaud, there may be too many lawyers and significantly fewer law firm jobs for them upon graduation.

Tuition at the law school in academic year 2012–13 was $41,618; tuition for 2013–14 will increase to $43,602. Students today pay more for one year's tuition than they paid for the entire law course of studies in 1991. As tuition increased, direct expenditures per student increased as well, but they still lagged substantially behind the average spent by other law schools. Assuming that next year's tuition does not increase, the total cost for the three-year program (in tuition and fees) would be $130,806. Students will pay most of that tuition through loans; the average loan indebtedness for Loyola law graduates, as reported on the school's website, was $115,393 for 2010–11. The monthly note on an $115,000 student loan to be paid back in ten years at 6 percent is $1,276 a month. Assuming a graduate earns the mean starting salary for the class of 2011, $78,653, she would have approximately $5,200 per month before taxes for living expenses. Assuming the median starting salary for the class of 2011, $60,000, those graduates would have $3,724 per month before taxes for living expenses.

This year, 2013, law schools face a substantial decrease in applicants,[10] probably in response to the low employment figures of the past years, the reduction in attorney compensation, and the substantial increase in law school tuition and debt, which may render solo practice or a practice that brings in the average attorney salary financially untenable.

While law firm employment opportunities have significantly dropped, however, the need for lawyers and legal assistance continues unabated. Significant numbers of populations have legal needs that fail to be met primarily because the cost of legal assistance is too high.

A number of other significant events have occurred since the turn of the century. In 2007, the Carnegie Foundation published its two-year study of legal education, the result of fieldwork at sixteen law schools, including class observations, and interviews with various faculty groups and students.[11] The Carnegie Report noted that legal education was professional education and that there should be a connection between the profession and professional education. It echoed some of the concerns articulated in the MacCrate Report, that law schools were not doing enough to integrate practice skills or learning styles. In addition, the Carnegie Report found that legal education did not sufficiently address professional identity and professional values; did not do a particularly good job at assessment; and that the three-year course of study reflected little sense of progression.

In 2007, large law firms dramatically increased associate compensation. The largest large firms offered $160,000 to their first-year associates. In comparison, in 2007, the average full professor of law salary was approximately $136,634.[12] Federal district court judges earned $165,000, and federal appellate court judges earned $175,000.[13] For a few years, the dramatic rise in associate compensation spurred strong interest in law schools. Law school enrollment thrived. This made it possible for the law school to bounce back during the post-Katrina years with a strong student enrollment.

The recession of 2008 eventually ceased, at least for a time, the substantial increase in disparity in compensation between the youngest members of the profession and the academy, but the pressures of practice increased dissatisfaction with practice at national firms, increasing competition for academic positions. In turn, the decline in student enrollment in recent years has created pressure for law schools to trim budgets, cutting back on academic positions.

In addition, the ABA relaxed accreditation standards in response to litigation by private law schools and the Department of Justice alleging antitrust violations. Over the course of the past three decades, the ABA has continued to revisit accreditation standards, making it easier for new law schools to become accredited. As of 2013, 202 law schools were ABA-approved, two of them provisionally. Of these, 176 are AALS member schools; an additional 24 are nonmember fee-paid AALS schools. Loyola is still one among four Louisiana-based schools; the opening of a fifth school scheduled for 2012 was postponed when its dean resigned.[14]

In the past few years, journalists and law professors have sharply scrutinized and criticized law schools and law school practices. Law schools and law school faculties have been assailed for charging too much tuition, not being transparent enough with employment figures, making too much money, and inadequately preparing students to pass the bar examination and to practice law.[15] Some, like Richard Susskind, have suggested that the profession is changing dramatically and that neither law firms nor law schools are ready for that change.[16] And, as always, there is a continuing desperate need for lawyers and legal services by masses of persons too poor to pay for them, and few entities ready or able to provide them.

Law is a discipline and profession that historically has provided a path to power. Loyola's law school, at its founding, opened that path for many denied access because of their religion, origin, or lack of resources. One of the challenges facing the law school as it celebrates its 2014 centennial is how to continue to provide that path for those for whom it is a challenge.

Although this story of Loyola University New Orleans College of Law explores many of the challenges that faced the law school, including internal academic and financial struggles and disputes, and its efforts, sometimes ineffectual, to integrate and reflect the racial, ethnic, and gender diversity of its geography and heritage, its undoubted success is reflected in its graduates, many of whom emerged as leaders of the bar, the judiciary, city and state government, the corporate world, the legal academy, and institutions of higher learning. Its future remains to be charted, but its past is graced by the life of its graduates.

NOTES

CHAPTER ONE

Epigraph 1: "Lawyer's Wife (2 a.m.)," *Times-Picayune,* October 4, 1914, reprinted from *Chicago News.*

Epigraph 2: Rev. P. A. Ryan, S.J., "The Beginnings of Loyola University, New Orleans," manuscript, p. 19, Loyola Archives.

1. "Not All England in Favor of War, Says Dr. Ahrens," *Times-Picayune,* October 4, 1914.

2. *Times-Picayune,* October 4, 1914, 25; *New Orleans Item,* October 4, 1914, 3, noting that 85 law students had enrolled, a much larger number than actually enrolled and completed the course of studies. The *New Orleans Item* carried an advertisement or notice in the October 2, 1914, paper announcing the opening of the law school on October 5, and noting that registration for the law and dental divisions of Loyola University began Monday, September 28, 1914 (7).

3. "The Weather," *Times-Picayune,* October 6, 1914.

4. "Church Protests against Gun-Toting Mass Meeting Grows out of Murder of Robert M. Denholme," *Times-Picayune,* October 5, 1914.

5. "Sheriff Tricks Angry Mob, Saves Negro Accused of Attempting to Rape White Woman," *Times-Picayune,* October 5, 1914.

6. *New Orleans Item,* October 6, 1914, 10.

7. "Predict Success in Law School of the Jesuits: Prominent Men Speak at the Exercises Opening," *Times-Picayune,* October 6, 1914.

8. *New Orleans Item,* October 6, 1914, 10.

9. "Bloodhounds Catch Planter's Slayer: Dogs Run down Negro Murderer of Hugh Russum: Fugitive Jailed," *Times-Picayune,* October 6, 1914.

10. I. A. Timmreck and Francis L. Janssen, S.J., "Loyola University New Orleans: A Compendium of Historical Information to Approximately 1974," manuscript, Loyola Archives; "Faculties Announced," *New Orleans Times-Democrat,* August 18, 1911.

11. O'Shanahan wanted to purchase the entire tract of land available for $75,000. The Jesuit consultors, the Jesuit advisory committee for the New Orleans area, however, cautioned against it. O'Shanahan later regretted it, "for in ten days I could have sold enough to pay for the entire tract I bought and put aside a sinking fund for the education of our young men" (Albert Biever, S.J., "Historical Sketch of the Church of the Most Holy Name New Orleans, 1892–1932" [New Orleans: The Parish, 1932], 10).

12. Biever's journal, "Reminiscence of Loyola University," contains several manuscripts housed at the Jesuit Provincial Archives. His journal doesn't identify which military conflict he is referring to, but the dates and references suggest the Franco-Prussian War, which broke out on July 19, 1870, when Napoleon III declared war on Prussia.

13. Biever, "Reminiscence."

14. Biever, "Reminiscence," 22.

15. Biever, "Reminiscence," 34. Mr. Koch did well after leaving the American South, and "on his arrival in Europe, he entered the Belgian province of the Society of Jesus for the Mission of Calcutta where he was ordained priest and named secretary to His Grace Archbishop Goethals. His biography which appeared recently shows him to have been a man of great holiness and learning." Father Biever's pointed commentary on Koch's success in the Church reveals his own attitude toward issues of race, to some extent reflective of the attitude of the Catholic Church at the time: he rejected overt racism and was plainly troubled by it but accepted its expression in the society in which he worked.

16. Biever, "Reminiscence," 44.

17. Biever, "Reminiscence," 46.

18. Biever, "Reminiscence," 48.

19. Biever, "Reminiscence," 48.

20. "Anonymous letters were received at the college threatening the Fathers with corporal punishment and even death. The priest however had also friends who rallied around them and who resolved to defend them even at the sacrifice of their lives" (Biever, "Reminiscence," 79). The threats of violence apparently were made by a group called the Lafayette Volunteers.

21. Biever, "Reminiscence," 79. His account was as follows: "The community had just finished the recital of the Litanies . . . when a number of men on horse-back rode up to the college. They called for Father Abbadie, the 'cure' and bluntly asked him whether it was lawful to lynch a negro who had insulted a white woman. Father Abbadie of course told them and that in a very authoritative manner, that they had absolutely no right to take this man's life but that they should hand him over to the lawfully constituted authorities and have him judged by the courts of the Parish. As they rode away, I heard one shout: 'Je t'ai dit de ne pas demander le cure, qu'il no le permettra pas.' As far as I remember the unfortunate negro was not lynched but was handed over to the sheriff of the parish and judged by the court."

22. Biever, "Reminiscence," 28.

23. Biever, "Reminiscence," 28.

24. Biever, "Reminiscence," 132, 142.

25. Biever, "Reminiscence," 150–54.

26. Biever, "Reminiscence," 46.

27. Biever, "Reminiscence," 35.

28. Timmreck and Janssen, "Loyola University New Orleans: A Compendium," 24–26.

29. Louisiana Act No. 136, July 10, 1912.

30. Loyola Scrapbook Journal, July 1904 to July 1922, Series I, Scrapbook 1, Loyola Archives.

31. Remarks by President of Loyola University, Meeting of Marquette Association, September 29, 1949, Marquette Assn. for Higher Education, History, 7.3–53.2, Loyola Archives.

32. Remarks by President of Loyola University, Meeting of Marquette Association, Septem-

ber 29, 1949, Marquette Assn. for Higher Education, History, 7.3–53.2, Loyola Archives. The Association brought in $84,555.61 to build Marquette Hall.

33. Biever, "Reminiscence," 66–68.

34. *New Orleans Times-Democrat,* May 20, 1912.

35. Ryan, "The Beginnings of Loyola University," 13.

36. Transylvania University is now a liberal arts college, still in Kentucky. Supreme Court Justices John Marshall Harlan and Samuel Freeman Miller are also Transylvania University graduates.

37. Nadia Moise, interview by author, March 23, 2013, New Orleans, notes on file with author.

38. Biever, "Reminiscence," 150–54.

39. Act No. 136. Father Biever's journal notes that Houma Catholics (a community southwest of New Orleans), represented by State Senator Butler, opposed granting the charter to Loyola, but that a last-minute effort by then archbishop Blenk and the New Orleans delegation led by Byrnes rescued the charter. Butler was successful in adding a clause to the provision of the charter that Loyola supporters perhaps rightfully considered a slight. Butler insisted that the charter be modified to read: "provided that Loyola University will reach the standards of other recognized Universities in the country" (Act. No. 136). Biever's journal records a conversation between him and St. Paul at the time where he asked St. Paul: "Do we accept the condition?" and St. Paul responds, "Yes" (Biever, "Reminiscence," 154). The conversation makes clear that St. Paul enjoyed Biever's respect and trust. It makes the subsequent fallout between Biever and Monahan over faculty compensation understandable.

40. Loyola Scrapbook Journal, July 1904 to July 1922, Series I, Scrapbook 1, Loyola Archives.

41. Slaughter-House Cases, 83 U.S. 36 (1873). At issue in the case was the state's ability to restrict the business of slaughtering animals in New Orleans to one entity. Conditions in the city were described as "noxious" and "offensive." Others described the city as "the dirtiest city in the United States." The Court rejected the butcher's challenge to the state-granted monopoly, but in doing so narrowly interpreted the Fourteenth Amendment, facilitating the undoing of Reconstruction and the post-Reconstruction birth of segregation and Jim Crow.

42. William Ivy Hair, *Carnival of Fury: Robert Charles and the New Orleans Race Riot of 1900* (Baton Rouge: Louisiana State University Press, 1976), 69.

43. Campbell Gibson and Kay Jung, "Historical Census Statistics on Population Totals by Race, 1790 to 1990, and by Hispanic Origin, 1970 to 1990, for Large Cities and Other Urban Places in the United States," U.S. Census Bureau (February 2005), table 19, "Louisiana—Race and Hispanic Origin for Selected Large Cities and Other Places: Earliest Census to 1990," www.census.gov/population/www/documentation/twps0076/twps0076.html.

44. Hair, *Carnival of Fury,* 70–71; Rachel L. Emanuel and Alexander P. Tureaud Jr., *A More Noble Cause: A. P. Tureaud and the Struggle for Civil Rights in Louisiana* (Baton Rouge: Louisiana State University Press, 2011), 4–5; Alice Moore Dunbar-Nelson, "People of Color in Louisiana," in *Creole: The History and Legacy of Louisiana's Free People of Color,* ed. Sybil Kein (Baton Rouge: Louisiana State University Press 2000), 3–41.

45. 1900 Census in Gibson and Jung, "Historical Census Statistics."

46. Italians, for example, generated a fair amount of hostility in the community. In 1891, eleven Italians were lynched publicly in New Orleans. Nicholas C. Borkowski, "The Mass Lynch-

ing of Italians in 1891 New Orleans: Marking Italians as Racially 'Dago,'" *Michigan Journal of History* 10, no. 2 (Fall 2014): 158–79; Adam Fairclough, *Race & Democracy: The Civil Rights Struggle in Louisiana 1915–1972* (Athens: University of Georgia Press, 1995), 6. By 1930, Italians were the single-largest group of immigrants to Louisiana (James G. Dauphine, *A Question of Inheritance: Religion, Education, and Louisiana's Cultural Boundary, 1880–1940 [Lafayette: Center for Louisiana Studies, University of Southwestern Louisiana, 1993],* 24). Although Italians were treated generously by the drafters of the 1898 Louisiana Constitution, with specific provision for the passing of literacy tests in one's "mother tongue," several convention delegates spoke derisively about them with references to the "Dago Privileged Voter" (*Official Journal of the Proceedings of the Constitutional Convention of the State of Louisiana, February 8, 1898* [New Orleans: R. J. Hearsey, Convention Printer, 1898], 122).

47. Hair, *Carnival of Fury,* 71–73.

48. Alecia P. Long, *The Great Southern Babylon: Sex, Race, and Respectability in New Orleans 1865–1920* (Baton Rouge: Louisiana State University Press, 2004), 10–15. On housing integration, see also Emanuel and Tureaud, *A More Noble Cause,* 11, 15.

49. Hair, *Carnival of Fury,* 118.

50. Scholars continue to debate the extent of influence the Spanish had on the city's governing structure and the Louisiana civil code, and scholars like Loyola law graduate and LSU emeritus law professor Robert Pascal contend that other scholars have tended to minimize the impact of the Spanish law, preferring to emphasize the impact of the French code instead. Much of the architecture of the French Quarter is actually Spanish. Even today, when one is much more likely to hear Spanish spoken on city streets than French, the state proclaims its French heritage in the welcome signs greeting travelers to the state with a "Bienvenu" but no "Bienvenidos."

51. James M. Woods, *A History of the Catholic Church in the American South, 1513–1900* (Gainesville: University Press of Florida, 2011), 372–73.

52. Mary Lou Widmer, *New Orleans 1900 to 1920* (Gretna: Pelican, 2007), 100.

53. Hair, *Carnival of Fury,* 13–14; T. Harry Williams, *Huey Long* (New York: Vintage, 1981), 183–88.

54. 163 U.S. 537 (1896).

55. Rebecca J. Scott, *Degrees of Freedom: Louisiana and Cuba after Slavery* (Cambridge: Harvard University Press, 2005), 88–93; Fairclough, *Race and Democracy,* 15.

56. Hair, *Carnival of Fury,* 137–38.

57. Fairclough, *Race and Democracy,* 9.

58. Fairclough, *Race and Democracy,* 9.

59. Woods, *Catholic Church in the American South,* 374–75.

60. Woods, *Catholic Church in the American South,* 355–56.

61. James G. Dauphine, *A Question of Inheritance: Religion, Education, and Louisiana's Cultural Boundary, 1880–1940* (Lafayette: Center for Louisiana Studies, University of Southwestern Louisiana, 1993), 3–4.

62. Jack Temple Kirby, *Darkness at the Dawning: Race and Reform in the Progressive South* (Philadelphia: Lippincott, 1972), 14; Dauphine, *A Question of Inheritance,* 24; Justin A. Nystrom, *New Orleans after the Civil War: Race, Politics and a New Birth of Freedom* (Baltimore: John Hopkins University Press, 2010), 215–16, 236–37.

63. Act of July 7, 1896; Amasa M. Eaton, "The Suffrage Clause in the New Constitution of Louisiana," *Harvard Law Review* 13 (December 1899): 279.

64. *Reference Biography of Louisiana Bench and Bar* (1922), 45.

65. *Proceedings 1898 Convention,* 9–10.

66. *Proceedings 1898 Convention,* 9–10.

67. Armantine M. Smith, "The History of the Women's Suffrage Movement in Louisiana," *Louisiana Law Review* 62 (2002): 509, 514–23; Carmen Lindig, *The Path from the Parlor: Louisiana Women 1879–1920* (Lafayette: Center for Louisiana Studies, University of Southwestern Louisiana, 1986), 37–40.

68. Smith, "Women's Suffrage Movement in Louisiana," 538–44; Lindig, *The Path from the Parlor,* 112–13, 131–38.

69. *Proceedings 1898 Convention,* 142.

70. John St. Paul, New Orleans, *Proceedings 1898 Convention,* 144.

71. Charles T. Soniat, New Orleans, *Proceedings 1898 Convention,* 145–46, and, generally, *Proceedings 1898 Convention,* 143–46.

72. Scott, *Degrees of Freedom,* 42–46.

73. State ex rel David Jordan Ryanes v. Jeremiah M. Gleason, Docket No. 14651, Transcript of Hearing, 37–38, Historical Archives of the Supreme Court of Louisiana, Earl K. Long Library, University of New Orleans.

74. State ex rel Ryanes v. Gleason, 112 La. 612, 36 So. 608 (1904). The court's reasoning was that an appeal is neither a matter of right nor a necessary element of due process of law, but a privilege that is entirely within the discretion of the state either to grant or to withhold. Since the Constitution did not provide for an appeal in cases where a citizen challenged the new qualifications provisions because they denied him the vote, the state's motion to dismiss "must prevail." The court's opinion took barely one page.

75. 238 U.S. 347 (1915).

76. 380 U.S. 145 (1965). Louisiana primarily relied on its white primary law until 1944, when the Supreme Court struck down a parallel Texas primary system.

77. *Proceedings 1898 Convention,* 9–10.

78. Dauphine, *A Question of Inheritance,* 6.

79. Bernard A. Cook, *Founded on Faith: A History of Loyola University New Orleans* (New Orleans: Loyola University, 2012), 19; 1848 charter in the House Diary of 1896, Provincial Archives. The first Catholic school established in New Orleans appears to have been a school for boys founded by the Capuchin order in 1725. The school had ceased to exist by 1731 (Roger Baudier, *The Catholic Church in Louisiana* [New Orleans: 1930], 199–203).

80. Baudier, *The Catholic Church in Louisiana,* 105.

81. Baudier, *The Catholic Church in Louisiana,* 88–89, 102–5.

82. Virginia Meacham Gould, "Henriette Delille, Free Women of Color, and Catholicism in Antebellum New Orleans, 1727–1852," in *Beyond Bondage: Free Women of Color in the Americas,* ed. D. B. Gaspar and D. C. Hine (Urbana: University of Illinois Press, 2004), 279.

83. Virginia Meacham Gould and Charles E. Nolan, "Mother Henriette DeLille (1812–1862): Servant of Slaves," in *Religious Pioneers: Building the Faith in the Archdiocese of New Orleans,* ed. Dorothy Dawes and Nolan (New Orleans: Archdiocese of New Orleans, 2004), 25, 30–32.

84. Woods, *Catholic Church in the American South,* 346.

85. Woods, *Catholic Church in the American South,* 300, 359.

86. Dauphine, *A Question of Inheritance,* 7–8.

87. Stephen J. Ochs, *Desegregating the Altar: The Josephites and the Struggle for Black Priests, 1871–1960* (Baton Rouge: Louisiana State University Press, 1993); Dolores Egger Labbe, *Jim Crow Comes to Church: The Establishment of Segregated Catholic Parishes in South Louisiana* (Lafayette: University of Southwestern Louisiana, 1971).

88. Woods, *Catholic Church in the American South,* 310–11; Dauphine, *A Question of Inheritance,* 8.

89. Woods, *Catholic Church in the American South,* 311; Dauphine, *A Question of Inheritance,* 7.

90. R. Bentley Anderson, *Black, White, and Catholic: New Orleans Interracialism, 1947–1956* (Nashville: Vanderbilt University Press, 2005), 3.

91. Anderson, *Black, White, and Catholic,* 5, quoting then archbishop Jansenns of New Orleans, who spearheaded segregation of church parishes; Emanuel and Tureaud, *A More Noble Cause,* 12–13; Woods, *Catholic Church in the American South,* 369.

92. Fairclough, *Race and Democracy,* 13–14.

93. Fairclough, *Race and Democracy,* 7. The Archdiocese of New Orleans remained hostile to black priests, either refusing to ordain them or banning them from conducting services in New Orleans.

94. Hair, *Carnival of Fury,* 71.

95. Long, *The Great Southern Babylon,* 102–4, 180–81.

96. John P. Dyer, *Tulane: The Biography of a University 1834–1965* (New York: Harper and Row, 1966), 5–15. The University of Louisiana in New Orleans began as a medical college founded by a group of physicians in 1835. The faculty provided medical services to patients at Charity Hospital in return for the cost of the lease of land on Common Street between Baronne and Philippa, which became known as University Place. In 1847, the Louisiana legislature established the college as the University of Louisiana; funding was haphazard, and the medical faculty resisted giving over their independence and autonomy to the new board of administrators (ibid., 19–23). It became Tulane University with a gift from Paul Tulane, a Princeton, New Jersey, resident with strong ties to New Orleans.

97. Emanuel and Tureaud, *A More Noble Cause,* 55.

98. Emanuel and Tureaud, *A More Noble Cause,* 54–56.

99. Committee of Examiners of the Supreme Court Minutes, 1898–1923, Louisiana Archives, Tulane University Library.

100. Robert Stevens, *Law School: Legal Education in America from the 1850s to the 1980s* (Chapel Hill: University of North Carolina Press, 1983), 24–28.

101. Stevens, *Law School: Legal Education in America,* 37.

102. Stevens, *Law School: Legal Education in America,* 37–38.

103. Stevens, *Law School: Legal Education in America,* 38, 27.

104. Stevens, *Law School: Legal Education in America,* 23.

105. Stevens, *Law School: Legal Education in America,* 27 (quoting Lewis Delafield, president of the American Social Science Association, in a speech at the Association's 1876 meeting, criticizing the view).

106. Stevens, *Law School: Legal Education in America,* 27 (quoting Lewis Delafield, president of the American Social Science Association, in a speech at the Association's 1876 meeting, criticizing the view).

107. Stevens gives an example of the stratification of law schools involving the law schools at Georgetown and Catholic University. Georgetown today is considered the leading Jesuit university in the country. In 1894, when Catholic University thought about providing for legal studies by importing the Georgetown program at the suggestion of the apostolic delegate (the pope's representative), both schools turned the transfer down with Catholic expressing concern at the part-time, evening program run at Georgetown, "frequented mostly by young men who were government employees during the day and had only the evening hours to fit themselves for professions" (Stevens, *Law School: Legal Education in America,* 76–77).

108. Ryan, "The Beginnings of Loyola University," 3, 7.

109. Ryan, "The Beginnings of Loyola University," 3.

110. Cook, *Founded on Faith,* 43.

111. Woods, *Catholic Church in the American South,* 364.

112. Emanuel and Tureaud, *A More Noble Cause,* 35, 34–53.

113. The *University Bulletin* for academic year 1913–14, 85–87, lists the members of both the Jesuit Alumni Association and the Marquette Association for Higher Education. Judge John St. Paul, as well as other members of the first law faculty at Loyola, served as members of these organizations.

114. Consultors' Minutes of December 28, 1911, Provincial Archives.

115. Consultors' Minutes of December 28, 1911, Provincial Archives.

116. Ryan, "The Beginnings of Loyola University," 17.

117. *University Bulletin,* 1913–14, 44.

118. Stevens, *Law School Legal Education,* 74–75.

119. Ryan, "The Beginnings of Loyola University," 10.

120. Father Moynihan's concerns proved accurate with respect to a medical school. Father Biever's vision originally included plans for a medical school. "Faculties Announced," *Times-Democrat,* August 18, 1911. Further consideration of the feasibility of starting a medical school, however, led him to abandon those plans largely due to the costs of offering a medical education and his sense that he would need a huge endowment (Biever, "Reminiscence," 159).

121. Robert Emmett Curran, *A History of Georgetown University: From Academy to University, 1789–1889* (Washington, D.C.: Georgetown University Press, 2010), 291–92. President Abraham Lincoln appointed Miller to the Supreme Court in 1862. Justice Miller was paid $250 in 1870-71.

122. Curran, *A History of Georgetown University,* 336–39.

123. Curran, *A History of Georgetown University,* 336.

124. Curran, *A History of Georgetown University,* 291.

125. Curran, *A History of Georgetown University,* 113.

126. Consultors' Minutes of July 6, 1915, Provincial Archives.

127. John St. Paul Jr. went on to serve as president of Loyola's Alumni Association. He was active in celebrating the school's fiftieth anniversary and donated a portrait of his father, John St. Paul, to the law school.

128. Recorded remarks of Reverend Father Otis, S.J., Founding of Law School File, Loyola Archives.

129. Biever, "Reminiscence," 80.

130. *University Bulletin,* 1913–14, 44.

131. *University Bulletin,* 1913–14, 45.

132. *University Bulletin,* 1913–14, 45.

133. *University Bulletin,* 1914–1915, 45, and generally available at www.archive.org/stream/loyolauniversi9141510yo#page/42/mode/2.

134. Cook, *Founded on Faith,* 55.

135. *University Bulletin,* 1916–17.

136. Fr. Minister's Diarium, vol. 1. 1904 to 1917, p. 121, Loyola Archives.

137. "Tropical Storm Expected to Hit near River Mouth," *Times-Picayune,* September 29, 1915.

138. "New Orleans Safe after Great Storm," *Times-Picayune,* September 30, 1915; "Relief Being Sent to Various Points Where Most Needed," *Times-Picayune,* October 4, 1915.

139. Consultors' Minutes of July 6, 1915, and August 25, 1915, Provincial Archives.

140. Loyola University New Orleans College of Law Records. By 1953, Ms. Allen was Alice Allen Daviau and had taken up residence in Los Angeles, California.

CHAPTER TWO

Epigraph: Susan K. Boyd, *Assuring a Qualified Bar: The ABA's First Section* (American Bar Association: 1993), 17, quoting Dean Harry S. Richards from the University of Wisconsin.

1. W. Lee Hargrave, *LSU Law: The Louisiana State University Law School from 1906 to 1977* (Baton Rouge: Louisiana State University Press, 1976), 17–19.

2. Timmreck and Janssen, "Loyola University New Orleans: A Compendium," 44.

3. In November 1921, the Board of Directors of Loyola noted that other universities were denying Loyola students academic credit earned at Loyola (Minutes, Loyola Board of Directors, November 22, 1921, Loyola Archives).

4. Association of Colleges and Secondary Schools of the Southern States ("Association"), to Father Walsh, Loyola, Accreditation, dated December 7, 1921, and November 4, 1922, Loyola Archives.

5. Alfred Zantzinger Reed, *Training for the Public Profession of the Law: Historical Development and Principal Contemporary Problems of Legal Education in the United States with Some Account of Conditions in England and Canada* (New York: Scribner's, 1921), 394–403.

6. Reed, *Training for the Public Profession of the Law,* 401–2.

7. Reed, *Training for the Public Profession of the Law,* 398–99.

8. Stevens, *Law School: Legal Education in America,* 97.

9. Loyola President Rev. Florence Sullivan, S.J., to Chairman of the Commission on Institutions of Higher Education, May 14, 1923, Loyola Archives.

10. Loyola's Responses to the 1923–24 Association Questionnaire, Loyola Archives. Louisiana uses the term "parish" for "county." Currently, Louisiana is organized into sixty-four parishes. The term dates back to the French and Spanish colonial period, which were both officially Roman Catholic.

11. Father Sullivan explained further what he called the "peculiar trait of our Law Faculty," since "the reward of teaching is the honor of the position and the good achieved; they take no salaries whatever, but the tuition fees are paid in to the University to form a Law fund for building and endowment" (Sullivan to Campbell, July 12, 1923, Loyola Archives).

12. Sullivan to Campbell, July 12, 1923, Loyola Archives.

13. Campbell to Sullivan, June 27, 1923, Loyola Archives.

14. Sullivan to Campbell, October 16, 1923, Loyola Archives.

15. Postscript to Sullivan to Campbell, October 16, 1923, Loyola Archives.

16. Rev. Francis X. Twellmeyer, S.J., Loyola's fourth president, died suddenly in the winter of his first year as president. His successor, the Reverend Florence Sullivan, S.J., served as dean of Loyola's College of Arts and Sciences from 1919 to 1925 and as a practical matter was involved in the communications to secure Loyola's accreditation even prior to his appointment as president of the University in 1925.

17. W. D. Hooper to Sullivan, December 16, 1929, Loyola Archives.

18. Oral Interview of Leon Sarpy by John Nelson, January 26, 1993, Loyola Law Library Archives.

19. The family of Branch K. Miller, a prominent New Orleans lawyer, donated his law library to the law school, as did the family of U.S. Supreme Court Chief Justice Edward D. White after his death. Other collections donated to the law school included that of Judge St. Paul, Judge Lamar Stephens from Georgia, Judge Charles Parlange, attorneys Thomas J. Semmes, J. M. Lapeyre, W. C. Staub, Charles T. Soniat, and from New York, Francis and Jerome Mullen (Margaret Carey, "Informal History of Loyola," manuscript, p. 7, Loyola Archives).

20. "Law School Meets New President," *Maroon,* April 16, 1924.

21. The *Handbook* for the law school's first year lists Father Ryan as vice president and lecturer on ethics, but it is not clear whether he ever actually offered the course.

22. The Society appears to have begun in 1923 and formed officially in 1924. In spring 1924, students formed the Alpha Phi Delta law fraternity. The following year students formed the Edwin Douglas White Chapter of Sigma Nu Phi.

23. Christenberry encountered resistance to his appointment as United States attorney, on the grounds that he had not been supportive of the indictments and prosecution of members of the Long organization (Nomination of Herbert W. Christenberry to be United States Attorney for the Eastern District of Louisiana, United States Senate, Hearings before a Subcommittee of the Committee on the Judiciary, United States Senate, 77th Cong., 2d sess., Saturday, January 10, 12, 1942). Christenberry's brother, Earl Christenberry, was secretary to Huey P. Long and later served as secretary to Governor Earl Long. Christenberry was accused of serving as a "dummy candidate" for a senatorial primary election of September 13, 1932, a common political practice of the time.

24. Margaret Carey notes, Folder 1.1–2.9, Loyola Archives.

25. *University Bulletin,* 1921–22, 114.

26. This LLM was discontinued in the 1927–28 academic year.

27. *University Bulletin,* 1919–20, 6.

28. *University Bulletin,* 1920–21, 109.

29. *University Bulletin,* 1920–21, 109.

30. *University Bulletin,* 1922–23, 9.

31. Boyd, *Assuring a Qualified Bar.*

32. Beverly Moran, "The Wisconsin Diploma Privilege: Try It and You'll Like It," *Wisconsin Law Review* (2000): 645, 647 (quoting Elihu Root et al., *Report to the Special Committee to the Section of Legal Education and Admissions to the Bar of the American Bar Association,* 46 REP. ANN. MEETING ABA 679, 688 [1921]); James P. White, "Symposium: Legal Education in an Era of Change," *Duke Law Journal* (1987): 292, 295.

33. La. Act. No. 113 of 1924 § 1. The act provided: "Be it enacted by the Legislature of Louisiana, That every applicant for admission to the Bar of this State, whether holding a diploma from a Law School or not, before being licensed to practice law shall be required to pass a satisfactory examination before the Committee of Bar Examiners of the Supreme Court, on such subjects and under such rules and regulations as are now, or may hereafter be, prescribed by the Supreme Court; provided, that applicants for admission to the bar who have not received a diploma from an approved law school be required to prove a course of study under the supervision of a reputable Louisiana lawyer for a period of not less than three years, providing further that the Court shall not prescribe a higher general Educational qualification than a High School Course or the equivalent thereof."

34. Boyd, *Assuring a Qualified Bar,* 31.

35. Boyd, *Assuring a Qualified Bar,* 31.

36. Boyd, *Assuring a Qualified Bar,* 38.

37. Father Sullivan to Dr. Kirkland, Southern Association of Colleges, dated November18, 1925, Loyola Archives.

38. Father Sullivan to Dr. Campbell, Southern Conference, May 14, 1923, Loyola Archives.

39. *University Bulletin,* 1924–25, 7. Kenny was transferred to Spring Hill College.

40. *University Bulletin,* 1924–25, 21. Loyola internal enrollment records are inconsistent. A dean's report on enrollment prepared in 1939 shows different numbers for certain years. The inconsistency in numbers may reflect the time at which the report was prepared.

41. *University Bulletin,* 1925–26, 7.

42. *University Bulletin,* 1925–26, 9. This represented a meaningful increase in tuition: $120 in 1925 purchased $1,631.31 in 2014 dollars.

43. *University Bulletin,* 1925–26, 15.

44. In 1929–30, the *University Bulletin* reports that Mr. Bonomo earned an LLB from Georgetown. At some point in the years preceding he must have completed the work.

45. Inspection Report of Herschel W. Arant, 1929, AALS Archive.

46. In 1990, Loyola invested the Leon Sarpy Distinguished Professor of Law in Kathryn Venturatos Lorio, a 1973 graduate of the law school.

47. J. Skelly Wright was the second law graduate to be appointed to the federal bench, although he graduated from the law program in 1934, after Ainsworth.

48. The Honorable Carl E. Stewart, Loyola class of 1974, currently sits as chief judge, United States Court of Appeals for the Fifth Circuit.

49. Judge Ainsworth's friends and family funded the Ainsworth lecture series. Guest lecturers included: Warren E. Burger, chief justice of the United States; William H. Webster, former judge of the U.S. Court of Appeals for the Eighth Circuit and former director of the FBI; John R. Brown,

chief judge of the U.S. Court of Appeals for the Fifth Circuit; Kenneth F. Ripple, judge of the U.S. Court of Appeals for the Seventh Circuit; Charles E. Roemer III, former governor of the State of Louisiana; Lewis F. Powell Jr., associate justice, retired, of the U.S. Supreme Court; John Minor Wisdom, senior judge of the U.S. Court of Appeals for the Fifth Circuit; Kenneth W. Starr, former U.S. solicitor general; Antonin Scalia, associate justice of the U.S. Supreme Court; Henry A. Kissinger, former U.S. secretary of state; Deanell Tacha, then judge on the U.S. Court of Appeals for the Tenth Circuit; Guido Calabresi, judge, U.S. Court of Appeals for the Second Circuit; and Patrick E. Higginbotham, judge on the U.S. Court of Appeals for the Fifth Circuit.

50. Inspection Report, 1929, H. W. Arant, to Executive Committee of the AALS, Loyola Archives and AALS Archives.

51. "Loyola Revises Teaching of Law," *Times-Picayune,* October 13, 1931.

52. A 1930 appendix to Standard Number 18 to Loyola's application to the Southern Association notes that someone at the AALS had suggested that in order to gain membership Loyola had to have a full-time dean from Harvard or Yale, and three or four full-time professors from Yale, Harvard, Pennsylvania, Columbia, Cornell, or Northwestern (Loyola Archives).

53. "Law School Dean Named at Loyola," *Times-Picayune,* May 8, 1932.

54. "Loyola Activity about to Start for New Session," *Times-Picayune,* October 11, 1932.

55. Inspection Report, 1932, H. C. Horack to Executive Committee of the AALS, AALS Archives. The author has not located an intervening report on an inspection apparently conducted by E. A. Gilmore in 1931.

56. "Going to Bar Convention," *Times-Picayune,* October 5, 1933.

57. CPI Calculator at http://data.bls.gov/cgi-bin/cpicalc.pl?cost1=175.00&year1=1934&year2=2014; U.S. Bureau of Labor Statistics, "Consumer Expenditure Survey," table 9, available at www.bls.gov/opub/uscs/1934–36.pdf. The same report provides retail prices of selected foods in U.S. cities for 1934 including a dozen eggs at thirty-three cents and a half gallon of milk at twenty-two cents.

58. Inspection Report, 1934, H. C. Horack to AALS, AALS Archives.

59. Minutes, Meeting of Board of Trustees, Loyola University, January 17, 1936, including letter from Southern Association of Colleges and Secondary Schools, December 20, 1935, recognizing Loyola as a full member of the organization, out of probationary or conditional membership status (Loyola Archives).

CHAPTER THREE

1. Cook, *Founded on Faith,* 129–30.

2. "Editorial," *Loyola Law Journal* 12, no. 2 (1931): 80–81. Long had already been elected to the U.S. Senate, *Maroon,* February 6, 1931.

3. Minutes of Meeting of the Board of Trustees, Loyola University, March 7, 1935, Loyola Archives (hereafter cited as Board minutes).

4. Williams, *Huey Long,* 492–521.

5. Williams, *Huey Long,* 492–521. It was not just the law school that was affected by Senator Long's push to enhance LSU, but the pharmacy and dentistry schools as well.

6. Board minutes, Loyola University, July 1, 1936, Loyola Archives.

7. Board minutes, July 1, 1936, Loyola Archives. The CPI Inflation Calculator at the Department of Labor calculates that $4,000 in 1936 had the same buying power as $68,460.43 in 2014. According to a report by the College and University Professional Association for Human Resources published in the *Chronicle of Higher Education,* the 2010 median law school dean salary was $278,454.

8. "Loyola Foresees Successful Year," *Times-Picayune,* August 30, 1936, 29.

9. Board minutes, May 4, 1937, Loyola Archives.

10. "Campaign to Ban Indecent Books Will Be Opening; Archbishop Rummel Urged All to Take Part in Drive," *Times-Picayune,* February 14, 1939.

11. Board minutes, January 10, 1938, Loyola Archives. The Board minutes refer to the Gamma Eta Gamma Legal Fraternity, likely an error, as the actual organization to be established was the Delta Theta Phi, National Legal Fraternity. *Law School Bulletin,* 1937–38.

12. Board minutes, October 3, 1938, Loyola Archives.

13. Board minutes, October 3, 1938, Loyola Archives. Although the Board minutes reference letters from Dean Connor, none of the letters appear in the archives. During this meeting, the Board considered a request from the law school to grant the degree of juris doctor, on which the Board deferred to the law school.

14. Subsequent law bulletins refer to the St. Thomas More Club as being founded by students in 1935.

15. *Law School Bulletin,* 1940–41. Throughout this period of time, the bulletins note that there is also a Law Sodality open to all Catholic law students.

16. Board minutes, March 7, 1939, Loyola Archives.

17. Board minutes, July 23, 1943, Loyola Archives. The student was from Honduras and claimed he was having difficulty obtaining air travel back to Honduras after graduation. The law school regent, Father Walsh, told the Board "he did not consider the reason sufficient for granting the student's request but that he should be told to remain until after the commencement exercises, and to leave as soon as he could thereafter either by boat or by plane or by train whenever he could secure passage." The Board was not unanimous, but the majority agreed with Father Walsh's recommendation.

18. Board minutes, April 3, 1940, May 8, 1940, Loyola Archives.

19. Dean Connor protested the criticism and reminded the Board that the only reason he had not spoken to Dr. Bonomo was because he'd been asked to "spare Professor Bonomo's feelings" (Board minutes, June 14, 1940, Loyola Archives).

20. Board minutes, June 14, 1940, Loyola Archives.

21. Law school deans exercised discretion in the hiring of various staff members. It appears from various dean's reports that the dean appointed clerical staff without formal approval of the Board but with full consultation with the regent. The same dean's reports, however, make it clear that spending out of law school moneys to paint the law school or conduct other similar repairs had to be approved by the president or the board.

22. Board minutes, May 8, 1940, Loyola Archives.

23. Board minutes, May 8, 1940, Loyola Archives.

24. Board minutes, May 30, 1940, Loyola Archives. Dean Connor had promised Mr. Pascal a salary of $2,500.

25. Board minutes, June 14, 1940, Loyola Archives.

26. Dean Connor to President and Board, June 5, 1940, Loyola Archives.

27. Father Twomey to Father Shields, May 18, 1948, Twomey Papers, correspondence, box 1, folder 4, Loyola Archives.

28. Board minutes, June 14, 1940, Loyola Archives.

29. Board minutes, September 23, 1940, Loyola Archives.

30. Dean's monthly report to the President, December 1938, January 6, 1939, Loyola Archives. Apparently initial funding for the Institute was to be disbursed equally among the three law schools "to be used in carrying out projects undertaken by the Institute." Louisiana Act 166 of 1938 (Chapter 4, Title 24, Louisiana Revised Statutes of 1950).

31. Janet Mary Riley and other law faculty, including Kathryn Venturatos Lorio and Dian Tooley in recent years, worked on LSLI projects.

32. James Thomas Connor, "Dean of Loyola's Law School Reports on the Recent Frisco Meeting: Connor Tells History of Group Organized to Solve Differences in National, State Legislation and Avoid Natural Mixups," *Sunday Item-Tribune,* New Orleans, August 6, 1939; James Thomas Connor, "Louisiana's Napoleonic Code Backs Civil Law in Conference of States: Group Must Carefully Distinguish between Legislation to Avoid Imposing Adverse Rules on Some States' Declared Public Policy," *Sunday Item-Tribune,* New Orleans, August 13, 1939; James Thomas Connor, "Careful and Diligent Work Goes into Making Uniform State Laws: Loyola Dean Traces Steps Followed by National Conference to Insure Fairness to All Sections in Promulgation of New Rulings," *Sunday Item-Tribune,* New Orleans, August 20, 1939.

33. Board minutes, Loyola University, January 17, 1936, Loyola Archives.

34. Dean's report to President for December 1939, January 4, 1940, Loyola Archives.

35. Dean's annual report to President from July 1, 1938, to June 30, 1939, Loyola Archives.

36. Dean's annual report to President from July 1, 1938, to June 30, 1939, Loyola Archives.

37. Dean's monthly report to the President for May 1939, June 1, 1939, Loyola Archives.

38. Dean's report to the President for October 1939, November 3, 1939, Loyola Archives.

39. An 1880 case arising in Louisiana that ended up before the U.S. Supreme Court on oven patents (Ball v. Langles, 102 U.S. 128 [1880]).

40. Edward Livingston, a New Yorker who took up life in Louisiana in 1804, played a meaningful role in drafting the Louisiana Civil Code of 1825 and served in Andrew Jackson's cabinet as secretary of state. He died in New York in 1836.

41. Loyola University, A Letter to the Alumni on the Progress of the School of Law, November 7, 1938, Dean's Reports File, Loyola Archives.

42. Board minutes, April 3, 1941, Loyola Archives, planning the move from Bobet to Thomas More Hall at 6333 St. Charles Avenue; Board minutes, May 28, 1941, Loyola Archives, discussing a temporary move to Biever Hall or Otis, while renovations were completed at Thomas More and discussing the planned renovations. Thomas More Hall was demolished in 1982 after the law school moved to Branch Knox Miller Hall in 1973.

43. Board minutes, May 28, 1941, Loyola Archives.

44. Board minutes, August 18, 1942, and October 5, 1942, Loyola Archives.

45. Board minutes, January 11, 1943, Loyola Archives.

46. "Loyola Students and Staff Honor Dr. James Connor: Law School Dean Ordered to Active Duty in State Guard Staff," *Times Picayune,* October 1, 1940, 12.

47. Board minutes, September 23, 1940, Loyola Archives.

48. Board minutes, May 28, 1941, Loyola Archives.

49. Board minutes, December 11, 1941, Loyola Archives.

50. Board minutes, December 11, 1941, and January 5, 1942, Loyola Archives.

51. Board minutes, January 5, 1942, Loyola Archives.

52. Board minutes, February 10, 1942, Loyola Archives. Law students who had started their second semester of the senior year and had been called to active service during that semester were allowed to graduate without actually completing their last semester of studies (Board minutes, June 11, 1943, Loyola Archives).

53. *Law School Bulletin,* 1942–43.

54. Board minutes, September 18, 1942, Loyola Archives.

55. Board minutes, February 14, 1942, Loyola Archives.

56. Board minutes, May 8, 1942, Loyola Archives, discussing specific salary and other recommendations made by the dean.

57. Dean's report to President, February 8, 1941, and June 25, 1941, Loyola Archives.

58. Board minutes, September 14, 1942, Loyola Archives.

59. Board minutes, October 5, 1942, Loyola Archives. The average loss in student enrollment reported was 28.7 percent, with a low of 2.4 percent in Arts and Sciences to the law school high of 52.4 percent.

60. Board minutes, November 2, 1942, and November 6, 1942, Loyola Archives.

61. Dean's report to President, June 25, 1941, Loyola Archives.

62. Board minutes, December 26, 1942, Loyola Archives.

63. Dean's report to President, February 11, 1943, Loyola Archives.

64. Board minutes, January 30, 1950, Loyola Archives.

65. Dean's report to President, June 2, 1942, Loyola Archives.

66. Dean's report to President, October 18, 1942, Loyola Archives.

67. Dean Connor to President and Board, June 5, 1940, Loyola Archives.

68. *Law School Bulletin,* 1940–41.

69. Dean's report to President, November 5, 1941, Loyola Archives.

70. Dean's report to President, November 5, 1941, Loyola Archives.

71. Dean's report to President, February 11, 1943, Loyola Archives.

72. Dean's report to President, October 15, 1945, Loyola Archives.

73. Dean's report to President, May 4, 1946, Loyola Archives.

74. Dean's report to President, January 7, 1947, Loyola Archives.

75. Dean's report to President, May 17, 1948. There were other problems with the building. Bernard Cook in his history of Loyola notes that in July 1951, newly installed Dean Papale appealed to have the windows and doors of Thomas More Hall screened because night school classes were "constantly disturbed by mosquitoes and swarms of bugs" (Board minutes, July 19, 1951, Loyola Archives). The Board approved Papale's request for $1,275 to do the screening. Cook includes this incident as an example of the Board's tendency to micromanage Loyola through the 1950s (Cook, *Founded on Faith,* 188). But the Board's tendency to micromanage, at least the law school, was a feature of life at Loyola before and after the 1950s.

76. Dean's report to President, April 30, 1949, Loyola Archives. The AALS was debating the

question of law librarian status and whether law librarians were part of the law faculty program or whether they were part of the "general librarians" schedule.

77. Board minutes, January 10, 1951, Loyola Archives.

78. Dean's report to President, January 7, 1947, Loyola Archives. Undoubtedly, the salary available must have had an impact as well.

79. Dean's report to President, June 2, 1942, Loyola Archives.

80. Dean's report to President, January 5, 1947, Loyola Archives.

81. Dean's report to President, April 30, 1949, Loyola Archives.

82. Annual dean's report 1939 to 1940, Loyola Archives. The total law school budget projected for 1940–41 was $33,375.

83. "Report of the Curriculum Committee on the School of Law of Loyola University New Orleans, Louisiana," submitted by H. James Yamauchi, S.J., December 31, 1963, Loyola Archives.

84. Dean's report to President, April 30, 1949, Loyola Archives.

85. Board minutes, March 18, 1948, Loyola archives. It is estimated that $5,400 had the same buying power as $53,305.39 in 2014 (Department of Labor CPI Inflation Calculator). Law school tuition was raised to $450 in 1951, to make up for what the University considered the difference between the tuition and the expense to the University to educate the student (Board minutes, August 28, 1951).

86. Board minutes, December 23, 1948, Loyola Archives. Arts and Sciences tuition, which had been $260, was raised to $350; Pharmacy went from $200 to $400; and Dentistry from $400 to $500.

87. Board minutes, July 25, 1949, Loyola Archives.

88. Board minutes, September 29, 1949, Loyola Archives. Although the Board cited other reasons for opting not to offer to match the USF salary offer, in all likelihood the salary proved determinative. Its first response to the problem was dismay at losing Miller. The reasons advanced in the September 29 minutes, coming after Miller's extremely successful deanship for numerous years, were unconvincing: "The adverse attitude of Miller towards the Napoleonic Code . . . and a certain offensive manner towards students." Dean Miller notified the president of his election to the Executive Committee of the AALS in his report of April 30, 1949. Miller became dean of Catholic University Law School, until stepping down as dean in 1968. He remained on the faculty until 1972 but continued to teach at Catholic as an emeritus professor until 1982.

89. Board minutes, September 29, 1949, and November 22, 1950, Loyola Archives. Papale began his deanship at a salary of $7,000.

90. Dean's report to President, May 1, 1950, Loyola Archives.

91. Dean's report to President, November 6, 1951, Loyola Archives.

92. Dean's report to President, May 1, 1950, Loyola Archives.

93. Board minutes, November 22, 1950, Loyola Archives. Recognizing "the need of stability of faculty," Loyola stated its policy as "to grant permanent tenure after a probationary period of seven years to all full-time teachers regardless of academic rank."

94. Walter P. Metzger, "The 1940 Statement of Principles on Academic Freedom and Tenure," *Law and Contemporary Problems* 53 (Summer 1990): 3; Richard Hofstadter and Walter P. Metzger, *Academic Freedom in the United States* (New York: Columbia University Press, 1955).

95. According to the U.S. Department of Education in 1998, nearly all universities and col-

leges had tenure systems (Andrea Berger, Rita Kirshstein, and Elizabeth Rose, *Institutional Policies and Practices: Findings from the 1999 National Study of Postsecondary Faculty, Institution Survey,* 31 NCES 2001–201 [2001], U.S. Department of Education, National Center for Education Statistics).

96. *Loyola University Faculty Handbook,* 1956, Loyola Law School Archives.

97. Dean's report to President November 6, 1951, Loyola Archives. This appears to have been the last report filed by a law dean from this period. It is not clear whether there continued to be reports, and the remainder have been lost, or whether the reports ceased to be made.

CHAPTER FOUR

Epigraph 1: Bush v. Orleans Parish School Board,138 F. Supp. 337, 341–342 (E.D. La. 1956).

Epigraph 2: Vernon X. Miller, Dean, to Rev. Joseph H. Fichter, November 6, 1947, Fichter Papers, box 52, folder 14, Loyola Archives.

1. The integration of Loyola's undergraduate campus did not proceed as peacefully. There was turmoil on that campus, and that story is told in Bernard Cook's *Founded on Faith: A History of Loyola University New Orleans.* That turmoil, and the turmoil that resulted from protests against the Vietnam War, became part of the events that led to changes in the governing structure of the University and stronger protection for faculty rights, described in chapter 5.

2. As legal historian Mary L. Dudziak described World War II: "[A] war against a racist regime carried on by a nation with segregated military forces" (Dudziak, *Cold War Civil Rights: Race and the Image of American Democracy* [Princeton: Princeton University Press, 2000], 7).

3. Korematsu v. United States, 323 U.S. 214 (1944); Adam Liptak, "A Discredited Supreme Court Ruling That Still, Technically, Stands," *New York Times,* January 27, 2014. It is possible that the American public had little consciousness of the Supreme Court's decision on the internment of the Japanese in U.S. camps. A search of the newspaper databases yields very few articles and media reports on the internment. In Louisiana, I've discovered no newspaper treatments of the decision in the *Korematsu* case during the war period. A number of articles, however, reported on the push to intern the Japanese and on the internment itself ("Ask That Coast Enemy Aliens Be Interned by U.S.: Produce Men Call for More to Prevent 'Open Shooting,'" *Times-Picayune,* January 23, 1942; "'I Want to Go—Since I Have To' Says Jap Exiled from West Coast," *Times-Picayune,* March 24, 1942; "Biddle Directs Internment for 1302 Aliens Held," *Times-Picayune,* May 3, 1942; "Civil Liberties Union Applauds Court Decisions," *Times-Picayune,* June 28, 1942; "Interned Aliens Paroled for Work," *Times-Picayune,* July 26, 1942; "Japanese Born in America May Prove Loyalty to U.S.; Army Service or War Job Offered Internees," *Times-Picayune,* April 18, 1943; "Recommend Japs Here Be Drafted," *Times-Picayune,* July 17, 1943; "FBI Will Probe Jap Camp Riot," *Times-Picayune,* November 11, 1943). Some articles acknowledged the role of racial bias in relationships between Japanese Americans and others, including the Ku Klux Klan, not in Louisiana but in other parts of the United States, like Detroit ("Dies Will Probe Racial Clashes; Reports Evidence Japs Are Promoting Prejudice," *Times-Picayune,* June 24, 1943; "Dies Will Probe JAP Influence upon WRA," *Times-Picayune,* June 24, 1943). The national press dealt with the internment similarly. The number of press reports is slight compared to war coverage and to articles dealing

with the internment by the Japanese of Americans ("New Policy on Interned Japanese Urged by Senate Military Affairs Committee," *New York Times,* May 8, 1943; Charles Hurd, "Relocated Japanese Favor East: Those Released from Internment Avoid Pacific Coast," *New York Times,* May 7, 1944; "Japan Charges U.S. Kills Six Internees—Files Protest over 'Incidents' at Tule Lake—More Trouble There," *New York Times,* June 8, 1944).

4. Board minutes, February 21, 1943, Loyola Archives. For a description of the program that took 4,000 of the interned of college age "from concentration camp to campus," see Allan W. Austin, *From Concentration Camp to Campus: Japanese American Students and World War II* (Urbana: University of Illinois Press, 2004). Loyola's Board notes a letter concerning relocation of Japanese students: "This letter stated that the War Reclamation Authority had approved Loyola for the education of Japanese who are American citizens and who have been removed from Combat Zones and who are now in concentration camps. The Board was unanimous in the opinion that we would not have these Japanese at Loyola. Some of the members of the board thought that the letter should not be answered and others thought that it should be answered with an unmistakable refusal. The Board voted not to answer the letter at the present time."

5. For a discussion of President Truman's handling of race issues, including his establishment of the Committee on Civil Rights, see Richard Kluger, *Simple Justice: The History of* Brown v. Board of Education *and Black America's Struggle for Equality* (New York: Knopf, 2004), 248–54. President Truman also appointed the first African American to a federal circuit court of appeal when he appointed William H. Hastie to the United States Court of Appeals for the Third Circuit (Kluger, *Simple Justice,* 270).

6. The NAACP's strategy is described in Richard Kluger's *Simple Justice.* For a treatment of the struggle in Louisiana, see Emanuel and Tureaud, *A More Noble Cause.*

7. Civil Rights Act of 1964 Title VI and amendments.

8. Cheryl V. Cunningham, "The Desegregation of Tulane University" (master's thesis, University of New Orleans, 1982) (J. Skelly Wright case).

9. Bentley Anderson, *Black, White, and Catholic: New Orleans Interracialism, 1947–1956* (Nashville: Vanderbilt University Press, 2005). Anderson, as a Jesuit, was granted access to closed files at the Provincial Archives. I was not granted access to closed files but did have access to any materials that had been cited already by Anderson or Cook in his Loyola history. See R. Bentley Anderson, "Prelates, Protest, and Public Opinion: Catholic Opposition to Desegregation, 1947–1955," *Journal of Church and State* 46 (2004): 617–44; and R. Bentley Anderson, "Black, White, and Catholic: Southern Jesuits Confront the Race Question, 1952," *Catholic Historical Review* 91, no. 3 (July 2005): 484–505.

10. Missouri ex rel. Gaines v, Canada, 305 U.S. 337 (1938). See Kluger, *Simple Justice,* 198–212.

11. Emanuel and Tureaud, *A More Noble Cause,* 127–31.

12. Emanuel and Tureaud, *A More Noble Cause,* 131; Warren Rogers Jr., "Tiny Law School Faces Stiff Test; Southern U. Inspection Due Soon," *Times-Picayune,* May 29, 1945.

13. Hargrave, *LSU Law,* 151.

14. "Professional Associations Drop the Color Bar," *New South* 5, no. 7 (July 1950). The professional associations of teachers, doctors, and dentists, however, continued to hold out.

15. Janet Mary Riley, "The Effect of Segregation Laws on Louisiana Library Association Activities," *Library Journal* 75, no. 16 (September 15, 1950): 1466–69.

16. Riley, "The Effect of Segregation Laws on Louisiana Library Association Activities," 1469. The Association continued to face problems, however, within its ranks. Interracial meetings were threatening to many members, as the 1950 incoming president suggested when she stated at a meeting that "she was sure no parish, especially in north Louisiana, would ever again vote a library tax, if they knew that their librarians would annually attend an interracial meeting" (Janet Riley to Sue Hefley, dated January 4, 1950, Janet Mary Riley Papers, box 41/2, Loyola Archives).

17. Janet Mary Riley Papers, box 41/2, Loyola Archives.

18. Board minutes, June 16, 1942, Loyola Archives.

19. Board minutes, June 16, 1942, Loyola Archives.

20. Board minutes, June 16, 1942, Loyola Archives.

21. Anderson, *Black, White, and Catholic,* 62.

22. Anderson, *Black, White, and Catholic,* 23; Vernon X. Miller, Dean, to Rev. Joseph H. Fichter, November 6, 1947, Fichter Papers, box 52, folder 14, Loyola Archives. Miller's letter was essentially a legal opinion on the segregation law of Louisiana.

23. Board Minutes, November 29, 1947, Loyola Archives. "The thought of the Board was that while we want to avoid any prejudice against the negro race, we feel that Father Fichter is moving entirely too fast in view of conditions here in the city and that he be advised to become more acquainted with local feeling before attempting such a project as a university function. If he intends it as an entirely private meeting over which he would preside, it might be tolerated" (ibid.). At some point, Father Fichter was allowed to offer his course, but the Board again resisted inviting African Americans to lecture: "The Board felt that Fr. Fichter had pushed the matter of racial relations much too far and without getting necessary authorization from the president and dean" (Board minutes, September 24, 1948, Loyola Archives).

24. Anderson, *Black, White, and Catholic,* 8.

25. Board minutes, March 16, 1948, Loyola Archives; Shields to Twomey, March 20, 1948, Twomey Papers, box 1, folder 3, Loyola Archives.

26. Dean's report to President, May 17, 1948, Loyola Archives. He also, Dean Miller added, "has done much to help me to plan toward our objectives in law school administration."

27. Anderson, *Black, White, and Catholic,* 27–31.

28. Anderson, *Black, White, and Catholic,* 30.

29. Board minutes, March 11, 1949, Loyola Archives.

30. Board minutes, March 11, 1949, Loyola Archives. See Board minutes, March 12, 1949, Loyola Archives.

31. Minutes of Meeting sponsored by the Sub-Committee on Race Relations, February 21, 1949, Fichter Papers, box 47, folder 16, Loyola Archives. Dean Miller served as chair of the subcommittee at least when it was first founded. The steering committee had met, initially, at the law school. Minutes of the initial 1949 meetings were recorded on School of Law letterhead and were prepared by Janet Mary Riley, law librarian at the time and soon to be Loyola Law faculty member. Later in September 1949, Dr. Miller was appointed the chair of the executive committee (CHR Minutes: Membership, Sep-Dec. 1949, Fichter Papers, box 47, folder 17, Loyola Archives). One of the letter-writing campaigns involved protesting minstrel shows sent to church pastors and the archbishop (CHR Minutes, November 27, 1949, Fichter Papers, box 47, folder 17, Loyola Archives).

32. Anderson, *Black, White, and Catholic,* 15–16.

33. "Bishop Tells Steps for Promoting Race Justice," *Catholic Action of the South,* February 28, 1952; "'Where Is Mystical Body?' Father Fichter Asks CHR," *Catholic Action of the South,* October 10, 1942; "Catholic Group Hits 'Organized Racism,'" *New Orleans Item,* June 11, 1956; "Law School Dean to Speak Here," *Times-Picayune* (noting that Loyola law dean Papale and Janet M. Riley were among the panelists set to discuss integration); "African Bishop Will Speak," *New Orleans States-Item,* April 28, 1950; "Desegregation Discussion Set," *Times-Picayune,* November 10, 1955 (Janet Riley again a panelist as well as Benjamin Johnson, one of the first African Americans to graduate from Loyola's law school). The commission also gave a prize for an essay on race. Mrs. Francis X. Waguespack was the winner, writing on the topic, "Why is an integrated school better than a segregated school?" ("Prize for Racial Essay Is Awarded," *Times-Picayune,* March 26, 1956).

34. "Delegates of 11 States Form CCA," *New Orleans States-Item,* April 9, 1956. The Citizens' Councils of America was formed "to preserve the reserved natural rights of the people and of the states, including primarily the separation of the races in our school and all our institutions involving personal and social relations, and the maintenance of the rights of the states to regulate public health, morals, marriages, education, peace and good order in the states, under the constitution of the United States" (ibid.; "Citizens' Council Differs with Group," *New Orleans Item,* May 25, 1956; "Council Head Asks FBI to Eye Charges," *New Orleans Item,* June 15, 1956; "Citizens Council Asks FBI to Probe Priest," *New Orleans States-Item,* June 14, 1956).

35. Vernon X. Miller, Dean, Loyola University School of Law, to various invitees, dated February 14, 1949, Fichter Papers, box 45, folder 5, Loyola Archives. The group's early activities involved attending an integrated monthly mass and communion breakfast at Loyola. Loyola's president, Thomas J. Shields, cautioned not to use the cafeteria. Father Shields did not defend racial prejudice, he explained in his letter to Father Fichter, "but on the contrary condemn the prejudice that forces this decision; nevertheless we have to adopt a course which will most expeditiously bring about the happy day when racial prejudice will be abolished" (Thomas J. Shields to Rev. Joseph Fichter, April 27, 1949, Fichter Papers, box 45, folder 5, Loyola Archives). The group moved its breakfast and mass to Xavier.

36. Board minutes, October 28, 1949, Loyola Archives.

37. Warren Rogers Jr., "Tiny Law School Faces Stiff Test; Southern U. Inspection Due Soon," *Times-Picayune,* May 29, 1945.

38. Cook, *Founded on Faith,* 165; Anderson, *Black, White, and Catholic,* 62–63. None of the original documents surrounding the Alexander application appear to have survived.

39. Twomey to Francis Lucey, Georgetown, June 9, 1949, Twomey Papers, box 19, folder 3, Loyola Archives.

40. Lucey to Twomey, July 26, 1949, Twomey Papers, box 19, folder 3, Loyola Archives.

41. Anderson, *Black, White, and Catholic,* 79–81; Cook, *Founded on Faith,* 174–75; Twomey to Rev. Dobson, October 18, 1950, Twomey Papers, civil rights, box 19, folder 3, Loyola Archives.

42. Sweatt v. Painter, 339 U.S. 629 (1950).

43. McLaurin v. Oklahoma State Regents for Higher Education, 339 U.S. 637 (1950).

44. "Sixty Years after Admitting Its First Black Member, the American Bar Association Elects an African American President," *Journal of Blacks in Higher Education* 35 (Spring 2002): 34–35.

45. Walter J. Leonard, "The Development of the Black Bar," *Annals of the American Academy of Political and Social Science* 407, no. 1 (May 1973): 134–43.

46. William G. Paul, "President's Message: Increasing Diversity," *American Bar Association Journal* (October 1990): 8.

47. "Proceedings 1950 Association of American Law Schools," *Handbook of the Association of American Law Schools* (1948–51): 20.

48. "Report of the Special Committee on Discrimination in Law School Admissions," *AALS Proceedings,* 1951, 278. The resolution was modified to have it go into effect two years after adoption.

49. *AALS Proceedings,* 1950, 22–45.

50. "Negro Sues over LSU's Rejection; Files Action for Admission as Law Student," *Times-Picayune,* September 14, 1951.

51. "Hearing Date Set for LSU Race Suit," *Times-Picayune,* September 20, 1950; "Testimony Given on Policy of LSU; Stoke, Clark Testify on Negro Admission Plea," *Times-Picayune,* September 28, 1950.

52. "Argument Heard in Wilson's Suit; Three-Judge Court Takes Case under Advisement," *Times-Picayune,* September 30, 1950.

53. "LSU Is Ordered to Admit Wilson; Must Open Law School to Qualified Negroes, Ruling," *Times-Picayune,* October 8, 1950; "LSU Law School Hit," *Times-Picayune,* October 10, 1950.

54. Hargrave, *LSU Law,* 151–53.

55. "Solon Proposes School Equality; Negro Court Ruling Brings Strong Suggestion," *Times-Picayune,* October 15, 1950.

56. "Letter to the Editor on 'No Louisiana Law,' Loyola University," *Times-Picayune,* October 18, 1950.

57. Hargrave, *LSU Law,* 153.

58. Anderson, *Black, White, and Catholic,* 91–95. Gumbel served as an officer of SERINCO while a student at Xavier (SERINCO minutes for July–December 1949, Fichter Papers, box 51, folder 8, Loyola Archives).

59. Gumbel to Shields, June 21, 1951, Provincial Archives. The original application and Papale's response were not located in the various archival collections, but the subsequent appeal and the president's response were available in the Provincial Archives.

60. Gumbel to Shields, June 21, 1951, Provincial Archives.

61. Letter from Francis Lucey, Georgetown Law School, June 15 1951, Twomey Papers, box 2, folder 2, Loyola Archives.

62. The difficulties inherent in this move were stated forcefully to Father Twomey when he sought to persuade Gumbel to return to Loyola to finish his law studies there, after Loyola decided to admit African Americans to the law school (Gumbel to Twomey, September 13, 1952, Twomey Papers, correspondence, civil rights, box 19, folder 10, Loyola Archives). Gumbel had to leave his home, his family, and a job, and had only been joined by this family at the close of his first year. To return home, he would have to relocate everyone including a young child that had just begun his first year in D.C. schools. His letter makes clear how hard it must have been for a Jesuit to understand exactly the difficulties a parent faced in moving a family. Gumbel's letter did much to help Twomey understand (Twomey to Gumbel, October 28, 1952, Twomey Papers, corre-

spondence, civil rights, box 19, folder 11, Loyola Archives). Twomey tried to persuade Alexander to return to New Orleans and Loyola as well (correspondence between Twomey and Alexander, Twomey Papers, correspondence, civil rights, box 19, folder 11, Loyola Archives).

63. Twomey to McCormick, September 18, 1951, Twomey Papers, box 19, folder 8, Loyola Archives.

64. McCormick to Twomey, November 29, 1951, Twomey Papers, correspondence, civil rights, box, 19, folder 8, Loyola Archives.

65. Dean's Report to President November 6, 1951. Dean Papale served as a member of the Special Committee on Racial Discrimination in the Law Schools of the Association of American Law Schools. In 1957, *Northwestern University Law Review* published an essay by Dean Papale entitled "Judicial Enforcement of Desegregation: Its Problems and Limitations" (52, no. 3 [July–August 1957]: 301–19). He was featured as a panelist or lecturer a number of times to defend integration and to urge others to support desegregation efforts ("Blasts Attacks on High Court," *New Orleans States-Item,* April 9, 1956; "Hepburn Talks on Interposition, Human Rights Unit Hears Emory Dean," *Times-Picayune,* April 9, 1956).

66. Twomey to McCormick, December 18, 1951, Twomey Papers, correspondence, civil rights, box 19, folder 9, Loyola Archives.

67. Report of the Special Committee on Discrimination in Law School Admissions, Association of American Law Schools, *Association Proceedings,* 1951, 278–300.

68. *AALS Proceedings,* 1951, 291.

69. *AALS Proceedings,* 1951, 19.

70. *AALS Proceedings,* 1951, 20–22.

71. Driscoll joined the Loyola Law faculty under Dean Miller in academic year 1950–51. He taught commercial law courses, criminal law, criminal procedure, and introduction to procedure.

72. *AALS Proceedings,* 1951, 22–23.

73. Only seventeen schools voted against the committee proposal (*AALS Proceedings,* 1951, 42–44).

74. A. W. Crandell, New Orleans Province, to Twomey, January 5, 1952, Twomey Papers, correspondence, civil rights, box 19, folder 9, Loyola Archives; letter from A. W. Crandell, July 14, 1952, noting a meeting scheduled for August 28–29, 1952, to discuss interracial relations in the Southern Province and develop a Province policy, Twomey Papers, correspondence, civil rights, box 19, folder 10, Loyola Archives. The policy that the province eventually adopted was that Loyola would integrate gradually.

75. Twomey to Donnelly, June 1, 1952, Twomey Papers, correspondence, civil rights, box 19, folder 10, Loyola Archives.

76. Letters from Dean Papale and Father Twomey make clear that the matter had been decided in August. Leflar to Papale, August 21, 1952 (referring to Papale letter of August 5, 1952 stating that Loyola law school will probably "admit a limited number of qualified negroes this fall"); and Twomey to Gumbel, August 30, 1952 (inviting Gumbel to return to New Orleans to take up legal studies at Loyola, something that Gumbel appears to have considered but in a moving letter communicated how difficult it would be for him and so refused), Twomey Papers, correspondence, civil rights, box 19, folder 10, Loyola Archives; Board minutes, September 6, 1952, Loyola Archives. The New Orleans Provincial had yet to work out the province policy and

for this reason "permission was obtained from Fr. Provincial to admit Negroes to the Loyola Law School" (ibid.). See Anderson, "Black, White, and Catholic: Southern Jesuits Confront the Race Question," *Catholic Historical Review* 91, no. 3 (July 2005): 484–505.

77. Father Twomey to Dr. Robert Shea, October 30, 1952, Twomey Papers, general correspondence, civil rights, box 19, folder 11, Loyola Archives.

78. Board minutes, March 29, 1953, Loyola Archives.

79. Ultimately, the Board rejected integration of the dental school (Board minutes, May 3, 1953, Loyola Archives).

80. Board minutes, May 23, 1954, Loyola Archives. The Board was split on admitting African Americans to the graduate program in education and deferred the decision to the Father Provincial. In response to the Father Provincial's directive, the University opened admission to African Americans to evening programs but not to day programs (Board minutes, November 1, 1954, Loyola Archives). A year later the Board agreed to allow an African American to attend summer school day classes (Board minutes, April 22, 1955, Loyola Archives).

81. Robert Leflar to Dean Papale, August 21, 1952, Twomey Papers, correspondence, civil rights, box 19, folder 10, Loyola Archives.

82. Twomey to Robert Shea, October 30, 1952, Twomey Papers, general correspondence, civil rights, box 19, folder 11, Loyola Archives.

83. Twomey to Bartholomew Lahiff, S.J., January 12, 1953, Twomey Papers, general correspondence, civil rights, box 19, folder 11, Loyola Archives.

84. Board minutes, June 16, 1955, Loyola Archives.

85. Board minutes, July 27, 1955, Loyola Archives.

86. Board minutes, July 27, 1955, Loyola Archives.

87. Twomey to Austin Morris, S.J., November 25, 1953, Twomey Papers, correspondence, box 2, folder 14, Loyola Archives.

88. Clem Kennington, "A Great Loss," *Legal Rag* 12, no. 3 (December 1969).

89. "23 School Boys Win Scholarships," *Times-Picayune,* June 15, 1927.

90. *Times-Picayune,* February 27, 1939. The reference is to Thomas E. Dewey, former governor of New York, who lost presidential elections to both Franklin Roosevelt and Harry Truman. In his early days as a prosecutor he built up a reputation for aggressively going after organized crime.

91. *Times-Picayune,* January 17, 1939, April 6, 1939, June 21, 1939.

92. Gilbert King, *The Execution of Willie Francis* (New York: Basic Civitas, 2008).

93. *Robinson v. California* (1962) incorporated the cruel and unusual punishment clause of the Eighth Amendment, and *Benton v. Maryland* (1969) incorporated the double jeopardy clause of the Fifth Amendment.

94. Louisiana, ex rel Francis v. Resweber, 329 U.S. 459 (1947); King, *The Execution of Willie Francis,* 176–205; Helen Patton Wright, *My Journey: Recollections of the First Seventy Years* (Chevy Chase: Posterity, 1995), 69–71.

95. Wright, *My Journey,* 69–71.

96. King, *The Execution of Willie Francis,* 171.

97. King, *The Execution of Willie Francis,* 172.

98. Liva Baker, *The Second Battle of New Orleans: The Hundred-Year Struggle to Integrate the Schools* (New York: Harper Collins, 1996).

99. Interview, August 2, 2013, Washington, D.C. (notes on file with author).

100. Baker, *The Second Battle of New Orleans,* 381.

101. "Blasts Attacks on High Court," *New Orleans States-Item,* April 9, 1956.

102. "Blasts Attacks on High Court," *New Orleans States-Item,* April 9, 1956.

103. Kim Lacy Rogers, *Righteous Lives: Narratives of the New Orleans Civil Rights Movement* (New York: New York University Press, 1993), 110–46.

104. Lombard v. Louisiana, 373 U.S. 267, 268–72 (1963).

105. Lolis Elie, interview by author, May 1, 2014, New Orleans (notes on file with author); see Rogers, *Righteous Lives,* 53–56.

106. State v. Goldfinch, 241 La. 958, 132 So. 2d 860 (1961).

107. *Lombard,* 373 U.S. at 267.

108. Amistad Research Center, Tulane University, John P. Nelson Papers, 1957–1977, www.amistadresearchcenter.org/archon/?p=collections/findingaid&id=64&q=&rootcontentid=38971#id38971. However, Armand Romain, a white attorney, had represented David J. Ryanes in his challenge to the 1898 Louisiana Constitution.

109. *Lombard,* 373 U.S. at 267, 268–69.

110. State versus Goldfinch, 241 La. 958, 132 So. 2d 860 (1961), *reversed,* 373 U.S. 267 (1963).

111. *Lombard,* 373 U.S. at 267. See Rebecca Fenton, "Loyola University New Orleans School of Law Commemorates the Fortieth Anniversary of the Landmark Decision in Lombard v. Louisiana," *Journal of Public Interest Law* 5 (2004): 63.

112. Fenton, "Loyola School of Law Commemorates," 67.

113. *Lombard,* 373 U.S. at 273–74.

114. Guillary v. Administrators of Tulane University of LA, 203 F. Supp. 855 (E.D. La. 1962), vacated, 212 F. Supp. 674 (1962).

115. Cook, *Founded on Faith,* 223.

CHAPTER FIVE

Epigraph: Robert Stevens, *Law School: Legal Education in America,* 209, 234.

1. Title IX of the Education Amendments of 1972, 20 U.S.C. §1681 *et seq.*

2. Mary Jude Goebel, "Law School Emphasizes Fair Hiring," *Code,* September 1984 (responding to concerns that law firms were discriminating against women in 1984).

3. "Diversity at Tulane Law School," Tulane University Law School, www.law.tulane.edu/tlsStudentLife/index.aspx?id=728. The first law school to admit women appears to have been the Union College of Law, now known as Northwestern School of Law, in Illinois in 1870 (Lani Guinier, Michelle Fine, and Jane Balin, *Becoming Gentlemen: Women, Law School, and Institutional Change* [Boston: Beacon, 1997], 116n38).

4. Hargrave, *LSU Law,* 36. See L. Marino, K. Tonnas, and J. Coulter, "Legal History—State's First Women Law Graduates," *Louisiana Bar Journal* 55 (August/September 2007), 107. Arabella Mansfield is credited as the first woman admitted to the practice of law in the United States; she was admitted to the Iowa bar in 1869. Ada A. Kepley was the first American woman to receive an accredited law degree, in 1870 (Cynthia Fuchs Epstein, *Women in Law,* 2nd ed. [Urbana: University of Illinois Press, 1993], 49–50).

5. Bradwell v. Illinois, 83 U.S. 130 (1873).

6. Barbara Miller Solomon, *In the Company of Educated Women: A History of Women and Higher Education in America* (New Haven: Yale University Press, 1985), 131. In fact, by 1920, six years after the law school's founding, no state prohibited women from being admitted to their bar (Joellen Lind, "Symbols, Leaders, Practitioners: The First Women Professionals," *Valparaiso University Law Review* 28 [Summer 1994]: 1327).

7. Epstein, *Women in Law,* 53; Karen Berger Morello, *The Invisible Bar: The Woman Lawyer in America from 1638 to the Present* (New York: Random House, 1986).

8. *Monroe News Star* 29, no. 24, Friday, January 3, 1941.

9. Cook, *Founded on Faith,* 170. Some programs at Loyola, like the pharmacy school, admitted women even before the law school, and other programs, like the school of education, admitted them in the 1930s. Bernard Cook concludes that by 1940 Loyola's day school was visibly co-ed, although the largest college, Arts and Sciences, still did not formally admit them (ibid., 116–17).

10. W. O. Hart, "Rights of Women in Louisiana," *Loyola Law Journal* 1, no. 1 (March 1920): 14–27; J. C. Hollingsworth, "Interpretation of Seven-Year Divorce Law," *Loyola Law Journal* 1, no. 1 (March 1920): 28–29; J. T. Convery, "The Right of the Unborn Child to Life," *Loyola Law Journal* 3, no. 1 (November 1921): 26; Florence Loeber, "Women under the Law in Louisiana," *Loyola Law Journal* 3, no. 1 (November 1921): 26–30. Loeber was described as "a distinguished member of the New Orleans Bar." The article summarized Louisiana law as it affected women and noted the changes that the state had made on the status of women, flowing in part from the adoption of the Nineteenth Amendment: "To-day, however, with women standing beside men in the various walks of life, with full political suffrage, each legislative year necessarily brings a decided broadening of these doctrines. A few years ago our women could hold no public office. . . . It is only within the recent years that any woman could even witness a will" (Loeber, "Women under the Law in Louisiana," 25). Loeber identified in the piece the disabilities faced by a married woman under Louisiana law; the *Journal* described her as "noted for her broad common sense view that the disabilities attaching to women under the law should be removed steadily, but gradually; that their rights should grow up as needs arise until the custom blossoms out in full strength and vigor," which may reflect the editor's views rather than the author's.

11. "The Female of the Species," *Loyola Law Journal* 2, no. 1 (November 1920): 25. The commentary is followed by a joke, similarly common for the journal at the time, on "Irrelevant Relations": "Lawyer—'So you want a divorce from your wife. Aren't your relations pleasant?' Client—'Mine are, but hers are the most unpleasant lot I ever met.'"

12. "Dedicated to the Graduating Class '22—The Day—The Class Reporter '22," *Loyola Law Journal* 3, no. 4 (October 1922): 3, 10.

13. Epstein, *Women in Law,* 219–36; Herma Hill Kay, "UC's Women Law Faculty," *University of California Davis Law Review* 36 (2003): 331n26; Herma Hill Kay, "Symposium: The Voices of Women: A Symposium on Women in Legal Education: The Future of Women Law Professors," *Iowa Law Review* 77 (1991): 8–9. Tulane University Law School hired Cynthia Ann Samuel, its first woman law professor, in 1975. Southern University Law Center hired its first woman faculty, Cynthia Picou, in 1976.

14. Marina Angel, "Law Stories: Reflections of Women in Legal Education: Stories from Four Decades of Section Chairs: Women in Legal Education III," *University of Missouri Kansas City Law Review* 111 (Spring 2012): 714; Marina Angel, "Women in Legal Education: What It's Like to

Be Part of a Perpetual First Wave, or the Case of the Disappearing Women," *Temple Law Review* 61 (Fall 1988): 801.

15. Hargrave, *LSU Law*, 46–47.

16. Riley was not the only woman to turn a librarian's position into a tenure-track teaching position. Marina Angel noted that one of the early chairs of the AALS Section on Women in Legal Education also started out as law librarian (Angel, "Law Stories," 711). Epstein noted the prevalence of women in law librarian positions (Epstein, *Women in Law*, 220).

17. Dean Miller began to look for someone to replace her at a starting salary of $175 a month (Dean's report to Father Shields, President, dated 10/15/1945) (Shields had just taken over from Father Roy, who was still serving as Loyola president on February 1945).

18. Letter from Mortimer Schwartz, Librarian and Assistant Professor of Law, University of Oklahoma Law Library, October 6, 1953, Janet Mary Riley Papers, box 22/2, Loyola Archives.

19. Janet Mary Riley Papers, box 21, Loyola Archives.

20. Cook, *Founded on Faith*, 191–209.

21. Cook, *Founded on Faith*, 197–98.

22. Discussions about the curriculum and other related matters are based primarily on the version of the *Law School Bulletin* in place at the time. I have also relied on the faculty papers of Dennis Rousseau and others in the Law School Archives, which contained many reports, memoranda and other materials that were very helpful in tracing some of the events during this period.

23. Janet Mary Riley Papers, AAUP Files, Loyola Archives. The American Association of University Professors (AAUP) formed in 1913 and issued its first publication in 1915, the *General Declaration of Principles*, recognizing academic freedom as a critical characteristic of universities and the institution of tenure as the most effective way to secure academic freedom to academics.

24. Janet Mary Riley Papers, box 4, Blouin File, Loyola Archives. In the view of Blouin and other faculty, he had earned tenure upon accepting his position on the faculty. In the view of the University, the decision to grant tenure came after some time in the faculty. Blouin was a popular teacher, but his publications, in the view of the University, did not merit tenure. References to decisions taken at the law school make clear that sometimes the University faculty preferred more popular teachers to professors who were strong scholars; in the case of the English department, however, Blouin's supporters made clear their preference for good teachers rather than good scholars.

25. Janet Mary Riley Papers, box 4, Blouin File, Loyola Archives.

26. *Loyola University Faculty Handbook* (rev. 1973), Loyola Law School Archives.

27. *Loyola University Faculty Handbook* (rev. 1973), p. 14, Loyola Law School Archives.

28. *Loyola University Faculty Handbook* (rev. 1973), pp. 14–15, Loyola Law School Archives .

29. *Loyola University Faculty Handbook* (rev.1981, effective August 16, 1982), 13–1, 6; 16–11, 6–4.

30. Louisiana Bar Foundation, Oral Histories, Janet Riley video, available at www.raisingthebar.org/ProgramsAndProjects/OralHistories.asp?Vid=Riley&Wiew=Janet Mary Riley#AN .

31. The problems women faced in the legal academy are legion and persist today (Christine Haight Farley, "Confronting Expectations: Women in the Legal Academy," *Yale Journal of Law and Feminism* 8 [1961]: 333; Guinier, Fine, and Balin, *Becoming Gentlemen*)

32. "Women Make Headway in Law School," *Legal Rag*, January 1969. Not all issues of

the *Legal Rag* or the *Code* have survived, and the editors did not use issue numbers or dates consistently.

33. "Women Make Headway in Law School," *Legal Rag*, January 1969, 3.

34. Edwin Lombard, "Black Attorneys," *Legal Rag* 12, no. 3 (December 1969).

35. See, e.g., Jim Murray, "BLSA Moot Team Third in Nation," *Code*, April 1984. Not all issues of the *Code* survived. Moreover, the editors of the *Code* chose not to report the date of issue, so it is sometimes difficult to tell the time period in which a particular issue appeared.

36. Letter from Gerald P. Bodet, then assistant professor of history, LSU, in New Orleans; letter from Maurice C. Hebert, January 12, 1967; Dean Papale to President Father Jolley, memorandum, September 14, 1966, President's Correspondence, Loyola Archives.

37. Jimmy Gelpi, "Letters Dear Editor," *Legal Rag*. no. 7 (1965): 3.

38. Remarks of Judge Robert Ainsworth to Faculty of School of Law, March 4, 1969.

39. The city first dropped out of the top-20 list in the 1980 census and has never returned to the status it enjoyed for most of the twentieth century.

40. U.S. Bureau of the Census, *Census of Population: 1970* (Washington, D.C.: U.S. Government Printing Office, 1973): tables 7 and 16.

41. U.S. Bureau of Census, *Census of Population: 1970*, 20–36, 20–147, table 45.

42. Herman Bastian, "Minority Recruitment," *Code* 3, no. 3, p. 6.

43. President Carter to Joseph Kavanaugh, December 12, 1984 (conveying approval of the *Code* policy statement and Loyola Code Policy Statement), President's Law School Correspondence 1984–85, Loyola Archives.

44. "Editorial—A Hope for the Future," *Code* 1, no. 1, p. 2.

45. "Editorial—A Hope for the Future," *Code* 1, no. 1, p. 2.

46. Bill Billeaud, "Students Grade Teachers," *Code* 1, no. 1, p. 2.

47. Raymond C. Vinet Sr., "Bomb Scare—The Anarchist Movement," *Code*, December 1970, 4.

48. "Opinion: Black Students Reply," *Code*, March 1971, 3.

49. Epstein, *Women in Law*, 219.

50. Rob Scirocco, "Assistant Dean Schwab Supports Minorities," *Code*, April 1978, 2.

51. "Briefs—Demand for Legal Education Growing," *Code*, February 1974, 3.

52. Janet Mary Riley, *Louisiana Community Property: Cases and Materials on Louisiana Property Law of Marriage* (Baton Rouge: Claitor's, 1972). See Gerard A. Rault Jr., "Book Review: *Louisiana Community Property: Cases and Materials on Louisiana Property Law of Marriage* by Janet Mary Riley," *Tulane Law Review* 46 (1972): 1082.

53. Corpus Christi Parish Credit Union v. Martin, 358 So. 2d 295 (La. 1978).

54. *Corpus Christi*, 358 So. 2d at 298. Or Id. at 298.

55. 1979 La. Acts No. 709 § 1, effective Jan. 1, 1980.

56. Kirchberg v. Feenstra, 609 F. 2d 727 (5th Cir. 1979).

57. "Effective Start for Women's Club," *Code*, April 1974, 7.

58. Bloom left Loyola in 1979 to join the Albany Law School faculty.

59. Bonnie DeNoux, "Barriers Lower for Women in Law," *Code*, October 1975, 1.

60. Bonnie DeNoux, "Barriers Lower for Women in Law," *Code*, October 1975, 3.

61. "Faculty News," *Code*, April 1976, 2.

62. Amy Lipp, "Women Review Impact of Laws," *Code,* April 11, 1979, 4; *Code,* Winter 1983, 2; M. J. McQueeny, "Joint Custody Aspects Explored at Conference," *Code,* February 1984, 3.

63. "Law Conference," *Code,* February 1978, 5.

64. Corpus Christi Credit Union v. Martin, No. 77–6078 (CDC, Orleans Parish, February 14, 1978), ruling article 2404 invalid under the federal constitution.

65. Roma Caramanica, "Legal Obstacles Face the Battered Woman," *Code,* November 17, 1978, 3. The spring 1981 conference featured "Women and Employment" ("Conference Draws 100," *Code,* Spring 1981, 5).

66. *AWLS Newsletter* 2, no. 3 (November 1978): 3, Loyola Archives.

67. Interview with Kathryn Lorio.

68. Mary E. Lockard, "Prof. Lorio Awarded Endowed Chair," *Code,* Fall 1992, 1, 3.

69. Kathryn Lorio, "Symposium: Reflections of Women in Legal Education: Stories from Four Decades of Section Chairs—Reflections: A Generation Later," *University of Missouri Kansas City Law Review* 80 (2012): 745.

70. "Macke Elected President: New S.B.A. Officers," *Code,* April 1976, 17.

71. Jerry Madere, "Miss Heriot Leaves Library," *Code,* September 1976, 2.

72. Dead File: Law Library 1978–1982, Loyola Archives. The University had been a selective depository for federal documents since 1942. Mary Lee Sweat and Stella Chiang to President Carter, memorandum, dated March 1, 1982, Dead File: Law Library 1978–1982, Loyola Archives.

73. A Proposal to Establish LEXIS Computerized Legal Research System in the Law Library, submitted by Win-Shin S. Chiang, Law Librarian, October 1979, pp. 2–3, Dead File: Law Library 1978–1982, Loyola Archives.

74. Dead File: Law Library 1983–84, Loyola Archives.

75. Law Library Consultant's Report, 1984, Dead File: Law Library 1983–84, Loyola Archives.

76. Law Library Consultant's Report, 1984, Dead File: Law Library 1983–84, Loyola Archives.

77. "Moot Court Board Arrives," *Code,* October 1973.

78. Brendan Brown to Father Francis Janssen, January 28, 1975, Loyola Archives.

79. Nate Fink, "Referendum Discussed," *Code,* February 1974.

80. Academic Unit Three Year Plan September 1982–August 1985, submitted to Standing Council for Academic Planning, Loyola University New Orleans, Louisiana, School of Law, April 8, 1982, p. 56, Dennis Rousseau Papers, Loyola Law School Archives.

81. Academic Unit Three Year Plan September 1982–August 1985, submitted to Standing Council for Academic Planning, Loyola University New Orleans, Louisiana, School of Law, April 8, 1982, p. 56, Dennis Rousseau Papers, Loyola Law School Archives.

82. U.S. Bureau of the Census, *1980 Census of Population* (Washington, D.C.: U.S. Government Printing Office, September 1981), table 58.

83. Bureau of the Census, *1980 Census,* tables 56, 58, and 82. 26. Two percent of Louisiana families had incomes in 1979 below 125 percent of the poverty level.

84. Dean Sponsler to Vice President for Academic Affairs, memorandum, September 10, 1984, on "Minority Recruitment and Retention," President's Law School Correspondence 1984–85, Loyola Archives.

85. Pamela Jackson, memorandum dated July 19, 1983, on "1982–83 Continuing Legal Education Seminar Series," President's Law School Correspondence 1984–85, Loyola Archives.

86. La. Sup. Ct. R. XXX, 8 La. Rev. Stat. Ann. (1988).

87. Bayless Manning, "Financial Anemia in Legal Education: Everybody's Business," *American Bar Association Journal* 55 (December 1969): 1123–28.

88. Mary Jude Goebel, "Burger at Law School," *Code,* September 1984; Mary Jude Goebel, "Students to See Burger via Closed Circuit TV," *Code,* October 1984. Something similar happened when the law school hosted former Russian president Mikhail Gorbachev in spring 1997. Gorbachev spoke to a standing-room-only audience, but neither law faculty nor law students were in the audience unless as an invited guest.

89. Dean Sponsler to Dr. Preston, memorandum, May 5, 1986, on "Law School Policy on Tuition Remission," President's Law School Correspondence 1986, Loyola Archives. Dean Sponsler acknowledged the potential loss of tuition revenue to Loyola, particularly when part-time faculty taught only one semester and even when they received the benefit during a year when they did not actually teach. His recommendation was to change the benefit to be conditional on having taught without compensation for three years before being entitled to the benefit.

90. Dean Sponsler to Dr. Preston and President Carter, memorandum, dated September 24, 1984, on "Results of the July 1984 Bar Examination," President's Law School Correspondence 1984–85, Loyola Archives; Dean Sponsler to Faculty, memorandum, September 30, 1985 (on "1985 July Louisiana Bar Exam Results" [Loyola again coming in third in the state]), President's Law School Correspondence 1985, Loyola Archives. Occasionally, Loyola came in second, as in the February 1984 bar exam, or even first, as in February 1985.

91. *Code,* November 1984, 1.

92. Carolyn McNabb, "Loyola Ranks Third on Bar Exam," *Code,* October 1986 (for the third year in a row).

93. "Editorials: Required Classes Drown Creativity," *Code,* October 1986.

94. Miles Trapolin, "Class Changes Suggested," *Code,* February 1986.

95. Mike Trapolin, "Incoming Students Must Take Poverty Law Class," *Code,* April 1986.

96. Trapolin, "Incoming Students Must Take Poverty Law Class," quoting Associate Dean Jim Klebba.

97. Maher v. Roe, 432 U.S. 464 (1977); San Antonio Independent School District v. Rodriguez, 411 U.S. 1 (1973); Dandridge v. Williams, 397 U.S. 471 (1970).

98. Guido Calabresi, *The Costs of Accidents: A Legal and Economic Analysis* (New Haven: Yale University Press, 1970); Guido Calabresi, "Some Thoughts on Risk Distribution and the Law of Torts," *Yale Law Journal* 70 (1961): 499; Richard A. Posner, *The Economics of Justice* (Cambridge: Harvard University Press, 1983); Richard A. Posner, *Frontiers of Legal Theory* (Cambridge: Harvard University Press, 2001). Law and economics led to other approaches including behavioral economics and games theory.

99. Modern tort law reflects cost-benefit analysis, but constitutional doctrine was impacted as well, perhaps most directly in modern procedural due process analysis as developed by the U.S. Supreme Court in the *Matthews v. Eldridge* case (Matthews v. Eldridge, 424 U.S. 319 [1976]).

100. Roberto Mangabeira Unger, *The Critical Legal Studies Movement* (Cambridge: Harvard University Press, 1983); Derrick Bell, *Race, Racism and American Law* (Boston: Little, Brown, 1973); Catharine MacKinnon, *Sexual Harassment of Working Women* (New Haven: Yale University Press, 1979); Catharine MacKinnon, *Feminism Unmodified* (Cambridge: Harvard University

Press, 1988); Jean Stefancic and Richard Delgado, *Critical Race Theory: An Introduction* (New York: New York University Press, 2001).

101. MacKinnon, *Sexual Harassment of Working Women;* MacKinnon, *Feminism Unmodified.* See Martha Chamallas, *Introduction to Feminist Legal Theory* (New York: Aspen Law and Business, 1999); and Nancy Levit and Robert R. M. Verchick, *Feminist Legal Theory* (New York: New York University Press, 2006).

102. Billie Tully, "Loyola Seeks Order of the Coif," *Code,* September 1986.

103. Francis Allen to the law school, Loyola Archives.

104. Billie Tully, "Coif Rejects Law School's Application," *Code,* February 1987.

105. Subsequently, in the late 1990s another faculty member similarly denied tenure initially by the Faculty Rank and Tenure Committee, moved the committee to reconsider its vote. That faculty member was more fortunate and successfully convinced the committee to reconsider its vote and change it, voting the second time to grant the professor tenure.

106. Frances Jones, "Spend Summer in Mexico," *Code,* October 1987.

107. Kevin Katner, "Viva Loyola Law in Mexico," *Code,* September 29, 1989.

108. Rick Bissell, "Sarah Weddington Speaks on Abortions," *Code,* November 1975.

109. Marisa Campagna, "Women Students Host Sarah Weddington," *Code,* February 1987.

110. Albert Nicaud, "Privacy Symposium Widely Attended," *Code,* April 1988.

111. Notes from Thomas Sponsler (on file with the author). See http://lpdb.la.gov/Serving%20The%20Public/Programs/Capital%20Post%20Conviction%20Project%20of%20Louisiana.php.

112. Sponsler went on to serve as dean of Albany Law School until his retirement in 2002.

113. Geri Flaum, "Street Law Program Kicks Off at Loyola Law," *Code,* April 1991.

114. Jim Mullen, "Faculty Diversification Blue," *Code,* November 1990; Melissa Nanni and Mike Villalobois, "Rebuttal to Faculty Diversification Blues," *Code,* November 1990.

115. Demetrie E. Ford and Louella P. Givens, "A Minority's View of Law School," *Code,* November 1989.

116. North Carolina Central was a public institution set up to provide a legal education to blacks in North Carolina in 1939, since segregation shut the doors of the University of North Carolina at Chapel Hill to blacks. At the time, North Carolina was accredited by the ABA but had not been granted AALS membership. AALS granted membership to the school in 2012.

117. ABA Section of Legal Education and Admissions to the Bar, available at www.americanbar.org/groups/legal_education/resources/aba_approved_law_schools/by_year_approved.html.

118. *Law School Bulletin,* 1991–92.

119. "504 New Lawyers Certified," *Times-Picayune,* November 3, 1991, 4G. Tulane's bar pass rate was 70 percent, LSU's was 78 percent, and Southern's was 38 percent.

120. Judith N. Collins, "NALP Research: Salaries for New Lawyers: An Update on Where We Are and How We Got Here," *NALP Bulletin,* August 2012, available at www.nalp.org/uploads/0812Research.pdf.

121. *Report of the Louisiana Bar Foundation, Conclave on Legal Education and Professional Development* [Garsaud Report] (1995), 107, 122.

122. Richard A. White, "Variations in the Success Rates of Minority and Nonminority Candidates in the AALS Faculty Appointments Register," *AALS Newsletter,* March 1996, available at

www.aals.org/services_newsletter_articles_3–96b.php. See also David Segal, "What They Don't Teach Law Students: Lawyering," *New York Times,* November 19, 2011.

123. Linda A. Bell, "UPS and Dowes: The Annual Report on the Economic Status of the Profession: Academic Salaries since the Early 1970s," *Academe* 85 (March–April 1999): 11; Maryse Eymonerie, "Diversity within Adversity: The Annual Report on the Economic Status of the Profession, 1991–92," *Academe* 78, no. 2 (March–April 1992): 7, 12.

124. *Legal Education and Professional Development—An Educational Continuum, Report of the Task Force on Law Schools and the Profession: Narrowing the Gap* (1992), American Bar Association Section of Legal Education and Admission [MacCrate Report].

125. MacCrate Report, 113.

126. MacCrate Report, 27–30.

127. MacCrate Report, 67–74.

128. Jennifer M. Gardner, "The 1990–91 Recession: How Bad Was the Labor Market?," *Monthly Labor Review* 117, no. 3 (June 1994), available at www.bls.gov/mir/1994/06/1451full.pdf.

129. "Lateral" is a term used to denote an individual who has experience or who has been out in practice for a term of years.

130. MacCrate Report, 76.

131. MacCrate Report, 79–80.

132. MacCrate Report, 121–25. The MacCrate Report then broke down each skill and value and discussed each in depth, formulating the different sets of skills that constituted each fundamental skill.

133. MacCrate Report, 112.

134. Louisiana Task Force on Women in the Courts Final Report 1992, Supreme Court of Louisiana, New Orleans.

135. Louisiana Task Force on Women in the Courts Final Report 1992, Supreme Court of Louisiana, New Orleans, p. 5.

136. Jeannette F. Swent, "Gender Bias at the Heart of Justice: An Empirical Study of State Task Forces," *Southern California Review of Law & Women's Studies* 6 (Fall 1996):1 (discussing task force reports from California, Colorado, Florida, Illinois, Maryland, Massachusetts, Michigan, Minnesota, Nevada, New Jersey, New York, Rhode Island, Utah, and Washington). See also Judith Resnick, "'Naturally' without Gender: Women, Jurisdiction, and the Federal Courts," *New York University Law Review* 66: 1682.

137. Louisiana Task Force on Women in the Courts, 113.

138. Louisiana Task Force on Women in the Courts, 114.

139. Louisiana Task Force on Women in the Courts, 31.

140. *Law School Bulletin*, 1992–93. The United States Supreme Court recognized sexual harassment as a form of sex discrimination in 1986. Meritor Savings Bank, FSB v. Vinson, 477 U.S. 57 (1986).

141. Bob McKnight, "Dean Sets Out Goals, Hopes," *Code,* November 7, 1990.

142. Amanda Winters, "What Has This School Done for You Lately?" *Code,* April 1991.

143. Angela Heath Waldhien, "Judge Louis Westerfield," *Code,* September 1994. Prior to taking up the deanship at Mississippi, Westerfield was appointed to serve on the Lousiana Court of Appeal for the Second Circuit in Shreveport, to fill the seat of departing Judge Carl E. Stewart,

also a Loyola Law graduate, who had been appointed to serve on the United States Court of Appeals for the Fifth Circuit.

144. From 1986 to 1989, the percentage of minorities at the law school fluctuated from 9 percent in 1989–90 to 11 percent in 1986–87. Prior to that, the percentage of minorities at the law school since 1974 was less than 10 percent, often falling as low as 5 percent (in 1977, 1978, and 1985) for the day division. In his first year as dean, the percentage of minorities went up to 15 percent, and in his last year it rose to 31 percent (Law faculty meeting, February 16, 1995, attachments).

145. Shea Watkins, "Loyola Ponders Loan Forgiveness," *Code,* March 1990. Gary Clements spearheaded the drive at LPILG to establish a loan-forgiveness program at Loyola (Sheila Watkins, "LPILG," *Code,* November 1990). Matthew Wolf, "Loan Forgiveness Program for Public Interest Grads in Place," *Code,* Spring 1992; Matthew Wolf, "First Recipient of Loan Forgiveness Honored at Luncheon," *Code,* Spring 1992.

146. Student Bar Association Report, October 25, 1993, Loyola Law School Archives.

147. Westerfield suffered a fatal heart attack in 1996, two years after leaving Loyola. Dean Bromberger established the Westerfield Fellows as a way to bring to the law school highly credentialed individuals interested in pursuing a career in teaching law to teach first-year students, while providing the Fellows time and resources to develop their scholarship and teaching competence. The majority of Westerfield Fellows have been invited to join tenure-track law faculty positions throughout the country.

CHAPTER SIX

1. Dean's monthly report to the President for September, 1939, October 3, 1939, Loyola Archives.

2. Dean's report to the President for October 1939, November 3, 1939, Loyola Archives.

3. *Law School Bulletin,* 1953–54, 12; "Loyola to Assist in Legal Program," *Times-Picayune,* February 12, 1953.

4. Stevens, *Law School: Legal Education in America,* 215.

5. "Poor May Get New Legal Aid," *Times-Picayune,* November 6, 1966; "Law, Poverty Program Near," *Times-Picayune,* November 5, 1966.

6. "A Proposal to the Council on Legal Education for Professional Responsibility, Inc. for Support of a Civil and Criminal Clinical Education Program submitted by Loyola University Law School," November 9, 1970, Loyola Archives–Law School Law Clinic.

7. Marcel Garsaud, interview by author, notes on file with author.

8. In 1969, the ABA proposed a "Model Practice Rule," which allowed students to practice law under the supervision of licensed attorneys (ABA Model Student Practice Rule § III). See George K. Walker, "A Model Rule for Student Practice in the United States Courts," *Washington and Lee Law Review* 37 (1980): 1101, 1104–5.

9. Gordon Gsell, "Justice Barham Calls for Student Legal Aid 'Army': Idea Is Proposed before Young Lawyers," *Times-Picayune,* May 1, 1971.

10. La.Sup.Ct.R.Vix-A (March 3, 1971), Current Minute Book, Supreme Court of Louisiana,

October 7, 1968–April 2, 1971. See Sam A. LeBlanc III, "Debate over the Law Clinic Practice Rule: Redux," *Tulsa Law Review* 74 (1999–2000): 219, 220–22.

11. "Court Rules Changed," *Code,* March 1971.

12. Frank Achary, "The Legal Clinic," *Code,* Fall 1972.

13. John Occhipinti, "Lemann Answers Swaim's Charges" *Code,* April 1974.

14. Letter from CLEPR of April 1, 1971; letter of June 7, 1971, President's Files, Loyola Archives; "School Given Grant of $25,000: Clinical Legal Studies to Begin at Loyola," *Times-Picayune,* April 8, 1971.

15. John Occhipinti, "Lemann Answers Swaims' Charges," *Code,* April 1974.

16. Notes of telephone message from Dean Garsaud to Father Carter, March 20, 1975, Law School Clinic, 1970–83, Loyola Archives.

17. Frank Schultz, "Law Clinic," *Code,* November 1974. Some law faculty criticized the clinic because of its cost and doubts about its benefit to the students.

18. Agreement between Louisiana Commission on Legal Education and Clinical Services and Loyola University of the South, April 1, 1978 (third year of grant for the clinic), Loyola Archives.

19. The grant was in the amount of $24,300. Telegram to President, Loyola, dated September 7, 1978, and correspondence in President's Law School General Correspondence File, Loyola Archives.

20. 1986 Self-Study, ABA Accreditation Reinspection Site Visit, November 1986, Loyola Archives.

21. Dean Garsaud to the President, dated June 29, 1978, President's Law School General Correspondence File, Loyola Archives.

22. Meg Copernoll, "New Professors Add Depth to Law Faculty: Nelson Named Clinic Director," *Code,* October 31, 1979.

23. Kenneth Beck, "Staff Grows with Gallagher, Regan," *Code,* October 1985.

24. Terry Herndon, "Is Public Education a Casualty of Reaganomics?," *New York Times,* November 15, 1981.

25. LSU Law School began to offer an immigration law clinic in spring 2009.

26. Evaluation of the Loyola University Law Clinic, Dr. Paul V. Murray, Department of Education, Loyola University, August 1983, Law School Clinic–1970–83, Loyola Archives.

27. Fed. Reg. 49, no. 115, 24469–70 (June 13, 1984).

28. Fed. Reg. 49, no. 115, 24470. The Legal Services Corporation is a Washington, D.C., nonprofit corporation chartered by the federal government in 1974 to provide free civil legal services to the poor.

29. Fed. Reg. 49, no. 115, 24470.

30. John Nelson to Dean Sponsler, memorandum, December 10, 1984 (description of the Loyola Law School Clinic), 9.

31. John Nelson to Dean Sponsler, memorandum, December 10, 1984 (description of the Loyola Law School Clinic), 13–17.

32. Stevens, *Law School: Legal Education in America,* 240–41.

33. The standard provided: "The law school shall afford to full-time faculty members whose primary responsibilities are in its professional skills program a form of security of position reasonably similar to tenure and perquisites reasonably similar to those provided other full-time

faculty . . ." (Standard 405[e], Council of the Section of Legal Education and Admissions to the Bar, ABA).

34. Thomas Sponsler to Vice President for Academic Affairs, memorandum, June 28, 1984, Proposed Standard 405(e) of the ABA Standards for Approval of Law Schools, Law School Accreditations 1981–86, Loyola Archives. Schools would be given two years to come into compliance with the plan.

35. Dean Garsaud to AALS, correspondence dated April 10, 1981, Law School Accreditations 1981–86, Loyola Archives.

36. *Faculty Handbook,* chap. 11A, adopted by Loyola's Board of Trustees on November 17, 1988.

37. Supplemental Appropriations Act, Legal Service Corporation, Pub. L. No. 99–88, 99 Stat. 305 (Aug. 15, 1985). The grant was for $4 million "to remain available until expended" (ibid.). Drake University School of Law in Des Moines, Iowa, received the same amount. See also Legal Services Corporation to President Carter, dated December 27, 1985, informing the University of the grant (Law School Poverty Law Center 1985, Loyola Archives). Michael S. Gallagher to Thomas Sponsler, memorandum on criteria for Gillis W. Long expenditures, November 17, 1985, McAulay Papers, Loyola Law School Archives.

38. Cong. Rec. H3974 (June 6, 1985).

39. Cong. Rec. H3974 (June 6, 1985).

40. Thomas Sponsler, e-mail interview by author (notes on file with author).

41. Supplemental Appropriations Act, Legal Services Corporation, Pub. L. No. 99–88, 99 Stat. 305 (Aug. 15, 1985).

42. Supplemental Appropriations Act, Legal Services Corporation, Pub. L. No. 99–88, 99 Stat. 305 (Aug. 15, 1985).

43. President Carter to Senator Hatfield, dated June 24, 1985, President's Files, Law School Poverty Law Center 1985, Loyola Archives). Father Carter sent letters to many senators and representatives thanking them for their support and informing them as to the specific measures and plans the law school had for use of the funds.

44. Michael Gallagher, S.J., to Dean Sponsler, memorandum, dated August 13, 1985, President's Files, Law School Poverty Law Center 1985, Loyola Archives.

45. Request for new position submitted to University Budget Committee for the School of Law, attached to Gillis Long submission, President's Files, Law School Poverty Law Center 1985, Loyola Archives. The supervising attorney had a great number of other duties as well. In addition, the grant supported the hiring of a legal secretary.

46. President's Files, Law School Poverty Law Center 1985, Loyola Archives. The first person to be hired for this position was Don Woodman (Miles Trapolin, "New Computers Aid Legal Studies," *Code,* April 1987).

47. Memorandum to Skills Committee, dated October 23, 1984, Loyola Law School Archives.

48. Report to the Skills Committee, from Pamela L. Ebel, Associate Dean for Special Programs, on Five-Year Report and Recommendations for the Skills Curriculum, August 27, 1990, McAulay Papers, Loyola Law School Archives.

49. Paul Guillotte Jr., "Skills Committee Presents Law Students' Concerns," *Code,* November 1987.

50. Guillotte, "Skills Committee Presents Law Students' Concerns."

51. Patricia Regan, "Clinic Receives Grant for Up-dating Tel-Law," *Code,* February 1987.

52. "Johnson Seeks Judiciary," *Code,* November 1988.

53. Kenneth Beck, "Staff Grows with Gallagher, Regan," *Code,* October 1985.

54. "Report to the Faculty on the Law Clinic: Educational Objectives, Teaching Methods and Administrative Policies," September 1990, McAulay Papers, Loyola Law School Archives.

55. Special faculty meeting minutes, March 31, 1992, and faculty meeting minutes, April 6, 1992.

56. Susan Finch, "Lawyer-Professor Has History of Advocacy," *Times-Picayune,* September 20, 1998.

57. Faculty meeting minutes, April 11, 1995.

58. Faculty meeting minutes, November 11, 1997.

59. Adam Glazer, "Note: The Implications of Changes to Louisiana's Law Clinic Student Practice Rule," *Georgetown Journal of Legal Ethics* 12, no. 751 (1999); LeBlanc, *Debate over the Law Clinic Practice Rule.*

60. LA. Sup. Ct. R. 20 (Limited Participation of Law Students in Trial Work). See Christian Leadership Conf. v. Supreme Court of Louisiana, 252 F. 3d 781 (5th Cir. 2001). See also Peter A. Joy, "Political Interference with Clinical Legal Education: Denying Access to Justice, *Tulane Law Review* 74, no. 235 (1999).

61. Chris Gray, "Court Reins in Student Lawyers," *Times-Picayune,* June 18, 1998; James Gill, "High Court Target of Disgust," *Times-Picayune,* June 28, 1998.

62. Supreme Court Rule XX, June 17, 1998, amended in 1999.

63. Mark Schleifstein, "Professors to Protest Curbs on Law Clinics—Supreme Court Restrictions Will Limit Legal Services for Poor People, They Say," *Times-Picayune,* January 5, 1999; Mark Schleifstein, "Professors Protest Law Clinic Rules—Access to Courts Restricted for Poor, Minorities, Critics Say," *Times-Picayune,* January 8, 1999.

64. Mark Schleifstein, "Groups File Suit to Challenge Limits on Law Clinics—Rules Violate Constitution, They Say," *Times-Picayune,* April 17, 1999.

65. Susan Finch, "New Law Clinic Rules Hot Topic at Forum," *Times-Picayune,* September 17, 1998; Susan Finch, "Business Had Hoped to Oust Incumbent," *Times-Picayune,* October 4, 1998.

66. Susan Finch, "Cusimano Facing Hurdle in Runoff," *Times-Picayune,* October 5, 1998.

67. Faculty meeting minutes, August 12, 2004.

68. Faculty meeting minutes, October 2004.

69. Louisiana Senate Bill 549. See Robert R. Kuehn and Bridget M. McCormack, "Lessons from Forty Years of Interference in Law School Clinics," *Georgetown Journal of Legal Ethics* 24 (2011): 59, 67; Adam Babich, "Controversy, Conflicts, and Law School Clinics," *Clinical Law Review* 17 (2011): 469.

70. "Opinion: Law Clinic Ban Dies a Good Death," *CityBusiness,* May 20, 2010, available at http://neworleanscitybusiness.com/blog/2010/05/20/opinion-law-clinic-ban-dies-a-good-death/.

71. Steven Griffin and Brian Bromberger, "Legislation Would Handcuff Law Clinics," *Times-Picayune,* May 1, 2010.

72. American Bar Association, Section of Legal Education & Admissions to the Bar, Standards for Approval of Law Schools, Standard 302(a)(4)(2011).

73. ABA Standard 303, Curriculum.

74. Diane Ried, "Two-Year Law Schools?" *Code,* April 1976.

CHAPTER SEVEN

1. Bernard A. Cook gives a full treatment of this period in his history of Loyola University, *Founded on Faith,* 193–211.

2. Academic Unit Three-Year Plan September 1982–August 1985, submitted to Standing Council for Academic Planning, Loyola University New Orleans, Louisiana, School of Law, April 8, 1982, Dennis Rousseau Papers, Loyola Law School Archives.

3. Moot Court Board to Father Michael F. Kennelly, S.J., memorandum November 14, 1973; Dean Garsaud to Very Rev. Michael F. Kennelly, S.J., President, dated November 14, 1973; John L. Eckholdt, Senior Vice President for Finance, to Mr. Ralph C. Rushing Assistant Controller, memorandum, dated November 15, 1973 (authorizing the transfer of funds to pay for the travel), Loyola Archives. Not all requests for contingency funds were granted. A request for contingency funds to cover a shortfall in the law review budget in 1976 was rejected; the president recommended that the deficit be covered "from within the existing budget" (Robert Preston, Vice President for Academic Affairs to Marcel Garsaud Jr., Dean, memorandum, September 17, 1976, subject Law Review Contingency Request). Financial decisions may have been squarely within the control of the University, but academic decisions remained with the law school.

4. "Law Strike Threatened," *Code,* December 1970.

5. Clem Kennington, "The President Speaks," *Code,* December 1970. Construction began in 1971. "Construction Contract Awarded," *Code,* April 1971.

6. Dave Breen, "Father Carter Meets with Law Students," *Code,* April 1973; "Father Carter: Another View of University Funding," *Code,* April 1973. A similar exchange occurred in 1975 ("Tuition Editorial Causes Flak," *Code,* November 1975; "Letter to the Editor" from Father Carter).

7. Father Carter to George Lange, President, SBA, dated April 2, 1973, President's Law School General Correspondence 1967–73, Loyola Archives.

8. Father Carter to George Lange, President, SBA, dated April 2, 1973, President's Law School General Correspondence 1967–73, Loyola Archives.

9. Dean Garsaud to Rev. James Carter, Provost, memorandum, March 1, 1972, in which he requests approximately an additional $35,000 a year. Dean Garsaud attached a letter from then Loyola president Jolley promising upon his employment as dean to "bring the level of faculty salaries . . . to a competitive position with the law schools in our area within a period of three years."

10. Michael Kennelly, President, to Father Carter, Provost, March 29, 1972, Loyola Archives.

11. Marcel Garsaud, Dean, to Rev. James C. Carter, President, memorandum, dated November 24, 1975, subject: Budget Requests and Advisory Council Meeting; and the president's reply (dated November 26, 1975, President's Law School General Correspondence 1974–76, Loyola Archives), discussing, among other things, the "overhead" charged to the law school, problems with law faculty raises, and the failure of the University to devote excess law tuition revenues back to the law school; see also memoranda dated November 10, 1975, from Dean Garsaud requesting

an additional law librarian; two new faculty positions; the creation of a teaching fellowship on an annual basis; and a "major and realistic increase in faculty salaries"; and the president's response of November 13, 1975, in which he notes that the budget requests are not timely and that law faculty and students are "still under the impression that law gifts and tuition ... [are] not being used for law education," and expresses concern over the future of the common law program, given the decline in law applications.

12. President Carter to Dean Garsaud, memorandum, dated February 20, 1981, on Faculty Hiring, President's Law School General Correspondence, Loyola Archives.

13. Rev. James C. Carter, Provost, to Dean Garsaud, memorandum, November 16, 1961, subject: "Opening of Classes for the Fall Semester," Loyola Archives.

14. Marcel Garsaud Jr., Dean, to Dr. Robert Preston, Vice President for Academic Affairs, memorandum, dated October 21, 1976.

15. Vice President for Academic Affairs to Dean Garsaud, memorandum, dated January 19, 1978, President's Law School General Correspondence, Loyola Archives.

16. Academic Unit Three Year Plan September 1982–August 1985, School of Law, submitted to Standing Council for Academic Planning (SCAP), Loyola University New Orleans, Louisiana, April 8, 1982, p. 2, Rousseau Papers, Loyola Law School Archives.

17. The 1979 inspection that culminated in a 1981 report found a student-faculty ratio of 1:33. It found faculty salaries too low when compared with national averages and also found insufficient support for faculty (Academic Unit Three Year Plan September 1982–August 1985, School of Law, submitted to Standing Council for Academic Planning (SCAP), Loyola University New Orleans Louisiana, April 8, 1982, pp. 20–21, Rousseau Papers, Loyola Law School Archives.

18. James C. Carter, President, to Law Student, February 16, 1982, President's Law School General Correspondence, Loyola Archives.

19. Richard McCormack, Chair, Committee on Tuition Increases, to President Carter, April 7, 1982, President's Law School Correspondence, box 17, folder 1, Loyola Archives.

20. President Carter to Richard McCormack, dated April 16, 1982, President's Law School Correspondence, box 17, folder 1, Loyola Archives.

21. Robert Preston, Vice President for Academic Affairs, to President Carter, memorandum, February 6, 1981, Loyola Archives.

22. Tom Sponsler to Rev. James C. Carter, S.J., memorandum, dated May 24, 1983, subject: memo of our discussion of March 28, 1983.

23. Tom Sponsler to Rev. James C. Carter, S.J., memorandum, dated May 24, 1983.

24. For a brief period between its move from Bobet to Thomas More Hall, the law school was housed at Biever Hall (Board Minutes, April 3, 1941, Loyola Archives [planning the move from Bobet to Thomas More Hall at 6333 St. Charles Avenue]; Board Minutes, May 28, 1941, Loyola Archive [discussing a temporary move to Biever Hall or Otis, while renovations were completed at Thomas More, and discussing the planned renovations]). The law school regent, Father Walsh, urged the president to "go into the plans more fully with the Dean and Acting Dean of the Law school." The law school wanted a two-story rather than a one-story structure. The president was concerned about the additional expense of building a two-story building. See also Board minutes, May 28, 1941, Loyola Archives. The naming of Thomas More Hall was the subject of a contest by the Alpha Sigma Nu Fraternity. Of the student-submitted names, the Board selected two

as winners: William Byrnes Hall and John St. Paul Hall. Unfortunately, the Board chose Thomas More Hall, presumably because More is the patron saint of lawyers (Board minutes, August 18, 1942, and October 5, 1942, Loyola Archives). Dean Connor, still serving in the Army, objected to the naming of Thomas More Hall on the grounds that St. Thomas More had practiced the common law, not the civil law "as it is followed in Louisiana" (Board minutes, January 11, 1943, Loyola Archives). The law school building houses a memorial to St. Thomas More, erected during the deanship of John Makdisi.

25. Dean Thomas Sponsler et al., to Rev. James C. Carter, S.J., memorandum, dated January 15, 1984, Preliminary Evaluation of Mathes Report, dated January 12, 1984, Rousseau Papers, Law School Archives. See also Dean Sponsler to Dr. Preston, Vice President Academic Affairs, memorandum, September 5, 1984, President's Law School Correspondence 1984–85, Loyola Archives.

26. Dean Sponsler to Dr. Preston, Vice President Academic Affairs, memorandum, September 5, 1984, President's Law School Correspondence 1984–85, Loyola Archives.

27. Report of Ad Hoc Committee on Law School/University Finances and the Five-Year Planning Committee by Chair, James M. Klebba, to Dean Westerfield, July 13, 1992, Rousseau Papers, Loyola Law School Archives.

28. "Budget Cuts to Affect Alumni Mailing," *Code,* Spring 1992.

29. Associate Dean for Student Services Katherine Schwab to Dean Louis Westerfield, memorandum, September 4, 1990, "Student Services, Placement, and Moot Court—Report," McAulay Papers, Loyola Law School Archives.

30. "The State of Instructional Resources Loyola School of Law," Don Woodman, Director, September 19, 1990, McAulay Papers, Loyola Law School Archives.

31. Prior to 1987, in fact, less than 10 percent of law school revenues were going to University overhead/general expenses. In 1985–87, for example, only 1.6 percent of law school revenues went to University overhead/general expenses.

32. James M. Klebba to Dean Louis Westerfield, memorandum, dated April 15, 1993, "A Proposal for Fiscal Autonomy for the Law School—A Formula-Based Budgeting Arrangement," Rousseau Papers, Loyola Law School Archives.

33. Faculty meeting minutes, February 22, 1995, March 9, 1995, and March 23, 1995.

34. Faculty meeting minutes, February 16, 1996, and March 12, 1996.

35. In addition, the law school would also pay the University any "recoveries" due from any grants awarded to the law school such as those for the Gillis Long Poverty Law Center.

36. The initiative had begun during Dean Westerfield's tenure as dean and proceeded under Interim Dean Garsaud's tenure. Makdisi made it clear, however, that he stood ready to enforce the rule (faculty meeting minutes, August 7, 1996). Makdisi also instituted a practice of visiting classes unannounced, unless the law faculty member objected. While this practice probably improved law faculty performance in the classroom, it created tension among tenured faculty.

37. Faculty meeting minutes, August 7, 1996.

38. Faculty meeting minutes, May 12, 1997.

39. Faculty meeting minutes, August 14, 1997 (attachments).

40. Faculty meeting minutes, November 11, 1997 (attachments).

41. Faculty meeting minutes, January 13, 1998; Faculty minutes, February 9, 1998.

42. Louisiana offers two testing sessions—the primary one in the summer is reported in this

discussion. The February bar exam generally draws fewer test takers, and I did not include those results in this discussion. There were variances throughout, but the February bar, for the most part, showed the Loyola drop below the statewide average except in February 1997.

43. Faculty meeting minutes, September 12, 2000.

44. Wendell Gauthier died in 2001 at the age of fifty-eight ("Wendell Gauthier, 58, Dies; Lawyer in Big Damage Suits," *New York Times,* December 12, 2001). Mr. Gauthier's family, together with Michael X. St. Martin, established the Gauthier–St. Martin Eminent Scholar Chair in Environmental Law, the only endowed chair at the law school. The Gauthiers were generous to Tulane University and LSU as well.

45. "The Big Four Who Battle Big Tobacco," *Bloomberg Businessweek,* June 15, 1997.

46. Verchick subsequently served in the Obama administration as deputy associate administrator for policy at the U.S. Environmental Protection Agency from 2009 to 2010. After a Fulbright-Nehru Environmental Leadership Award served in India as a visiting scholar at the Center for Policy Research in New Delhi, he returned to Loyola, where he continues to teach environmental law courses. He also serves as Senior Fellow at Tulane University's Disaster Resilience Leadership Academy in Tulane's School of Social Work.

47. M. Isabel Medina, "Justifying Integration of Domestic Violence throughout the Law School Curriculum: An Introduction to the Symposium," *Loyola Law Review* 47, no. 1 (Spring 2001). The entire volume is devoted to articles produced for the symposium.

CHAPTER EIGHT

1. Coleman Warner, "Loyola Law School Chooses New Dean," *Times-Picayune,* May 8, 2003, B-3.

2. Shortly after hiring Brian Bromberger to lead the law school, Father Knoth was the subject of an investigation into possible inappropriate conduct. He resigned shortly thereafter, and an interim president was appointed while a presidential search was conducted and Father Wildes selected as Knoth's permanent replacement. Father Knoth had spearheaded substantial invigoration of, and fund-raising for, the University as a whole. Knoth's adeptness at communication facilitated change at the institution and helped usher it into modernity.

3. President's Convocation Address, Fall 2004, available at http://president.loyno.edu/sites/president.loyno.edu/files/convocation-20040823.pdf.

4. "ABA Approves Southern Plans for Part-Time Evening School," *Baton Rouge Advocate,* June 17, 2004.

5. Coleman Warner and Bruce Nolan, "University to Honor Landrieu family—But Church May Have Quarrel with Loyola," *Times Picayune,* May, 5, 2005; Coleman Warner and Bruce Nolan, "Loyola Unfazed by Church Criticism—Archbishop Opposes Honoring Landrieus," *Times-Picayune,* May 13, 2005.

6. Cook, *Founded on Faith,* 238.

7. *Times-Picayune,* August 26, 2005.

8. Mark Schleifstein, "Katrina Puts End to Lull—Storm's Western Path Puts N.O. on Edge: Hurricane Lashes South Florida, Leaves Six People Dead," *Times-Picayune,* August 27, 2005.

9. Gordon Russell, "Nagin Orders First Ever Mandatory Evacuation of New Orleans," *Times-Picayune,* August 28, 2005; Christine Hauser and Thomas J. Lueck, "Mandatory Evacuation Ordered for New Orleans as Storm Nears," *New York Times,* August 28, 2005.

10. Douglas Brinkley, *The Great Deluge: Hurricane Katrina, New Orleans, and the Mississippi Gulf Coast* (New York: Harpers Collins, 2006); Jed Horne, *Breach of Faith: Hurricane Katrina and the Near Death of a Great American City* (New York: Random House, 2006); John McQuaid and Mark Schleifstein, *Path of Destruction: The Devastation of New Orleans and the Coming Age of Superstorms* (New York: Little, Brown, 2006). See U.S. Congress, Senate, Committee on Homeland Security and Government Affairs, 109th Cong., *Hurricane Katrina: A Nation Still Unprepared* (Washington, D.C.: U.S. Government Printing Office, 2006).

11. The surge of water brought by the storm together with faulty design and construction of levees built to protect the greater metropolitan New Orleans area resulted in a number of breaches along the Industrial Canal levee, which flooded the Ninth Ward, a predominantly poor, black area of the city; St. Bernard Parish, a predominantly white area; and New Orleans East. Breaches at the Seventeenth Street Canal and the London Avenue Canal flooded and devastated predominantly white, middle-class, and wealthy parts of the city—the Lakeview area, parts of Old Metairie, and parts of uptown New Orleans, including Tulane University—as well as financially, racially, and ethnically diverse areas of the city like Broadmoor, Gentilly, and Mid-City (M. Isabel Medina, "Confronting the Rights Deficit at Home: Is the Nation Prepared in the Aftermath of Katrina? Confronting the Myth of Efficiency" *California Western Law Review,* 43 [2006]: 11).

12. Allison Plyer, "Facts for Features: Katrina Impact," New Orleans, The Data Center, 2014, available at www.datacenterresearch.org/about-us/.

13. *Hurricane Katrina and New Orleans Universities,* AAUP Report, May–June 2007.

14. Interview and written recollections of Barbara Wilson (on file with the author).

15. Brian Huddleston, "A Semester in Exile: Experiences and Lessons Learned during Loyola University New Orleans School of Law's Fall 2005 Hurricane Katrina Relocation," *Journal of Legal Education* 57, no. 3 (September 2007): 319–48.

16. One of the characteristics of the operation of the Houston program was a cessation of faculty governance. The first meeting of the year was held on August 23, before the hurricane. Some law faculty met in Houston during this period. Normal faculty meetings resumed in spring 2016.

17. Five law professors were exempted from teaching that fall: Professors Algero, Ciolino, Viator, Wallace, and Woods. Ciolino assisted the law school set up a temporary web page.

18. "Law Students Working within the Post-Katrina Legal Landscape: The Student Hurricane Network Annual Report October 2005–October 2006," ed. Laila Hlass, Morgan Williams, Josie Beets, Laurence Spollen, Kesav Wable, Jeremy Pfetsch, and Anna Arceneaux (copy of report with author).

19. Coleman Warner, "Loyola Still Weighing Storm-Related layoffs—President to Study Enrollment Statistics," *Times-Picayune,* November 15, 2002.

20. Brian Bromberger to faculty and staff, November 30, 2005.

21. John Pope, "Loyola Plans to Lay off Dozens—About 4,000 Students Expected Next Semester," *Times-Picayune,* December 7, 2005.

22. University Senate minutes, April 6, 2006, available at www.loyno.edu/universitysenate/sites/loyno.edu.universitysenate/files/Senate_min_40606.pdf.

23. University Senate minutes, Thursday, May 11, 2006, available at www.loyno.edu/universitysenate/sites/loyno.edu.universitysenate/files/20060511minutes.pdf.

24. University Senate minutes, April 20, 2006, available at www.loyno.edu/universitysenate/sites/loyno.edu.universitysenate/files/SenateMinutes04–20–06.pdf.

25. Jean-Paul Arguello, "Pathways Lawsuit Settled," *Maroon*. July 15, 2010.

26. *Hurricane Katrina and New Orleans Universities*, AAUP report, May–June 2007.

27. Loyola University New Orleans, AAUP, Approved by Committee 6/3/11, available at www.aaup.org/NR/rdonlyres/FEBA813E-E50A-421F-87F8–4AADF3F7A1D7/0/LOYOLAUNIVERSITYNEWORLEANS.pdf.

28. John Pope, "Censure of Loyola and UNO Is Lifted by National Education Group," *Times-Picayune*, June 13, 2011.

29. Scott T. Whittaker and Dona K. Renegar, "The Cause and Effect of Recent Changes to the Louisiana Bar Examination," *Louisiana Bar Journal* 61, no. 2 (August/September 2013): 90–96.

CONCLUSION

1. Garsaud Report, 29.

2. Garsaud Report, 32.

3. Garsaud Report, 83.

4. Garsaud Report, 97.

5. Garsaud Report, 101.

6. Garsaud Report, 107.

7. "Median Private Practice Starting Salaries for the Class of 2011 Plunge as Private Practice Jobs Continue to Erode," press release, Association for Legal Career Professionals, July 12, 2012, available at www.nalp.org/classof2011_salpressrel. The NALP reported the mean starting salary for the class of 2011 as $78,653, a drop of $14,000 from the 2009 mean starting salary. The NALP rate is likely to be much higher. Graduates may not realize they are going to be in solo practice until after they graduate and take the bar; at that point, they may not be reporting their employment status to their law schools. Nonetheless, the NALP claims to be basing its numbers on a 93 percent reporting rate. Class of 2011 National Summary Report, available at www.nalp.org/uploads/NatlSummChart_Classof2011.pdf.

8. "Median Private Practice Starting Salaries for the Class of 2011 Plunge as Private Practice Jobs Continue to Erode," press release, Association for Legal Career Professionals, July 12, 2012, available at www.nalp.org/classof2011_salpressrel.

9. "Search Wage Data for Your County," *ABA Journal* (March 2011), available at www.abajournal.com/magazine/article/search_wage_data_for_your_country; Rachel M. Sahorsky, "What America's Lawyers Earn," *ABA Journal* (March 2011), available at www.abajournal.com/magazine/article/what_americas_lawyers_earn/.

10. "LSATS Administered," Law School Admission Council, available at www.lsac.org/lsacresources/data/lsac-volume-summary.

11. William M. Sullivan, Anne Colby, Judith Welch Wegner, Lloyd Bond, and Lee S. Shulman, *Educating Lawyers: Preparation for the Profession of Law* (San Francisco: Jossey-Bass, 2007).

12. Scott Smallwood, "Faculty Salaries Rise by 3.4%; Law Professors Still Earn the Most," *Chronicle of Higher Education,* March 10, 2006, available at http://chronicle.com/article/Faculty-Salaries-Rise-by-34-/10320.

13. "Salaries of Federal Judges, Associate Justices, and Chief Justice since 1968," United States Courts, available at www.uscourts.gov/judgesAndJudgeships/JudicialCompensation/PaychartsTables.aspx.

14. Sam Favate, "Louisiana Law School Loses Dean before Grand Opening," *Wall Street Journal,* September 20, 2012.

15. Brian Z. Tamanaha, *Failing Law Schools* (Chicago: University of Chicago Press, 2012).

16. Richard Susskind, *The End of Lawyers? Rethinking the Nature of Legal Services* (Oxford: Oxford University Press, 2010).

BIBLIOGRAPHY

BOOKS

Anderson, R. Bentley. *Black, White, and Catholic: New Orleans Interracialism, 1947–1956*. Nashville: Vanderbilt University Press, 2005.

Austin, Allan W. *From Concentration Camp to Campus: Japanese American Students and World War II*. Urbana: University of Illinois Press, 2004.

Baker, Liva. *The Second Battle of New Orleans: The Hundred-Year Struggle to Integrate the Schools*. New York: HarperCollins, 1996.

Baudier, Roger. *The Catholic Church in Louisiana*. New Orleans: Catholic Church, 1939.

Bell, Derrick. *And We Are Not Saved*. New York: Basic, 1987.

———. *Race, Racism and American Law*. 1973. 4th ed. New York: Aspen Law and Business, 2000.

———. *Shades of Brown*. New York: Teachers College Press, 1980.

Billings, Warren M., ed. *The Historic Rules of the Supreme Court of Louisiana 1813–1879*. Lafayette: Center for Louisiana Studies University of Southwestern Louisiana, 1985.

Boyd, Susan K. *The ABA's First Section: Assuring a Qualified Bar*. Chicago: American Bar Association, 1993.

Calabresi, Guido. *The Costs of Accidents: A Legal and Economic Analysis*. New Haven: Yale University Press, 1970.

Carter, Hodding, ed. *The Past as Prelude: New Orleans 1718–1968*. New Orleans: Tulane University, 1968; distributed by Pelican.

Chamallas, Martha. *Introduction to Feminist Legal Theory*. New York: Aspen Law and Business, 1999.

Cook, Bernard A. *Founded on Faith: A History of Loyola University New Orleans*. New Orleans: Loyola University New Orleans, 2012.

Cummins, Light Townsend, and Glen Jeansonne, eds. *A Guide to the History of Louisiana*. Westport: Greenwood, 1982.

Curran, Robert Emmett. *A History of Georgetown University: From Academy to University, 1789–1889*. Washington, D.C.: Georgetown University Press, 2010.

Dauphine, James G. *A Question of Inheritance: Religion, Education, and Louisiana's Cultural Boundary, 1880–1940.* Lafayette: Center for Louisiana Studies, University of Southwestern Louisiana, 1993.

Dawes, Dorothy, and Charles Nolan. *Religious Pioneers: Building the Faith in the Archdiocese of New Orleans.* New Orleans: Archdiocese of New Orleans, 2004.

Delgado, Richard, ed. *Critical Race Theory: The Cutting Edge.* Philadelphia: Temple University Press, 1995.

——. *The Rodrigo Chronicles: Conversations about America and Race.* New York: New York University Press, 1995.

Delgado, Richard, and Jean Stefancic. *Critical Race Theory: An Introduction.* New York: New York University Press, 2001.

Dudziak, Mary L. *Cold War Civil Rights: Race and the Image of American Democracy.* Princeton: Princeton University Press, 2000.

Dunbar-Nelson, Alice Moore. "People of Color in Louisiana." In *Creole: The History and Legacy of Louisiana's Free People of Color,* edited by Sybil Kein. Baton Rouge: Louisiana State University Press, 2000.

Durkin, Joseph T. *Georgetown University: First in the Nation's Capital.* New York: Doubleday, 1964.

——. *Georgetown University: The Middle Years (1840–1900).* Washington, D.C.: Georgetown University Press, 1963.

Dyer, John P. *Tulane: The Biography of a University 1834–1965.* New York: Harper and Row, 1966.

Emanuel, Rachel L., and Alexander P. Tureaud Jr. *A More Noble Cause: A. P. Tureaud and the Struggle for Civil Rights in Louisiana.* Baton Rouge: Louisiana State University Press, 2011.

Epstein, Cynthia Fuchs. *Women in Law.* 2nd ed. Urbana: University of Illinois Press, 1993.

Fairclough, Adam. *Race and Democracy: The Civil Rights Struggle in Louisiana, 1915–1972.* Athens: University of Georgia Press, 1995.

——. *Teaching Equality: Black Schools in the Age of Jim Crow.* Athens: University of Georgia Press, 2001.

Fischer, Roger A. *The Segregation Struggle in Louisiana 1862–77.* Urbana: University of Illinois Press, 1974.

Frystak, Shannon. *Our Minds on Freedom: Women and the Struggle for Black Equality in Louisiana, 1924–1967.* Baton Rouge: Louisiana State University Press, 2009.

Gould, Virginia Meacham. "Henriette Delille, Free Women of Color, and Catholicism in Antebellum New Orleans, 1727–1852." In *Beyond Bondage: Free Women of Color in the Americas,* edited by D. B. Gaspar D. C. Hine, 271–85. Urbana: University of Illinois Press, 2004.

Gould, Virginia Meacham, and Charles E. Nolan. "Mother Henriette DeLille (1812-1862): Servant of Slaves." In *Religious Pioneers: Building the Faith in the Archdiocese of New Orleans,* edited by Dorothy Dawes and Nolan, 25–36. New Orleans: Archdiocese of New Orleans, 2004.

Guide to the Louisiana Judiciary. Baton Rouge: Louisiana Governmental Studies, 1995.

Guinier, Lani, Michelle Fine, and Jane Balin. *Becoming Gentlemen: Women, Law School, and Institutional Change.* Boston: Beacon, 1997.

Hair, William Ivy. *Carnival of Fury: Robert Charles and the New Orleans Race Riot of 1900.* Baton Rouge: Louisiana State University Press, 1976.

Hargrave, W. Lee. *LSU Law: The Louisiana State University Law School from 1906 to 1977.* Baton Rouge: Louisiana State University Press, 2004.

Hofstadter, Richard, and Walter P. Metzger. *Academic Freedom in the United States.* New York: Columbia University Press, 1955.

Jacobson, Matthew Frye. *Whiteness of a Different Color: European Immigrants and the Alchemy of Race.* Cambridge: Harvard University Press, 1998.

Kein, Sybil, ed. *Creole: The History and Legacy of Louisiana's Free People of Color.* Baton Rouge: Louisiana State University Press, 2000.

Kemp, John R., ed. *Martin Behrman of New Orleans Memoirs of a City Boss.* Baton Rouge: Louisiana State University Press, 1977.

Kennedy, Duncan. *Legal Education and the Reproduction of Hierarchy: A Polemic Against the System.* New York: New York University, 2004. Originally self-published as a pamphlet in 1983.

King, Gilbert. *The Execution of Willie Francis: Race, Murder, and the Search for Justice in the American South.* New York: Perseus, 2008.

Kirby, Jack Temple. *Darkness at the Dawning Race and Reform in the Progressive South.* Philadelphia: Lippincott, 1972.

Kluger, Richard. *Simple Justice: The History of* Brown v. Board of Education *and Black America's Struggle for Equality.* New York: Knopf, 2004.

Labbe, Dolores Egger. *Jim Crow Comes to Church: The Establishment of Segregated Catholic Parishes in South Louisiana.* Lafayette: University of Southwestern Louisiana, 1971.

Leavitt, Mel. *A Short History of New Orleans.* San Francisco: Lexikos, 1982.

Levit, Nancy, and Robert R. M. Verchick. *Feminist Legal Theory.* New York: New York University Press, 2006.

Lindig, Carmen. *The Path from the Parlor: Louisiana Women 1879–1920.* Lafayette: Center for Louisiana Studies, University of Southwestern Louisiana, 1986.

Long, Alecia P. *The Great Southern Babylon—Sex, Race, and Respectability in New Orleans 1865–1920.* Baton Rouge: Louisiana State University Press, 2004.

MacCrate, Robert, ed. *Legal Education and Professional Development—An Educational Continuum.* Chicago: American Bar Association and West Publishing, 1992.

MacKinnon, Catharine A. *Feminism Unmodified.* Cambridge: Harvard University Press, 1988.

——. *Sexual Harassment of Working Women.* New Haven: Yale University Press, 1979.

McKinney, Louise. *New Orleans: A Cultural History.* Oxford: Oxford University Press, 2006.

Miller, Arthur Selwyn. *A "Capacity for Outrage": The Judicial Odyssey of J. Skelly Wright.* Westport: Greenwood, 1984.

Mohr, Clarence L., and Joseph E. Gordon. *Tulane: The Emergence of a Modern University, 1945–1980.* Baton Rouge: Louisiana State University Press, 2001.

Morello, Karen Berger. *The Invisible Bar: The Woman Lawyer in America: 1638 to the Present.* New York: Random House, 1986.

Nelson, John. *Loyola Law School Clinic.* New Orleans: Loyola University, 1984.

Nystrom, Justin A. *New Orleans after the Civil War: Race, Politics, and a New Birth of Freedom.* Baltimore: John Hopkins University Press, 2010.

Ochs, Stephen J. *Desegregating the Altar: The Josephites and the Struggle for Black Priests 1871–1960.* Baton Rouge: Louisiana State University Press, 1990.

Padberg, John W., S.J., ed. *The Constitutions of the Society of Jesus and Their Complementary Norms.* St. Louis: Institute of Jesuit Sources, 1996.

Peltason, J. W. *58 Lonely Men Southern Federal Judges and School Desegregation.* Urbana: University of Illinois Press, 1971.

Posner, Richard A. *The Economics of Justice.* Cambridge: Harvard University Press, 1983.

——. *Frontiers of Legal Theory.* Cambridge: Harvard University Press, 2001.

Powell, Lawrence N. *The Accidental City.* Cambridge: Harvard University Press, 2012.

Reed, Alfred Zantzinger. *Historical Writings in Law and Jurisprudence: Training for the Public Profession of the Law.* Buffalo, NY: Hein, 1986.

——. *Training for the Public Profession of the Law: Historical Development and Principal Contemporary Problems of Legal Education in the United States with Some Account of Conditions in England and Canada.* New York: Scribner's, 1921.

Rogers, Kim Lacy. *Righteous Lives: Narratives of the New Orleans Civil Rights Movement.* New York: New York University Press, 1993.

Scott, Rebecca J. *Degrees of Freedom: Louisiana and Cuba after Slavery.* Cambridge: Harvard University Press, 2005.

Smith, J. Clay, Jr. *Emancipation: The Making of the Black Lawyer 1844–1944.* Philadelphia: University of Pennsylvania Press, 1993.

Solomon, Barbara Miller. *In the Company of Educated Women.* New Haven: Yale University Press, 1985.

Stevens, Robert. *Law School: Legal Education in America from the 1850s to the 1980s.* Chapel Hill: University of North Carolina Press, 1983.

Sullivan, William M., Anne Colby, Judith Welch Wegner, Lloyd Bond, and Lee Shulman. *Educating Lawyers: Preparation for the Profession of Law.* San Francisco: Jossey-Bass, 2007.

Susskind, Richard. *The End of Lawyers? Rethinking the Nature of Legal Services.* Oxford: Oxford University Press, 2010.

Tamanaha, Brian Z. *Failing Law Schools.* Chicago: University of Chicago Press, 2012.

Tyler, Pamela. *Silk Stockings & Ballot Boxes: Women & Politics in New Orleans, 1920–1963.* Athens: University of Georgia Press, 1996.

Unger, Roberto Mangabeira. *The Critical Legal Studies Movement.* 1983. Cambridge: Harvard University Press, 1986.

Wheeler, Marjorie Spruill. *New Women of the New South: The Leaders of the Woman Suffrage Movement in the Southern States.* New York: Oxford University Press, 1993.

Widmer, Mary Lou. *New Orleans 1900 to 1920.* Gretna: Pelican, 2007.

Williams, T. Harry. *Huey Long.* New York: Vintage, 1981.

Woods, James M. *A History of the Catholic Church in the American South.* Gainesville: University Press of Florida Press, 2011.

Wright, Helen Patton. *My Journey: Recollections of the First Seventy Years.* Chevy Chase, MD: Posterity, 1995.

ARTICLES

Angel, Marina. "Law Stories: Reflections of Women in Legal Education: Stories from Four Decades of Section Chairs: Women in Legal Education III." *University of Missouri Kansas City Law Review* 111 (Spring 2012): 714.

———. "Women in Legal Education: What It's Like to Be Part of a Perpetual First Wave or the Case of the Disappearing Women." *Temple Law Review* 61 (Fall 1988): 801.

Babich, Adam. "Controversy, Conflicts, and Law School Clinics." *Clinical Law Review* 17 (2011): 469.

Bell, Linda A. "Ups and Dowes: The Annual Report on the Economic Status of the Profession: Academic Salaries since the Early 1970s." *Academe* 85 (Mar.–Apr. 1999): 11.

Berger, Andrea, Rita Kirshstein, and Elizabeth Rose. *Institutional Policies and Practices: Findings from the 1999 National Study of Postsecondary Faculty, Institution Survey* 31 NCES 2001–201 (2001). U.S. Department of Education, National Center for Education Statistics.

Borkowski, Nicholas C. "The Mass Lynching of Italians in 1891 New Orleans: Marking Italians as Racially 'Dago.'" *Michigan Journal of History* 10, no. 2 (Fall 2014): 158.

Calabresi, Guido. "Some Thoughts on Risk Distribution and the Law of Torts." *Yale Law Journal* 70 (1961): 499.

Eaton, Amasa E. "The Suffrage Clause in the New Constitution of Louisiana." *Harvard Law Review* 13 (December 1899): 279.

Eymonerie, Maryse. "Diversity within Adversity: The Annual Report on the Economic Status of the Profession, 1991–92." *Academe* 78, no. 2 (Mar.–Apr. 1992): 7.

Farley, Christine Haight. "Confronting Expectations: Women in the Legal Academy." *Yale Journal of Law and Feminism* 8 (1961): 333.

Fenton, Rebecca. "Loyola University New Orleans School of Law Commemorates the Fortieth Anniversary of the Landmark Decision in Lombard v. Louisiana." *Journal of Public Interest Law* 5 (2004): 63.

Gardner, Jennifer M. "The 1990–91 Recession: How Bad Was the Labor Market?" 117 *Monthly Labor Review* 117, no. 3 (June 1994). Available at www.bls.gov/mir /1994/06/1451full.pdf.

Glazer, Adam. "Note: The Implications of Changes to Louisiana's Law Clinic Student Practice Rule." *Georgetown Journal Legal Ethics* 12 (1999): 751.

Hart, W. O. "Rights of Women in Louisiana." *Loyola Law Journal* 1, no. 1 (March 1920): 14.

Hollingsworth, J. C. "Interpretation of Seven-Year Divorce Law." *Loyola Law Journal* 1, no. 1 (March 1920): 28.

Huddleston, Brian. "A Semester in Exile: Experiences and Lessons Learned during Loyola University New Orleans School of Law's Fall 2005 Hurricane Katrina Relocation." *Journal of Legal Education* 57, no. 3 (September 2007): 319.

Joy, Peter A. "Political Interference with Clinical Legal Education: Denying Access to Justice. *Tulane Law Review* 74, no. 1 (1999): 235.

Kay, Herma Hill. "Symposium: The Voices of Women: A Symposium on Women in Legal Education: The Future of Women Law Professors." *Iowa Law Review* 77 (1991): 8.

———. "UC's Women Law Faculty." *University of California Davis Law Review* 36 (2003): 331.

Kuehn, Robert R., and Bridget M. McCormack. "Lessons from Forty Years of Interference in Law School Clinics." *Georgetown Journal of Legal Ethics* 24 (2011): 59.

LeBlanc, Sam A., III. "Debate over the Law Clinic Practice Rule: Redux." *Tulane Law Review* 74 (1999–2000): 219.

Leonard, Walter J. "The Development of the Black Bar." *Annals of the American Academy of Political and Social Science* 407, no. 1 (May 1973): 134.

Lind, Joellen. "Symbols, Leaders, Practitioners: The First Women Professionals." *Valparaiso University Law Review* 28 (Summer 1994): 1327.

Loeber, Florence. "Women under the Law in Louisiana." *Loyola Law Journal* 3, no. 1 (November 1921): 26.

Lorio, Kathryn. "Symposium: Reflections of Women in Legal Education: Stories from Four Decades of Section Chairs—Reflections: A Generation Later." *University of Missouri Kansas City Law Review* 80 (2012): 745.

Manning, Bayless. "Financial Anemia in Legal Education: Everybody's Business." *American Bar Association Journal* 55 (December 1969): 1123.

Marino, L., K. Tonnas, and J. Coulter. "Legal History—State's First Woman Law Graduates." *Louisiana Bar Journal* 55 (August/September 2007): 107.

Medina, M. Isabel. "Confronting the Rights Deficit at Home: Is the Nation Prepared in the Aftermath of Katrina? Confronting the Myth of Efficiency." *California Western Law Review* 43 (2006): 11.

——. "Justifying Integration of Domestic Violence throughout the Law School Curriculum: An Introduction to the Symposium." *Loyola Law Review* 47, no. 1 (Spring 2001):1.

Metzger, Walter P. "The 1940 Statement of Principles on Academic Freedom and Tenure." *Law and Contemporary Problems* 53 (Summer 1990): 3.

Moran, Beverly. "The Wisconsin Diploma Privilege: Try It and You'll Like It." *Wisconsin Law Review* (2000): 645.

Papale. A. E. "Judicial Enforcement of Desegregation: Its Problems and Limitations." *Northwestern University Law Review* 52, no. 3 (July–August 1957): 301.

Paul, William G. "President's Message: Increasing Diversity." *American Bar Association Journal* (October 1990): 8.

Riley, Janet Mary. "The Effect of Segregation Laws on Louisiana Library Association Activities." *Library Journal* 75, no. 16 (September 1950): 1466.

"Sixty Years after Admitting Its First Black Member, the American Bar Association Elects an African American President." *Journal of Blacks in Higher Education* 35 (Spring 2002): 34.

Smith, Armantine M. "The History of the Women's Suffrage Movement in Louisiana." *Louisiana Law Review* 62 (2002): 509.

Walker, George K. "A Model Rule for Student Practice in the United States Courts." *Washington and Lee Law Review* 37 (1980): 1101.

White, James P. "Symposium: Legal Education in an Era of Change." *Duke Law Journal* (1987): 292.

Whittaker, Scott T., and Dona K. Renegar. "The Cause and Effect of Recent Changes to the Louisiana Bar Examination." *Louisiana Bar Journal* 61, no. 2 (August/September 2013): 90.

INDEX